AIKIDO RANDORI

Tetsurō Nariyama

Published by Shodokan

ISBN 978-0-9566205-0-7

First edition July 2010

Copyright © Shodokan

All rights reserved. No part of this publication may be reproduced or transmitted in any form or by any means without the written permission of the author.

Notice
The information in this book is meant to supplement proper coaching from bona fide instructors. Take full responsibility for your safety and the safety of others. All forms of physical activity pose some inherent risks. Do not take risks beyond your level of experience, skill and fitness. Seek medical advice before using this practice system.

Japanese words used in this book
Japanese words are explained the first time they appear in the text. Subsequently, they may be used interchangeably with equivalent English terms for the sake of readability or where they are commonly understood.

Spelling is based on the revised Hepburn method with long vowels distinguished from short ones by means of a macron, o (short) and ō (long) for example. Exceptions are for words such as aikido, judo and others that can be found in an English dictionary.

Japanese names are written with the given name followed by the family name.

General note
References to he/him/his are to be read as including references to she/her/her.

Photographs
The images in this book are selected mostly from sequences of photographs of demonstrations at normal speed and are intended to give an impression of each technique. The reader should refer to the accompanying text for detailed descriptions and important points.

Demonstrations are by:
    Tetsurō Nariyama
    Eiji Nishii
    Jonathan Cameron
    Ryūichi Ōmori
    Shinnosuke Sakai
    Kazuyoshi Fujimoto
    Tetsuya Nariyama
    Kentarō Sugano
    Takaaki Oyama

CONTENTS

Aim of this book vi
Introduction vii
Structure of this book viii

PART 1 BASICS 1
   Warm-up and cool-down 2
   Principles and concepts 3
      The principle of natural posture 3
      The principle of non-resistance 4
      The principle of breaking balance 5
      Maai 6
      Metsuke 6
      Seichūsen 7
      Tegatana 8
      Tōitsuryoku 8
      Idōryoku 8
   Tandoku kihon dōsa 9
      Unsoku 9
      Tegatana dōsa 14
   Sōtai kihon dōsa 23
      Tegatana awase 23
      Seichūsen no bōgyo 24
      Gasshō uke 26
      Tegatana no bōgyo 29
      Shōtei awase 31
      Hiriki no yōsei 32
      Go no sen no kuzushi 36
   Ukemi 48
      Kōhō ukemi 49
      Yoko ukemi 53
      Zenpō kaiten ukemi 57
      Tobi ukemi 59

PART 2 TOSHU 63
   Atemi waza 64
      Kihon atemi waza 65
      Tantō atemi waza 76
      Developing atemi waza skills 78
         Hontai no tsukuri 79
         Shōki no tsukuri 87
         Tsukuri from tai sabaki 91
      Timing opportunities against tantō tsuki 101

   Kansetsu waza 116
      Kihon hiji waza 116
      Tantō hiji waza 128
      Kihon tekubi waza 129
      Tantō tekubi waza 138
      Kihon uki waza 141
      Tantō uki waza 148
      Developing kansetsu waza skills 148
         Tegatana no tsukuri 151
         Nigiri gaeshi no tsukuri 162
         Hiji mochi no tsukuri 176
      Timing opportunities against tantō tsuki 187
   Kihon ura waza 193
      Against atemi waza 194
      Against kansetsu waza 202
   Combinations 212

PART 3   TANTŌ 219
      The tantō and tantō tsuki 220
      Developing tantō tsuki skills 221
   Tantō kaeshi waza 225
      Aigamae katate dori 226
      Gyakugamae katate dori 236
      Tantō kaeshi waza 244
         Using the hand holding the tantō 245
         Using the empty hand 256

PART 4   APPLICATION 269
   Stages of practice 271
      Renzoku tai sabaki 275
      Kakari geiko 279
      Hikitate geiko 280
      Randori geiko 281

PART 5   A PAPER BY KENJI TOMIKI 283

PART 6   REGULATIONS FOR RANDORI 287

AIM OF THIS BOOK

It is widely known that competitive aikido was created by Kenji Tomiki (1900-1979). His hard work and research in the latter years of his life concluded in the creation of a systematic practice method for randori (competitive practice within the limits of certain rules) in aikido.

The aim of this book is to describe this practice system along with an explanation of the underlying principles and a clarification of the historical and theoretical foundations of competitive aikido.

The result is a detailed work of reference to benefit your randori practice. Furthermore, it will improve your level of kata (practice of prearranged techniques) and give you a deeper insight into aikido in general.

It is hoped that this book will provide some useful advice for those people familiar with aikido and randori. Those who are beginners will get a very good idea of what is involved. It is not intended to teach you everything about randori, a large part of which is about intuition, experience and experiment. However, it will give you a solid foundation and guide you in the right direction.

INTRODUCTION

Aikido randori is a competitive practice followed within the Japan Aikido Association (JAA) and allied organizations around the world. Judo and kendo are well known for incorporating competitive practice and, as an extension, competitions. Competitive aikido is less well known but is equal to both as a contemporary budo from historical, technical and educational viewpoints.

There are two ranges when looking at the possibilities of attack and defence in jujutsu. The first is a close grappling distance where the hips and legs are used to throw. The second is a greater range where the participants are separated and an opponent attacks by striking (armed or unarmed) or moving in to grasp. With these two different ranges it is necessary to have two kinds of randori.

Jigorō Kanō (1860-1938) created Kōdōkan judo as a modernization of the old styles of jujutsu. He created an unarmed randori system of training using nage waza (throwing techniques) and katame waza (restraining techniques) at close range.

Atemi waza (striking techniques) and kansetsu waza (joint techniques) were excluded from judo randori but were included by Tomiki into a distinct randori system. This operates at an intermediate range between judo and kendo and has a mixed format with one person using a sponge rubber knife and the other person unarmed.

One purpose of randori is to take the place of the real fights of old in developing technique and character. It is not the same of course but it provides a glimpse of reality in a safe, controlled environment letting us use techniques against an opponent who is resisting.

The full experience of participants totally free to attack and defend within the randori framework is clearly not suitable for everyone. However, this forms only the final, tiny part of a comprehensive training method involving kata and randori. This practice system will always fit to your level of ability when applied properly and with the correct attitude allowing people of all levels to practise together for mutual benefit.

STRUCTURE OF THIS BOOK

This book is organised into six parts. Part one explains the principles of aikido and describes the basic movements and drills to learn essential skills. These are grouped into solitary exercises and those that require a partner. A separate section for learning how to fall correctly is also included.

Randori is a competitive practice between two people, one empty handed and the other holding a sponge rubber knife. Parts two and three are therefore organized according to these two roles which are called toshu and tantō respectively.

Part two deals with the toshu side. There are 17 techniques defined for randori with toshu allowed to use any of them on their own, in combinations or as counter techniques. These are presented in two groups, atemi waza and kansetsu waza, with an explanation of practices targeted to developing the skills and timing required in each. The basic counter techniques are also described along with some workable combinations.

Part three describes the requirements for tantō and their practice methods. Tantō is allowed to stab and apply a limited range of counter techniques to toshu's attacks in certain circumstances. The skills required by tantō are, on the surface, different from those of toshu but from a deeper technical viewpoint it can be seen that they have much in common.

Part four draws together the toshu and tantō sides into an applied training method described as a series of separate drills developing step by step from a basic level to full randori practice.

Part five is a translation of Tomiki's last paper to the Japanese Academy of Budo. It concerns the importance of correct application in aikido techniques.

Part six contains the current regulations used in randori competitions.

PART 1

BASICS

Judo and aikido have their origins in the old styles of jujutsu, so it is not unexpected that they have common principles. Jujutsu developed alongside kenjutsu (swordsmanship) and we can say that sword principles have also been absorbed into aikido.

The basics of aikido are brought together with these principles in mind to improve the fundamental skills necessary for correct practice. They are the secret to a solid foundation in aikido so, after a suitable warm-up, always practise them thoroughly at the start of the technical part of your training sessions.

The basic movements and practices comprise those that are done alone and those with a partner. Ukemi (breakfalls) are also included here as they are essential for a comprehensive practice of randori.

Techniques, drills, and practices in this book are generally described for a right handed person. However, it is important that you make efforts to practise equally on both left and right hand sides from the basic practices through to final application. This is particularly true when you take the role of toshu as you may have no choice in which hand your opponent holds the tantō (the knife and the person holding it are both referred to as tantō but the context determines the intended meaning).

WARM-UP AND COOL-DOWN

An adequate warm-up is essential to prepare your body for useful practice. The goals of your warm-up are improved muscular elasticity, greater efficiency in the respiratory and cardiovascular systems, improved perception and coordination, a shorter reaction time and better concentration.

A warm-up should start with low intensity exercises and progress to the intensity of the main part of the practice session. The basic drills described below are mainly a way to develop aikido skills but are also an extension of the general warm-up into a specific one with movements more closely resembling the practice that follows.

Once the main part of your practice has ended it is time for the cool-down. The aim is to gradually reduce the intensity until you stop sweating and are breathing normally. You should include movements that slow down your physiological functions and enhance recovery. Once you are breathing normally you can do some stretching and then finish with walking which helps to calm you down.

There are many good books describing effective warm-ups and cool-downs that include appropriate stretching. You are encouraged to find the exercises suitable for your age, health, physical characteristics and level of fitness.

PRINCIPLES AND CONCEPTS

Aikido has much in common with other Japanese budo. Three fundamental principles from judo are:
- shizentai no ri (principle of natural posture)
- jū no ri (principle of non-resistance)
- kuzushi no ri (principle of breaking balance)

Other concepts and terminology used in aikido are also outlined here and mentioned later where they are particularly relevant.

THE PRINCIPLE OF NATURAL POSTURE

Posture in general is known as shisei and differs from one fighting method to another. The kind of posture used in aikido is referred to as shizentai (natural posture) which is called mugamae (neutral stance) in its simplest standing form.

This is adopted when you stand with your head and body upright, your feet side by side about shoulder width apart (Tomiki referred to 'issoku chō' meaning the length of one of your feet as the distance between them) with your weight spread equally. Your legs are not stiff, but also not physically lax, so you retain the springiness that gives you the potential to move. Your chest and shoulders are relaxed with your arms hanging naturally by your sides. Your mouth is lightly closed and your eyes looking forward as they naturally should.

This neutral stance has a deeper significance though. If we disregard the outward form the idea is of a posture unbiased in any direction that allows for immediate, effective offence and defence.

These basic conditions of an ideal stance from which you can freely adapt to any attack also apply when you have one foot forward. This is known as migigamae (right stance) with the right foot forward and hidarigamae (left stance) with the left foot forward.

To adopt either of these stances step forward from mugamae so that your feet stay the same distance apart with your front foot pointing forward and your rear foot at an angle of about 60°. The distance between the feet

Top: mugamae
Bottom: migigamae

varies slightly according to the individual but the underlying concept of freedom of movement is the most important point. Keep the rest of your body as for mugamae. Facing your opponent in such a balanced, stable stance makes it easy to defend against his attacks and to initiate your own techniques.

The hanmi stance with one foot forward and your torso turned significantly is used effectively when avoiding an opponent's attack or moving to grasp his arm but it is not a basic posture. It should not be used initially as this implies you have already committed yourself to move in one direction.

Mushin mugamae
In the period of Japanese history when fighting methods were used on battlefields the intention was to kill. Warriors constantly faced death so they had to be always mentally prepared. In peaceful times the aim was self-defence but the same attitude of mental preparation reflecting in a natural physical posture ready against any attack became normal in everyday life. This continued in the development of Japanese budo with techniques from standing and customary kneeling positions.

Mushin mugamae describes this kind of clear, calm presence of mind and physical posture to defend against any attack. It is unchanged from the fights on the battlefields of old to competitive budo in a dojo today.

Training to perfect your techniques is said to be the same as training your mind and spirit. In kenjutsu (from the Book of Five Rings) and jujutsu (from the Heavenly Scroll of Kitō-ryū Jūjutsu) the belief is that study of their principles will ultimately lead you to a true natural posture (mugamae) as the manifestation of a clear mind and calm spirit (mushin).

THE PRINCIPLE OF NON-RESISTANCE

This is from a defensive viewpoint of a flexible body not opposing force directly with force. In other words, rendering an attack ineffective or reducing its effect by quick, controlled footwork and body movement.

Jujutsu was formerly called wajutsu, with 'wa' meaning accord, implying that you are acting in accordance with your opponent. By being flexible in your posture, movements, mental attitude and thoughts you can move freely and adapt to his actions. However, if you lose your balance or concentration you also lose this potential.

In terms of forces this means yielding to an opponent's attack when it is advantageous to do so. If someone physically stronger pushes you then you will be pushed back even if you use all of your strength. However, if you move back and remain balanced when pushed you can retain full control of your body. The same idea applies if you are pulled.

In randori you use this principle to avoid a tantō tsuki (stab with a knife) when separated from an opponent. You also use it to neutralise his power if he is holding your arm and trying to apply a technique.

However, it is not always applicable. You can oppose an opponent's force momentarily in situations where you may lose the initiative if you give way to his attack. This is often the case when applying counter techniques for example. We can view this as conforming to another fundamental concept from judo called seiryoku zenyō (maximum efficiency, minimum effort).

Moving in a natural posture indicates that your actions against a force follow this principle. Falling safely to avoid a hard impact when you are thrown is also consistent with this idea. Finally, there is also a relation to rhythm. Close observation of aikido reveals a succession of motion followed by rest followed by motion and so on. To be successful in your timing you need to adjust your rhythm to that of your opponent.

THE PRINCIPLE OF BREAKING BALANCE
From an attacking viewpoint this is creating a chance to apply a technique by taking advantage of your opponent's disrupted posture. It requires the application of the principles of natural posture and non-resistance so we can see that these are all closely related.

Before a successful technique can be used an opponent must be in a position where his balance is broken or he is momentarily immobile. There are two ways to achieve this: by breaking his balance as he moves or by taking advantage of his immobility at the instant he starts or stops a movement.

When a person moves, as in the first case, you have opportunity to break his balance particularly when he is attacking as he will be applying a force and that can make him vulnerable. If you pull when he pushes (or push when he pulls) then he is likely to lose his balance. At the same time, you retain full control of your body and full power whereas he is in a weak position and his useful power is momentarily reduced.

In the second case, when a person starts to move or just as he finishes a movement there is a split second in which he is immobile leaving him in a vulnerable position even though he is balanced. This immobility also occurs when someone in the process of losing his balance reacts naturally to regain it and tenses up, or when a person is surprised by an unexpected movement.

Not only is it physically difficult for someone to apply a technique when unbalanced but that person is also liable to lose concentration. On the other hand, retaining your posture, mobility and presence of mind in these situations increases your chance of applying a technique.

Breaking an opponent's balance will always make a throw work more efficiently regardless of an opponent's physical size and strength. Both opportunities for breaking balance require a finely tuned sense of timing to anticipate or read his movements. With poor timing the best case will result in an inefficient technique and the worst case will result in being thrown or stabbed.

MAAI

Maai is a concept relating to the space between you and your opponent but it is not simply the physical distance that separates you. It includes your position relative to him (which determines the angle of attack), the speed at which you can cover that distance, and also the rhythm.

The distance between you and your opponent is the same for both of you so finding maai that is beneficial only to you is difficult. Your aim is to get to a position where it is easy for you to attack but at the same time easy to defend or, in other words, hard for your opponent to attack. Your body position and ability to manipulate and control maai are what give you an advantage and are based on good footwork.

Maai has been studied in kenjutsu for many years and the concept of 'issoku ittō no maai' was formed. This depends on the weapon(s) used but in all cases it means the distance that you are capable of covering to attack and reach an opponent with one step. Likewise it is the distance that you need to be able to successfully defend against an attack.

Finding and maintaining an advantageous maai is difficult in a constantly changing situation such as randori. Good judgment of distance, speed of movement and accurate timing are therefore important. Tai sabaki (coordinated and controlled body movement) is used to find the positions that give you an advantage.

Issoku ittō no maai is the correct start position for the techniques and drills described in this book unless otherwise stated.

METSUKE

Metsuke is your visual and mental focus. It is the fixing of your gaze on one particular point without letting your focus and attention become too absorbed, and remaining alert to all movements, however slight, within your field of vision. In modern terms this amounts to peripheral vision but it also includes a combination of concentration and awareness.

The point of focus is often the opponent's eyes where you are also trying to read his thoughts. Do not let your gaze wander to the area you may be intending to attack for example as this betrays your intentions to your opponent who may be able to take the initiative.

The pictures on the facing page show a simple exercise to understand and practise metsuke.

Stand face to face with a partner with your arms and fingers extended towards each other so that your middle fingers are just touching (picture 1). Drop your hands. Your partner spreads his hands and feet (picture 2). Maintain eye contact and point to his fingers or toes as he moves them in a random sequence (picture 3).

SEICHŪSEN

Seichūsen is the centre line of your body that divides you into left and right halves. You are mechanically strongest when pushing or pulling along this line keeping your elbows in close to your body. Stability is reduced when your centre is moved away from its natural position and your balance is eventually broken when it is moved outside the extent of your feet.

When considering your centre and that of your opponent together, the line that connects the two is important. It relates to the direction you face or the angle in relation to him which is part of the concept of maai. Aim to always direct your centre towards his but avoid being on his centre line so that you have an advantage.

In kenjutsu the aim is to protect yourself by keeping your sword in your centre while controlling and opening your opponent's centre for attack. Aikido uses the same idea with defence against a knife strike using tegatana (hand blade). Your centre line is the most effective place to use tegatana in defence or when applying techniques while using quick footwork and good posture.

TEGATANA

Aikido uses weapons concepts in an empty-handed format which, in randori, takes the form of an unarmed person defending against a tantō tsuki. The randori practice system encourages the development of skills based on these concepts. In kenjutsu a sword is used and in aikido we use tegatana. This refers to the base of the little finger on the edge of the hand when the fingers are held together and extended. In a broad sense it refers to the hand blade or forearm as it is often used in randori.

Tegatana functions in defence as a shield by blocking or parrying an attack. However, this does not prevent a further attack again so grasping your opponent's arm is also necessary. When attacking, it is used to push or pull so always have in mind either grasping your opponent's arm or preparing for a technique.

Tegatana is used most effectively when it is in your centre with your power concentrated through it while using quick footwork and maintaining a strong and mobile posture.

TŌITSURYOKU

Tōitsuryoku is the concentration of your power through one point. Its effective use requires body movement from a stable posture rather than simple muscular strength.

In defence, you control an attack by avoiding it and using your tegatana with an extended arm. In attack, focussing your power through your arm combined with body movement is a step in your development of skills for atemi waza and kansetsu waza.

A reference to an extended or straight arm throughout this book does not mean an arm that is locked straight. Your arm should be slightly flexed, similar to the way it curves when held relaxed by your side or like the gentle curve of a Japanese sword, giving it some springiness and flexibility.

IDŌRYOKU

In simple terms this is movement from one place to another. In terms of aikido we can consider it to be the coordinated, controlled and effective movement of your whole body across the tatami. Tomiki said that idōryoku exists from start to finish in every technique. Controlling maai, avoiding an attack, closing the distance, breaking balance, positioning yourself for a technique and the final application all require idōryoku. Movements should be made with a purpose and confidence through light, fast footwork.

In aikido, movement tends to be through a shuffling motion keeping one foot in front of the other rather than normal walking where the feet pass by each other. Over one or two steps it is as fast as walking but presents less of an opening for attack.

TANDOKU KIHON DŌSA

Tandoku kihon dōsa are basic solitary practices that comprise unsoku (foot movements) and tegatana dōsa (hand blade movements).

UNSOKU

Between judo, kendo and aikido there are a variety of names for different foot movements. Excluding ayumi ashi which is similar to walking, they have a common principle which is to not cross one foot in front of the other. This kind of movement is used frequently and we shall refer to it as tsugi ashi.

An example of this is the following movement from hidarigamae, standing with your left foot forward. Push off with your right leg and slide your left foot forward. Once you have finished pushing with your right leg slide your right foot forward so that your feet come to rest at the same time and you are in a natural posture once again.

This kind of movement can of course be in any direction with either foot forward or the feet side by side. The aim is to always slide your feet and avoid crossing one foot in front of the other to minimise the time that you are open to attack and maximise your potential for offence and defence.

Your upper body remains erect and your lower body moves freely in all movements. Your knees are slightly bent and springy, weight slightly on your toes and your centre low. Move smoothly and swiftly retaining the potential, after every movement, to move again in any direction.

The basic practice of footwork is formed into unsoku with eight directions of movement: forward and backward, left and right, front and back corners. These are grouped into three sets with each set having a count from one to eight. When practising these, each count is followed as soon as possible by a fast movement.

Do not underestimate the value of studying and practising your footwork as the quality of your aikido depends greatly on it.

1. Forward and backward

Start in mugamae (picture 1).

Push forward with your right leg and slide your left foot forward. Draw your right foot quickly up behind your left foot so that you come to rest in hidarigamae (picture 2).

Reverse the previous movement by pushing back with your left leg and sliding your right foot back. Follow with your left foot to finish again in hidarigamae (picture 3).

Repeat the previous movement (picture 4).

Push forward with your right leg and slide your left foot forward. Bring your right foot forward to return to your start position (picture 1).

Repeat these movements but with your right foot forward.

2. Left and right

Start in mugamae (picture 1).

Push off with your right leg and slide your left foot to the left followed quickly by your right foot. Your feet come to rest at the same time so that you finish in mugamae (picture 2).

Push off with your left leg and slide your right foot to the right followed quickly by your left foot. Finish in mugamae in your start position (picture 3).

Repeat the previous movement (picture 4).

Push off with your right leg and slide your left foot to the left followed quickly by your right foot to return to the start position (picture 1).

Repeat these movements in the reverse order.

3. Corners

Start in mugamae (picture 1, opposite).

Push off with your right leg and slide to your front left corner. Follow quickly with your right foot and turn 90° to face to the right. Your feet come to rest at the same time so that you finish in mugamae away from your original centre line and forward from the start position (picture 2).

Return to the start position by reversing this movement pushing off with your left leg and sliding your right foot first (picture 3).

Repeat the previous movement so that you turn 90° to face to the left and finish in mugamae away from your original centre line and forward from the start position (picture 4).

Return to the start position by reversing this movement pushing off with your right leg and sliding your left foot first (picture 5).

Slide your right foot to your rear left corner and push off with your left leg. Follow quickly with your left foot so that you turn 90° to face to the right and stand in mugamae away from your original centre line and behind the start position (picture 6).

Return to the start position by reversing this movement pushing off with your right leg and sliding your left foot first (picture 7).

Slide your left foot to your rear right corner and push off with your right leg. Follow quickly with your right foot so that you turn 90° to face to the left and stand in mugamae away from your original centre line and behind the start position (picture 8).

Return to the start position by reversing this movement pushing off with your left leg and sliding your right foot first (picture 1).

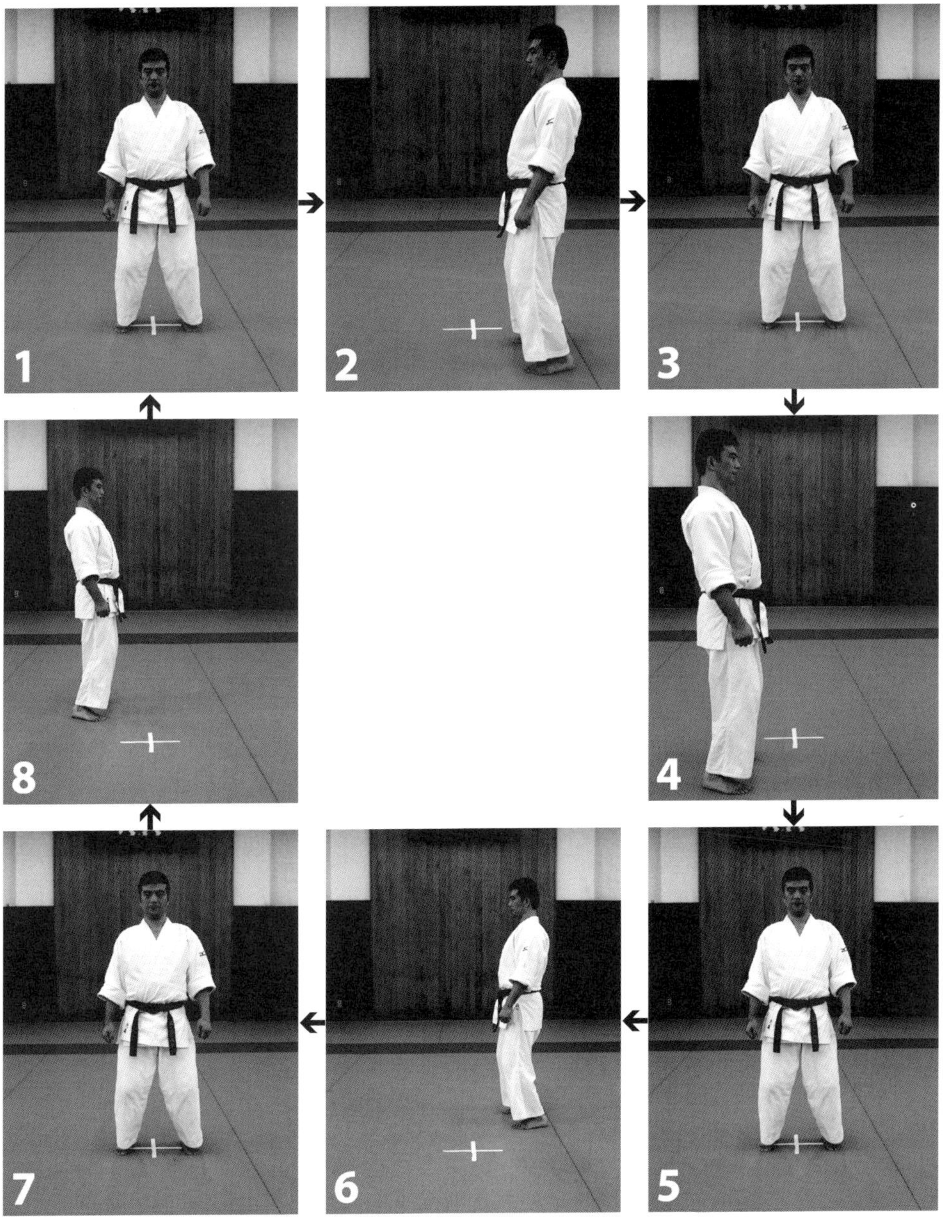
1
2
3
4
5
6
7
8

TEGATANA DŌSA

Sōkaku Takeda of Daitō-ryū Aiki-jūjutsu (the origin of aikido) spent much of his life devoted to the study of kenjutsu so Tomiki held the opinion that sword principles were absorbed into jujutsu and consequently into aikido. Attack and defence in kendo is with a sword and in aikido we use tegatana in a similar way. Adding metsuke and maai to tegatana dōsa we find ourselves with a kind of empty handed equivalent to kendo.

Tegatana dōsa incorporate the principles of seven sword cuts and comprise five sets of movements (each with a count from one to eight) to teach basic tegatana usage. They are:
1. shōmen no uchikomi, shōmen no tsukikomi
2. kiri kaeshi
3. maki zuki
4. kesa uchi
5. tenkai no uchikomi, tentai no uchikomi

In all of these it is important to keep your arm extended with your fingers straight and together. Each one uses movements with your whole arm and requires an awareness of the position and orientation of your hand. Coordinate your arm movement with your footwork and body movement making your actions smooth and precise ensuring your hand moves or finishes on your centre line.

Applications of tegatana dōsa can be found in all aikido techniques and the practices described in this book so it is important to understand them. Te sabaki is the general term used to describe the use of the hands.

1. Shōmen no uchikomi, shōmen no tsukikomi

Start in mugamae (picture 1 opposite). Bring your left hand into your centre with the fingers pointing down and hand blade towards you (picture 2). The subsequent hand movements are all with your hand blade on your centre line.

Raise your hand until it is above your head (picture 3). Keep your elbow down.

Tsugi ashi forward with your left leg in front as you bring your arm down so that your fingertips are at eye level and hand blade facing away from you (picture 4). This is the shōmen no uchikomi movement.

Tsugi ashi back bringing your arm down low with your fingers pointing down and hand blade towards you (picture 5).

Tsugi ashi forward bringing your hand back up to eye level (picture 6). This is the shōmen no tsukikomi movement.

Lower your arm as you move back to your start position stepping back with your right foot first (picture 1).

Repeat these movements with your right hand and right foot forward.

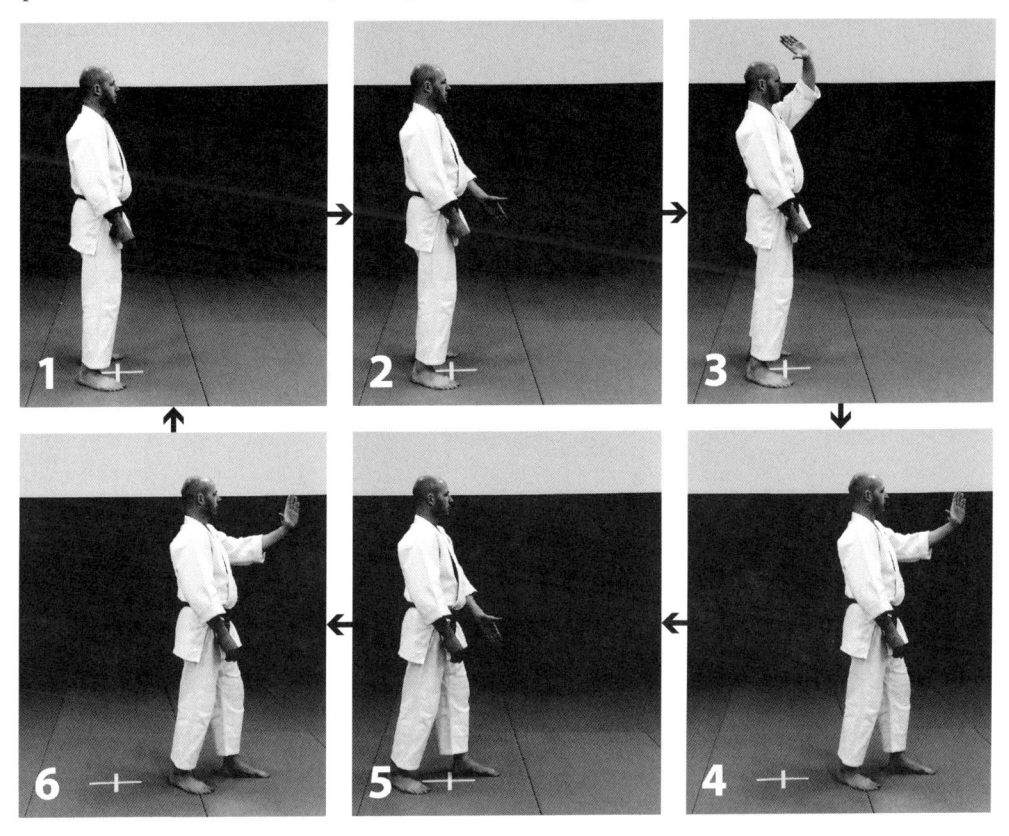

The pictures below show the hand movement on the centre line. Left to right, these pictures correspond to pictures 2, 3 and 4 (and 6) above.

2. Kiri kaeshi

Start in mugamae (picture 1). Turn your left hand palm up and, with your arm slightly to your left, raise it above your head (picture 2).

Tsugi ashi forward with your left leg in front. At the same time turn your hand in the opposite direction as you bring it down by the right side of your head (picture 3) and forward until it finishes in your centre (picture 4) with your hand blade at an angle.

Bring your hand back in a curve to your right until it is above your head as you tsugi ashi back (pictures 5 and 6).

Continue the curved arm movement to your left side and bring your hand forward again until it finishes on your centre line with your hand blade at an angle as you tsugi ashi forward (pictures 7 and 8).

Lower your arm and move back to your start position stepping back with your right foot first (picture 1).

Repeat these movements with your right hand and right foot forward.

The positions in pictures 4, 6 and 8 are shown below (left to right) viewed from the side.

3. Maki zuki

Start in mugamae (picture 1 overleaf). Bring your left hand, with fingers pointing down and hand blade towards you, into your centre (picture 2 overleaf).

Move your arm up in a curved, clockwise movement as you make a tsugi ashi forward with your left foot. Finish with your hand on your centre line at shoulder height with your palm facing away from you and thumb turned down slightly (pictures 3 and 4 overleaf).

Make a tsugi ashi movement back while bringing your hand back down on the same curved path so that it is low and in your centre with your fingers pointing down and hand blade towards you (pictures 5 and 6 overleaf).

As you tsugi ashi forward continue the anti-clockwise movement up until your hand is again on your centre line with palm up and at shoulder level (pictures 7 and 8 overleaf).

Bring your arm down at the same time as you step back to your start position, stepping back with your right leg first (picture 1 overleaf).

Repeat these movements with your right hand and right foot forward.

The positions in pictures 4 and 8 overleaf are shown on the right viewed from the side.

17

4. Kesa uchi

Start in mugamae (picture 1 opposite). Turn the palm of your left hand up and raise it straight up on your centre line to finish at shoulder level. At the same time step forward with your right foot slightly to the left of centre and with your toes turned a little to the left. Your right leg is bent and left leg is straight (picture 2 opposite).

Turn your hand over (picture 3 opposite). Drop your arm straight down close to your body and turn to face the opposite direction (pictures 4 and 5 opposite) raising your hand to shoulder level with your palm facing away from you and thumb pointing down. Keep your hand in your centre as you turn and finish with your left leg bent and right leg straight.

Drop your elbow so that your hand blade is angled down (picture 6 opposite). Turn to face the opposite direction using your hand blade as if making a cut (picture 7 opposite). Your hand stays in your centre as you turn but is away from your body.

Finish with your hand at shoulder level in your centre with palm turned up (picture 8). Your right leg is bent and left leg is straight.

Lower your hand and step back to your start position (picture 1 opposite).

Repeat these movements starting with your right arm and left leg forward.

The positions in pictures 2, 4, 5 and 7 are shown from left to right overleaf viewed from a perpendicular position.

19

5. Tenkai no uchikomi, tenkai no tsukikomi

Start in mugamae (picture 1). Bring your left hand, fingers pointing down and hand blade towards you, into your centre while stepping forward with your right foot so that your toes are slightly turned to the left and in front of the toes of your left foot (picture 2).

Turn your thumb down (picture 3) and turn to your left to face in the opposite direction. As you turn bring your hand over the top of your head leading with your hand blade (picture 4). As your hand comes down on your centre line to eye level, step back with your left foot. Your hand reaches its final position as you complete your step back (picture 5).

Lower your hand so that you are back in mugamae facing your original position (picture 6).

Repeat these movements starting with your right arm and left leg forward so that you return to your start position.

The position in picture 2 viewed from the front is shown on the right.

This first half of the movement is tenkai no uchikomi.

Sweep your right foot back and to the left about 45° and step back with your left foot. At the same time, bring your left hand to your right side and up above your head on your centre line with your hand blade uppermost (pictures 2 and 3 overleaf). Your hand finishes moving as your left foot stops.

Make a tsugi ashi movement forward still on the 45° line while bringing your hand down on your centre line until it is at eye level (picture 4 overleaf).

Step back to your start position with your left foot first (picture 1 overleaf).

Repeat these movements with your right arm moving to your right side to finish in the same place as you started.

This second half of the movement is tentai no uchikomi.

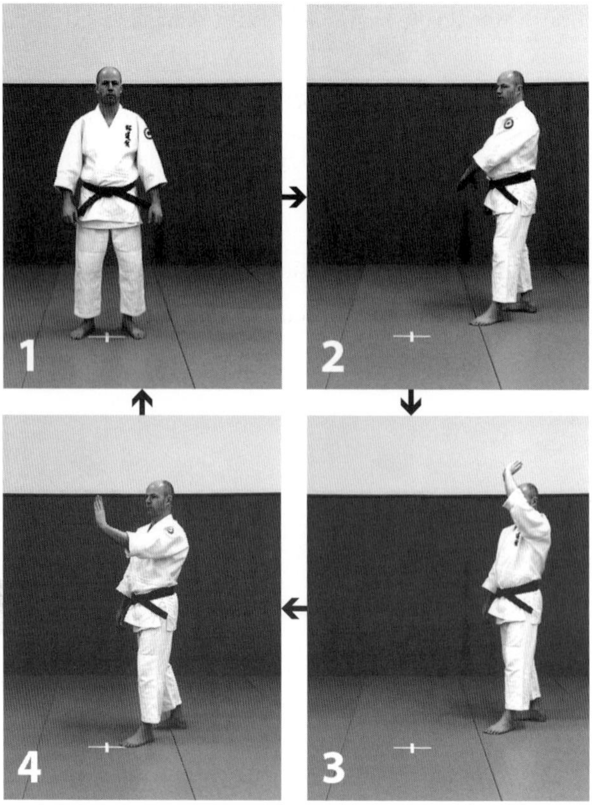
1
2
3
4

SŌTAI KIHON DŌSA

These are basic practices that involve two people. The six practices and balance breaking movements described here are central to good aikido. They target the development of essential skills and also teach an understanding of underlying principles that give you an insight into budo.

If you practise them thoroughly on left and right sides during every lesson you will quickly see the benefits and avoid bad habits that are difficult to alter later on.

TEGATANA AWASE
Procedure
The top right picture shows the start position.

Stand in migigamae with your right arm raised and extended. Your fingers are straight and held together so that your hand blade is towards your partner but held very slightly to the left of centre. The point at the base of your hand blade just on the back of your wrist is in contact with the same point on your partner's hand (bottom right picture). It is this point of contact that is kept in your centre. Your fingertips are on the line of sight between you and your partner.

The aim is to move freely using tsugi ashi in different directions and at different speeds maintaining the original distance between you and your partner and remaining in a correct posture.

Neither you nor your partner directs the movements. You are both free to move in any direction and at varying speeds but you must adapt to your partner's movements at the same time.

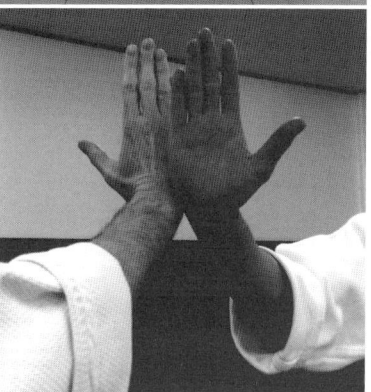

Coaching points
1. A disruption to your posture or an uncontrolled break in maai is considered a loss in terms of budo. Deviating from a natural posture, taking your hand out of your centre line, bending your arm or breaking the maai including taking your hand blade out of your partner's centre in this practice must also be considered a loss.

2. Your arm remains extended at all times. Tegatana awase translates as having the hand blades together but there is no pressure between your hands. The light contact allows you to be

sensitive to your partner's movements and to react to them with speed and precision.

3. Use metsuke to focus on your partner's eyes or a point nearby but at the same time keep his footwork visible in your peripheral vision.

4. The footwork used is an extension of unsoku with tsugi ashi movements in different directions and at varying speeds. Any movement by your partner is matched by a similar movement with your whole body.

5. If your partner pushes towards you, quickly adapt to his movement and move back rather than going against his force. The light hand contact and footwork to nullify your partner's push are not only an application of the principles of natural posture and non-resistance but a way to start understanding the principle of breaking balance.

The depth of this simple looking practice and the principles it encompasses allow you to experience the essence of budo.

Progression
1. From the start position one person closes his eyes. The other person is then responsible for all movements. The person with his eyes closed determines the movements of the other person through the light hand contact and reacts quickly to them.

2. From the start position lower your arms and then continue as for the basic version of this practice. The difference is that you must judge the maai visually. Stop at the end of the practice and raise your hands without adjusting your posture to judge whether you have successfully maintained the correct distance and direction of facing. This practice has a direct application in randori where you and your opponent are separated and constantly moving to control and take advantage of the maai.

3. As above but you are free to change from migigamae to hidarigamae and vice versa. Your partner does not have to change his stance when you change yours but you must maintain the maai.

SEICHŪSEN NO BŌGYO

This practice builds on the previous one. The format is the same but with the addition of certain 'attacks' from your partner against which you have a fixed response. His attacks are not real but they resemble attacks with the purpose of creating opportunities for you to practise in a certain way to learn specific skills.

Procedure
While moving freely as in the previous practice, your partner makes one of two possible attacks. When you are both in migigamae with your right hands together the two attacks are: closing his left hand into a fist and drawing it up and to his left side as if preparing to strike, or bringing

Preparation for a strike   Preparation for a kick

his left knee forward as if starting a front kick.

The instant either of these attacking movements start, push off with your left leg and drive forward focussing your power through your right arm on your centre line. Seichūsen no bōgyo translates as a centre line defence and it is along your partner's centre line that you push to break his balance backwards. He keeps his arm straight unless he has to bend it to prevent himself from falling.

Coaching points

In addition to the points from the previous practice, the following should be noted:

1. Your partner makes his attacks at random and can choose to attack with his arm or leg. For safety, when he attacks with his leg he keeps his toes in contact with the tatami, only brings his knee forward as far as his other knee and ensures there is no power in his leg movement.

2. Your partner must be stationary when he makes his attacking movement. So, he must stop his movement immediately before initiating his attack.

3. When your partner draws his hand back he is preparing to push forward with his back leg so he transfers his weight onto it. When he brings his back leg forward to start a kick his weight is on his front foot. In both cases his balance is more easily broken backwards.

4. Use metsuke to see his attack as soon as it starts and move quickly to close the distance. To make your push strong you need a stable posture and powerful movement concentrated through your extended arm. Drop your centre and drive through with your whole body while maintaining an upright posture.

This practice develops keen senses and fast movement. You must recognise an attacking movement and react to it keeping the time between your thought and action to a minimum and follow with a fast, decisive movement.

Tomiki explained this practice from kendo and judo aspects. In the case of kendo there is a position called tsubazeriai where the participants are close to each other with the tsuba (guards) of their shinai (bamboo swords) locked together. With the rules from a long time ago this was no opportunity to rest. One small lapse in concentration could mean your opponent pushing you to the floor and removing your head guard. This idea of taking advantage of your opponent's immobility the moment he lets his mind wander is used in this basic practice.

In the early days of judo there were players who would drop to one knee or adopt a bent posture to prevent them from being thrown. At the time, Jigorō Kanō talked about this kind of posture, which is unacceptable in budo, and the effectiveness of shizentai. One of his ideas was of the ability to deal with any kind of attack.

With his goal of preserving the whole range of jujutsu techniques in judo, if an opponent is at grappling distance and strikes or kicks it is difficult to defend effectively with a bad posture. However, if you have a correct posture and face your opponent you can feel his subtle movements and respond to them instantly. Kanō explained this to Tomiki and warned him strongly against adopting a poor posture.

From both points of view, a natural upright posture facing your opponent and using metsuke are important in seizing the opportunity to break his balance. This exercise will help you to develop these skills.

One example of applying these ideas in aikido randori is in using atemi waza at the instant tantō starts to make his attack when you are separated from him. Quick thinking and quick movement are essential.

Another example is controlling tantō's stab using your hand blade on his wrist or elbow at the instant he starts his movement. This uses the same timing opportunity to close the distance from where it is possible to grasp his arm and continue into kansetsu waza.

GASSHŌ UKE

This practice gets its name from the position your hands adopt in your defence which is a little like that used when praying. In the previous exercise there is only one defensive movement whichever of the two attacks is used. This exercise is more complex because you not only have to make a decision when to defend but also which defence to use according to the attack. In this case, the choice is whether to use your hands in a high position or a low position.

Procedure
Stand separated at a distance where your partner can strike you by making one movement to

reach you (issoku ittō no maai). He moves around freely and you react to his movements to maintain the range. At this distance you can see all of his movements using metsuke.

He attacks at random with yokomen uchi (angled downward hand blade strike) to either temple or a front kick using his back leg. When he attacks bring your hands together with

Top: right hand yokomen uchi to the left temple.
Middle: right hand yokomen uchi to the right temple.
Bottom: front kick using the rear leg.
Similar attacks with the left hand and right foot are also used.

your arms extended and hand blades towards him as you tsugi ashi forward. With both arms extended equally your hands are in your centre.

Against yokomen uchi swing your extended arms up so that your hand blades are 15-20cm from his face with the fingertips on the line of sight between you allowing eye contact to be maintained. Keep your hands on his centre line whichever arm he uses to attack and to whichever side he attacks (pictures below left and centre).

Against a kick lower your body by bending your knees, keeping your torso upright and bringing your hands to knee height in your centre. The aim is to keep your hands on your partner's centre line rather than on top of his leg (picture below right).

You both withdraw to the original distance after you have made your defence and continue the practice. Separate your hands, bring your arms to your sidesd and return to a natural posture.

Coaching points
1. You are both free to stand with either foot forward and also to change stances at any time.

2. When you are attacking stand with your right foot forward for the right hand yokomen uchi attacks. Raise your hand to your right to attack the left temple or raise it to your left to attack the right temple. The opposite applies for your left hand. The kick is a front kick with your back leg whichever stance you are in.

3. When kicking there is an issue of safety because the person defending makes a deep movement forward. There must be no power in the kick, keep the toes of the foot with which you are kicking in contact with the tatami and bring your knee no further forward than your other knee. Think of this as less of a kick and more of a movement intended to get a specific response from your partner.

4. The attacking movements are quick and light. When you block his attack he stops his movement so that there is no hard contact between his arm or leg and your arm. He should break the rhythm of his attacks, randomly using either arm or either leg and moving freely in

different directions or changing stances between each attack.

5. Maintain eye contact and use metsuke to see all of his movements. When you defend against his kick keep your line of sight horizontal in front of you so you can see as much of his body as possible.

6. To get the correct hand position place the palms of your hands together with the fingers straight and together. Cross your thumbs and then turn your fingers up, so that your hand blades are facing away from you, and extend your arms. The palms of your hands will start to move apart as your arms straighten but keep your hands tightly together so that there is no gap between them (pictures below).

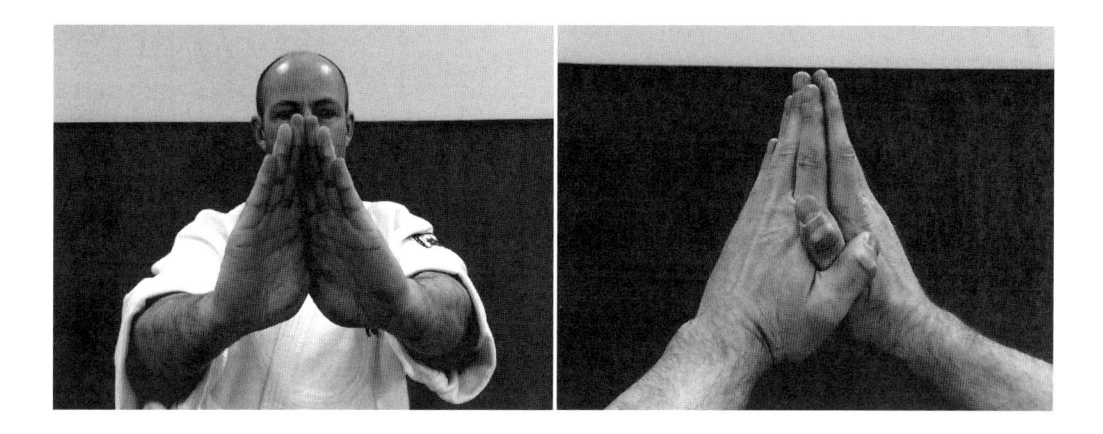

7. Your focus is on movement towards your partner's centre rather than aiming to block his arm or leg.

The principle used in this exercise is that of attacking your opponent's centre line while protecting your own as in kendo. Through this practice you gain an appreciation of your centre, your partner's centre and the line that connects them which means an awareness of the direction you are facing.

You also move in a natural posture, keep correct maai, use metsuke to see the attacks, improve your reaction speed and develop a fast movement which are all required in randori.

TEGATANA NO BŌGYO
This is an extension to the previous practice. The attacking movements are the same but the options for defence are increased which again builds on the complexity. Tegatana no bōgyo translates as a hand blade defence, using the tegatana of one hand instead of two as above.

Procedure
From the same situation and attacks as in the previous practice there are three possible responses.

Consider standing in migigamae in which case you would use your right hand.

Against a yokomen uchi attack with either hand to your left temple turn your palm up and raise it straight up to about shoulder height in your centre so that your hand blade is towards your partner's arm. Your arm is slightly bent but your fingers are extended and pointing towards his face (top picture).

If the attack is with either hand to your right temple raise your arm straight up to about shoulder height in your centre turning your hand so that your hand blade is towards your partner's arm (middle picture).

If he attacks with a kick move your hand onto your centre line and make a deep forward movement as in the previous exercise. Hold your hand so that your hand blade and elbow are down. Use your hand blade on top of your opponent's leg but keep your hand in your centre (bottom picture).

After defending you both withdraw to the original distance in a natural posture and continue the exercise.

Coaching points
1. The two hand positions adopted against the yokomen uchi attacks are the same as the finishing positions in the maki zuki movement from tegatana dōsa. The aim is to move your hand directly to its finish position in his centre (and yours) rather than moving as if to block his arm.

2. As in the previous exercise the attacking movements are there to elicit a specific response from your partner. This is particularly true in the case of a kick which is very powerful even for an unskilled person. Do not consider this exercise in terms of realistic self-defence, think about the principles as in the previous exercise and learn to use tegatana against fast attacks in a situation with constantly changing maai.

3. You should use right and left hands to defend. Whichever hand you use stand with the

same side foot forward. To avoid excessive footwork defend several times on one side and then change your stance once to defend using the other hand.

4. Your defence will involve a slight movement to the side and a turn of your body to avoid being struck because you are using only one hand to defend. Keep your hand in your centre and maintain a correct posture.

Using tegatana to deal with an opponent's tantō tsuki in randori at a separated distance makes great use of this principle. It is one of the most fundamental and yet most important skills in randori.

SHŌTEI AWASE

This is a practice for tōitsuryoku. It improves your posture and movement focussing through one point of contact in your centre to transmit your power to an opponent. The name of this exercise comes from the hand position where the lower part of the palm of your hand (shōtei) is in contact with that of your partner.

Procedure

Stand with your left foot forward and right arm extended in front of you so that your hand is in your centre and palm facing away from you. Keep your elbow down so that the U shape between your thumb and index finger is uppermost. Your partner adopts the same position (picture below left).

Your hands make contact so that the line of force along your arms is straight. The only contact is down the little finger and edge of your hand, across the bottom of your hand and up to the end of the thumb (picture below right). Close your hand very slightly to avoid your palms touching together.

Your partner pushes forward from the start position. He forces you back by pushing off with his right leg. As he does this stay generally relaxed and sink to maintain your position. If you feel your arm bending, your shoulder being pushed back, torso twisting or anything else that compromises your posture you must yield and quickly take a tsugi ashi back to settle into a stable posture again. When this happens your partner keeps his balance and moves forward to maintain the contact between your hands. Repeat this movement several times before changing and moving in the opposite direction.

Use your whole body to push and maintain a good posture with an upright torso. Slide your front foot forward as you push and quickly follow with your rear foot when your partner moves back so that you are never in danger of losing your balance and always able to move again.

Coaching points
1. Stability and mobility are both essential in aikido so do not spread your feet too far apart so that you are unable to move well yourself even though it is difficult for someone to move you.

2. Do not dip your elbow so that you redirect your partner's force upwards. You must keep his force straight along the length of your arm and through your body to make the practice effective for both of you.

3. Do not lean forward because the risk of losing your balance increases. Push forward with your hips so that your torso is upright and you can move forrward quickly to maintain your balance if your hand slips or your partner pulls his hand away.

4. Maintain a relaxed springiness in your body to absorb his force. If you stiffen up then it will be easier for him to move you and you will also be less mobile.

5. Using opposite hand and foot in this practice ensures that your hips stay square and your hand stays in your centre.

6. If, when you are pushing forward, your partner is technically superior or much more powerful then he must not just stand in one place. He must control his movement back so that you can continue to make maximum effort as you move. Likewise, if you are being pushed and are much less powerful or technically inferior, your partner should gradually increase the pressure until your posture is compromised at which point you quickly move back.

Transmitting your force through your hand is most effective when it is in your centre. Combined with body movement this is the best method of applying techniques. Atemi waza and kansetsu waza as a rule use this principle so train towards this. Two examples are shōmen ate where you are pushing on your opponent's jaw and oshi taoshi where the force is on the inside of his elbow.

HIRIKI NO YŌSEI
This is also a tōitsuryoku exercise but adds an element of timing. Normally, when practising techniques your timing is aided by being able to see your opponent's movement. In this practice your visual cue is removed and your timing is based purely on the feeling of the attack.

Procedure
Stand with your left foot forward in a natural posture but with your right hand slightly behind you. Your arm is relaxed and your hand lightly closed. Face forward so you cannot see your partner who stands directly behind you (picture 1 overleaf).

He also stands with his left foot forward. This distance between his toes and your heel is about 15cm. He grasps your wrist with both hands, left hand uppermost, and lifts straight up with extended arms (picture 2 overleaf).

Open your hand and extend your fingers as soon as you feel his grip. At the same time straighten your arm, close the gap between your arm and your body, bend both knees and drop your upper body 5-10cm straight down so that your weight is concentrated down your arm. This action stops his lift (picture 3 overleaf).

Once you have controlled his lift keep your arm in the same place with your fingers pointing down and turn towards your partner maintaining the pressure against his lift. Your arm is no longer vertical after you have turned but it is still in your centre. At this point, it is difficult to move your hand because he is holding your arm so turn your elbow down instead while keeping your arm extended (picture 4 overleaf).

Push off with your left leg so that your direction of movement is just to the right of his body. Drive your arm down slightly until his arms are alongside his body and then start to push up (picture 5 overleaf).

Slide your right leg forward to maintain your balance and good posture as you push. Bring your left hand in front alongside your right hand but do not let them touch. Make a second tsugi ashi movement if you need to and continue to raise your hands until they are in front of and above your head. Finish in a stable posture (picture 6 overleaf).

Coaching points
1. Your partner stands at a distance behind you where he can lift with extended arms. If he stands too close he is not only breaking the maai but also making this practice very difficult or impossible for you. He lifts your arm straight up rather than pulling it towards him and then lifting.

2. When you drop to stop his lift make sure that your shoulders are level and that you drop your body straight down keeping your torso upright by bending your knees equally. Do not sit back so that your weight is predominantly on your back leg. If he lets go of your arm you must remain balanced.

3. When he is trying to lift he is applying a force vertically along your arm. After you have turned he pushes rather than lifts but the direction of the force is still along your arm.

4. When you turn to face your partner do not let your weight transfer to your back foot. You

must ensure that you continue to apply pressure through your arm. Your back leg is straight and front leg is bent.

5. Push against his arms on a line as close to his body as possible. This direction is the most difficult for you because his arms are close to his body and he is strong in this position. However, this is intentional as the aim of the practice is to develop a powerful movement.

6. Keep your arm extended when you push and do not dip your elbow or bend your arm. The direction of the push is along the arc his hands would naturally take if he was to swing his extended arms behind him.

The direction of the initial lift

The direction of the lift after your turn

Your arm after your turn

Your arm after turning your elbow down

The direction of your hand movement

Your final arm position

GO NO SEN NO KUZUSHI

It is not easy or efficient to complete a technique without affecting an opponent's posture. There are two ways to do this:

1. By breaking his balance

This can be achieved by actively assisting in breaking his balance by pulling when he pushes or pushing when he pulls. Alternatively, if you avoid as he attacks his balance can be broken through his own movement. Either way he is left unbalanced and unstable.

2. By taking advantage of his immobility

This can occur through his movement as in tantō tsuki for example. At the moment he stabs, his front foot comes down onto the tatami and he is committed to placing it in one spot. For a split second he is unable to make a further movement and, although balanced, he is immobile and consequently vulnerable to an attack.

This can also occur through your movement. A reaction from your attempt to apply a technique for example can cause his body to tense which has the same result. This immobility is called kochaku and the instant that it occurs is referred to as kochaku shunkan.

The opportunity to apply a balance break in the first case is while your opponent is moving so you have more time than in the second case where the chance occurs at a momentary pause in his movement.

The first method is practised in the set of movements described here. The second method is introduced later.

To understand this practice a little better from the point of view of timing it helps to know about sen (initiative, advantage). This is used in the following general terms regarding timing in response to an attack:

- sen sen no sen – outwardly this has the appearance of an attack but it is in fact a defence. It is when your opponent has decided to attack but you take the initiative and make your defensive movement before he turns his thought into action.
- sen – defending as your opponent physically prepares his attack. For example, when he raises a sword in preparation to cut.
- go no sen – defending as the attack occurs. For example, as he brings a sword down to make a cut.

The timing used here is go no sen because your movement occurs as uke (the person on whom the technique is applied) grasps. This can be considered a little too late in terms of budo but if you apply movements based on tegatana dōsa at the moment he grasps then it is possible to take the advantage and break his balance to nullify his attack.

There are eight balance breaks in this practice, each one based on one of the movements from tegatana dōsa. These are grouped into pairs: jōdan (high), chūdan (middle), gedan (low) and kōhō (from behind) as shown in the table opposite.

Kuzushi	Uke's attack	Tegatana dōsa
jōdan	aigamae katate dori	kiri kaeshi
jōdan	gyakugamae katate dori	kiri kaeshi
chūdan	aigamae katate dori	maki zuki
chūdan	gyakugamae katate dori	maki zuki
gedan	aigamae katate dori	kesa uchi
gedan	gyakugamae katate dori	kesa uchi
kōhō (uchi)	kōhō ryōte dori	tenkai uchi komi
kōhō (soto)	kōhō ryōte dori	tenkai uchi komi

These are developed further as part of the kansetsu waza skills but are described here as they are also a basic practice for every lesson.

It is important for uke to be light and relaxed to allow you to practise the correct form and timing. Uke always starts from a distance from where he can reach to grasp your wrist with one tsugi ashi.

Practise on left and right sides. The grasps when practising on the right hand side are:

- aigamae katate dori – uke grasps your right wrist with his right hand
- gyakugamae katate dori – uke grasps your right wrist with his left hand
- kōhō ryōte dori – uke grasps your right wrist with his right hand and then steps behind you to grasp your left wrist with his left hand

Jōdan
Timing, coordinated hand and footwork, body movement and use of the centre line are all important parts in every one of these balance breaking movements. However, the two jōdan kuzushi require a finer degree of control over the timing and maai than the others. This is because you move back as uke moves towards you and make two quick hand movements just as he is taking his grip on your wrist.

Your aim is to not to let him settle into a stable posture as he steps to grasp your wrist. His step and his grasp occur at the same time so as he places his foot down make sure you are already moving back and starting to break his balance.

<u>Aigamae katate dori</u>
You both stand in migigamae. Uke steps forward with his right foot to grasp your right wrist with his right hand.

Start to move by stepping back with your left foot as he moves towards you and turn your thumb down.

Without stopping, immediately bring your right foot back and turn your hand in the opposite direction just as uke takes his grip on your wrist so that your hand blade is on the inside of his forearm.

Draw your arm up on your centre line as you finish your tsugi ashi back. Without stopping, continue taking small steps back and slightly to your right as if you are moving on the arc of a large circle. Keep your hand in your centre with your arm extended so you are using body movement to pull uke forwards rather than the strength of your arm.

Stop after several steps so that you are still facing him with your extended arm in your centre at about eye level. He releases his grip and you both lower your hands.

The close-ups of the hand movements below show the initial position (picture 1), turning your hand down the instant before uke grasps (picture 2) and turning it in the opposite direction as he grasps resulting in your hand blade being on the inside of his forearm (picture 3).

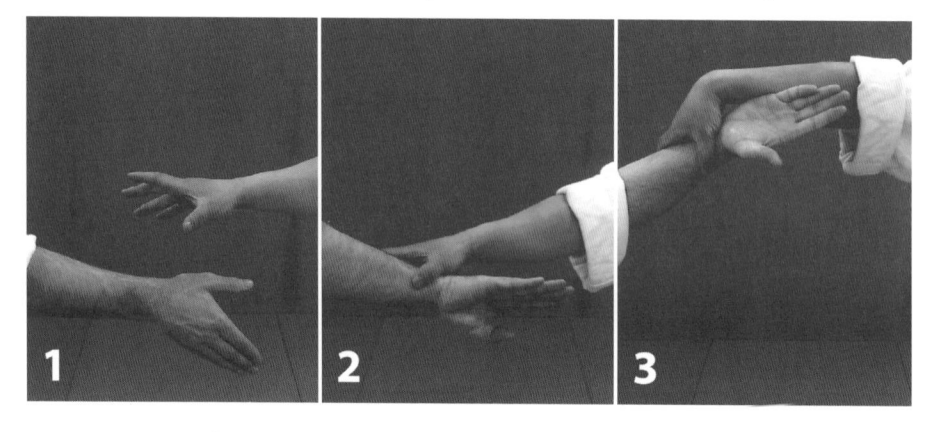

Gyakugamae katate dori

Stand in migigamae, uke stands in hidarigamae. He takes one tsugi ashi forward to grasp your right wrist with his left hand.

Start to move by stepping back with your left foot as he moves towards you and turn your palm up.

Without stopping, immediately bring your right foot back and turn your hand in the opposite direction just as uke takes his grip on your wrist. Bring your hand up on your centre line as you finish your tsugi ashi.

Without stopping, continue taking small steps back and slightly to your left as if you are moving on the arc of a large circle. Keep your hand in your centre with your arm extended and using body movement to pull uke forwards. Your elbow is down and your fingers point up.

Stop after several steps so that you are still facing uke with your arm extended and in your centre at about eye level. He releases his grip and you both lower your hands.

The close-ups of the hand movements below show the initial position (picture 1), turning your hand the instant before uke grasps (picture 2) and turning it in the opposite direction as he grasps resulting in your hand blade being on the inside of his forearm (picture 3).

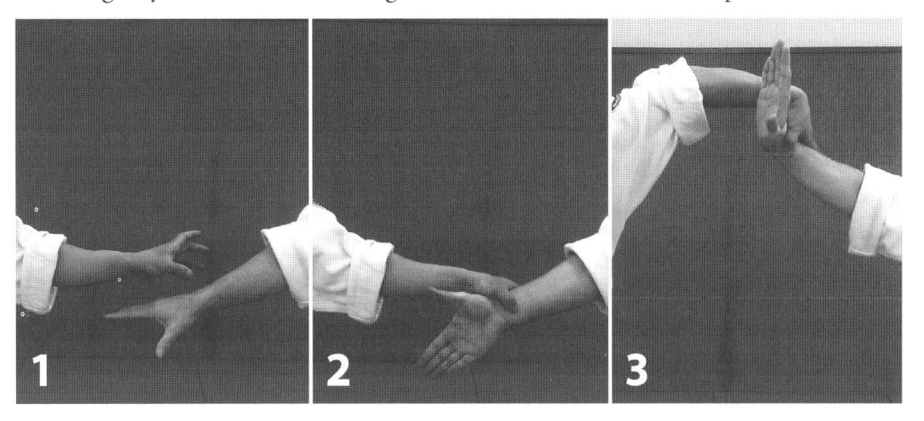

Chūdan
Your position relative to uke is important in the two chūdan kuzushi. You must ensure that you make a deep movement to finish behind him so that you can exert an effective force through your arm which is held in your centre.

Aigamae katate dori
You both stand in migigamae. He takes one tsugi ashi forward to grasp your right wrist with his right hand.

Turn your thumb down the instant before he grasps your wrist.

After he has grasped turn your hand in the opposite direction by bringing your elbow down so that your thumb is uppermost. Keep your arm extended in front of you and in your centre as you turn your elbow down and slide forward with your right foot so that it is about level with his right foot.

Step forward with your left foot keeping your right arm extended in front of you. When your hand gets past his body direct your hand to his centre line behind him and up towards his head as you start to turn to face in the opposite direction. Keep your hand in your centre as you turn. Finish with your hand at eye level, your fingers extended and together, and your hand blade facing away from you.

Make several tsugi ashi movements forward before stopping. Uke releases his grip and you both lower your hands.

The close-ups of the hand movements below show the initial position (picture 1), the instant after uke has grasped (picture 2) and after turning your elbow down to bring your hand back to its original orientation (picture 3). This forces his arm into a weaker position by turning his elbow away from his body.

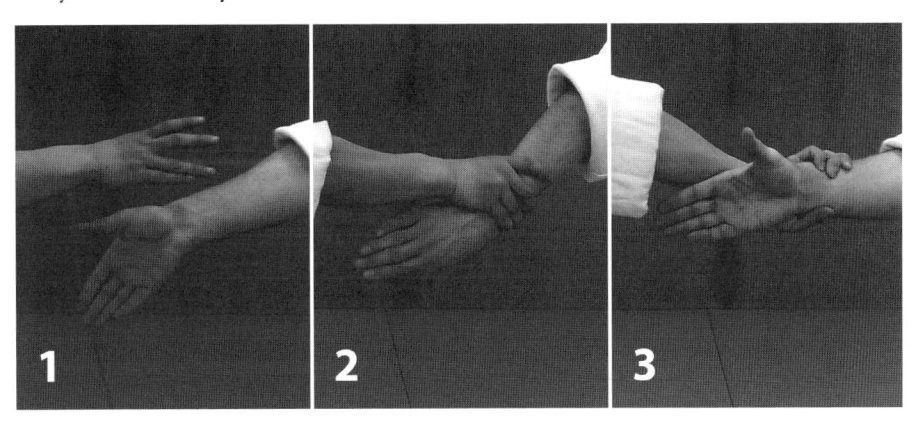

<u>Gyakugamae katate dori</u>
Stand in migigamae, uke stands in hidarigamae. He takes one tsugi ashi forward to grasp your right wrist with his left hand.

Turn your palm up the instant before he grasps your wrist.

After he has grasped turn your hand in the opposite direction so that your thumb is uppermost.

Keep your arm extended in front of you and in your centre as you turn your hand and slide forward with your right foot so that it is about level with his left foot.

Slide your right foot forward again keeping your right arm extended in front of you. When your hand gets past his body direct it to his centre line behind him and up towards his head as you start to turn to face in the opposite direction. Keep your hand in your centre as you turn.

Finish with your hand at eye level with your palm facing way from you and your thumb slightly pointing down and your left foot forward.

Keep your left foot forward and make several tsugi ashi movements forward before stopping. Uke releases his grip and you both lower your hands.

The close-ups of the hand movements overleaf show the initial position (lower picture 1), the instant after uke has grasped (lower picture 2) and after turning your hand back again (lower picture 3) so that his elbow is turned away from his body leaving him with a weaker grip.

Gedan

The idea behind uke's attacks in the gedan kuzushi is that he grasps your wrist and pushes your arm down so that your hand is pinned against your body. He is not expected to push in this practice but you should be aware of the how this makes him vulnerable to losing balance in a downward direction.

<u>Aigamae katate dori</u>
You both stand in migigamae. Uke takes one tsugi ashi forward to grasp your right wrist with his right hand.

Turn your palm up the instant before he grasps your wrist.

After he has grasped turn your hand over as you draw it towards you with your arm extended. At the same time step forward with your left foot slightly to his right and start to turn to face in the opposite direction so that your arm is close to you with your hand in your centre. Keep your hand open and on the top of his wrist.

Keep turning, bend your knees and drop your body with your weight transferred through your arm. Apply pressure with the heel of your hand as you continue to draw uke forward by pushing your arm away from you and bringing it up in front to shoulder height. Finish with your hand in your centre with the palm facing away from you and your thumb pointing down slightly.

Uke maintains his grip and moves through until his arm is extended and he is arching back as much as possible. He releases his grip to finish.

The close-ups of the hand movements overleaf show the initial position (picture 1), the instant after uke has grasped (picture 2) and after turning your hand back over the top of his wrist as you move towards him so that your hand is in your centre (picture 3).

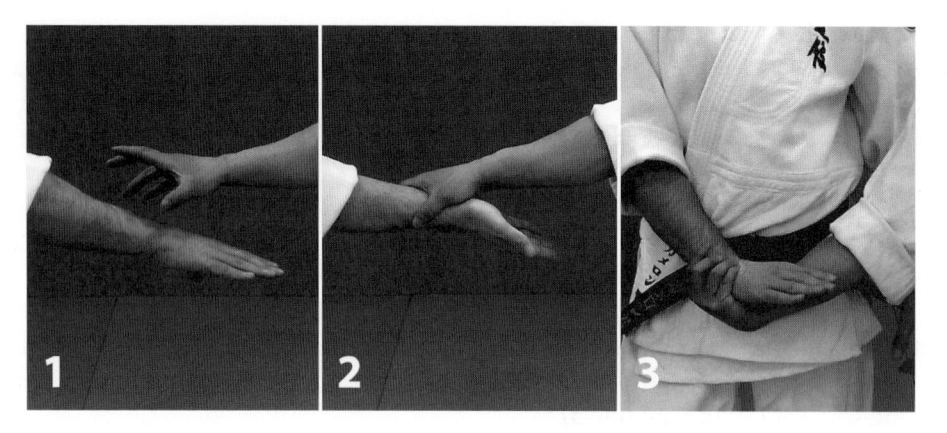

Gyakugamae katate dori

Stand in migigamae, uke stands in hidarigamae. He takes one tsugi ashi forward to grasp your right wrist with his left hand.

The instant before he grasps your wrist, turn your thumb down.

Turn your little finger down and draw your hand towards you keeping your arm extended. At the same time, make a tsugi ashi movement forward and slightly to his left and start to turn to face in the opposite direction so that your arm is close to you and your hand is in your centre.

Keep turning, bend your knees and drop your body with your weight transferred through your arm. Apply pressure with the back of your wrist as you continue to draw uke forward by pushing your arm away from you and bringing it up in front of you to shoulder height. Your hand is palm up and in your centre.

Uke maintains his grip and moves through until his arm is extended and he is arching back as much as possible. From this position you may step back with your left foot. Uke releases his grip to finish.

The close-ups of the hand movements show the initial position (picture 1), the instant after uke has grasped (picture 2) and after turning your hand again as you move towards him so that your hand is in your centre (picture 3).

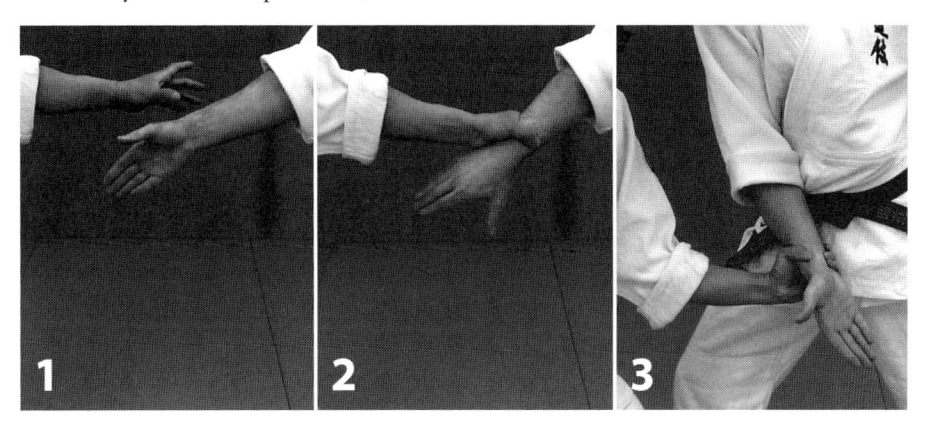

Kōhō

The attacks for both of these movements are the same. The first movement is an uchi (inside) movement in which you turn towards uke. The second one is a soto (outside) movement in which you turn away from uke.

Kōhō ryōte dori (1)

You both stand in migigamae. Uke takes one tsugi ashi movement forward to grasp your right wrist with his right hand. He then steps round behind you to grasp your left wrist with his left hand.

As he grasps your right wrist turn your thumb down and draw your hand towards you. As he moves to grasp your left wrist turn and face to your left so that he is now standing behind you.

Keep your left hand on the front of your leg and sweep your left foot forward and round turning your body to the right. Do this just as he is about to grasp your left wrist.

Your right hand is in your centre after you have turned. Keep your elbow down and lift your arm straight up above your head. Turn to your right to face the opposite direction and bring your arm down to eye level in your centre.

Make several tsugi ashi movements before stopping. Uke's balance is broken in the direction that draws him onto his toes.

He releases his grip and you both lower your hands.

Kōhō ryōte dori (2)
You both stand in migigamae. He takes one tsugi ashi movement forward to grasp your right wrist with his right hand. He then steps round behind you to grasp your left wrist with his left hand.

As he moves to grasp your right wrist make a small tsugi ashi movement towards him and draw your right hand into your body turning your hand blade down.

As he steps round to grasp your left hand raise your right hand on your centre line, keeping your elbow down and fingers up, until it is above your head.

Turn to your left to face to opposite direction and as you finish your turn throw your right hand and right side of your body forward keeping your torso upright. Leave your right hand out in front of you so that his balance is thrown forward and bring your left arm up into contact with his upper arm.

46

Without stopping, turn the left side of your body forward and step forward deeply with your left foot slightly to your left so that your upper arm pushes into his body just below his arm pit.

Drop your left arm and turn your thumb down as you do this. Uke lets go of your wrist as his balance is thrown forward.

UKEMI

At first sight ukemi (breakfalls) appear simply to be a way of falling safely when a technique is applied. It is of course very important to be able to fall with the least chance of injury particularly in randori due to its unpredictable nature. However, there are other reasons for becoming proficient in ukemi.

It is impossible to defend effectively against a technique unless you understand how it is applied. In addition, it is not possible to excel in applying techniques without a thorough understanding of ukemi. So, experiencing ukemi gives you an insight into the mechanics and timing involved in a throw. Also, the more skilled your ukemi become the more dynamic a technique can be applied which helps others to improve.

If you are afraid of being thrown it is difficult to achieve a high level of skill and understanding in aikido. Build your confidence to overcome these fears by learning to fall correctly by yourself to start with and then by being thrown during practice. You will then be unafraid of attacking or being attacked and can enjoy the complete aikido experience.

Do not become preoccupied with winning in competition. If you enter a contest with the sole idea of not losing you are immediately going to be stiff and defensive which is an unsuitable state for good aikido. The same situation occurs if you are practising with the intent of not being thrown and that is no position from which to learn.

In randori your aim is to develop speed and free movement. Concentrate on acquiring the skills you need without bothering about being thrown. You will then be able to use them in attack and defence as the opportunities arise.

Learning ukemi follows a simple progression. Start by practising alone in low positions with less movement and progress to higher positions with more movement. Start slowly and gradually increase the speed. Then you can practise being thrown by a partner starting slowly again and carefully increasing the speed and intensity. It is important that ukemi form part of almost every practice session.

KŌHŌ UKEMI

This is used when you are pushed backwards. It is the most commonly used ukemi and the one that is learned first.

It is particularly important when doing this ukemi to learn how to avoid injury to your head and spine. To protect your head tuck your chin down on to your chest to avoid your head falling back and hitting the tatami as you roll. To protect your spine sit down completely onto the heel of the foot with which you step back (or both heels when doing this at a slower pace) before rolling. The aim is to make these movements without thinking.

Step 1 – supine
Lie on your back with your legs bent and feet apart. Raise your head off of the tatami and keep your chin down towards your chest. Extend your arms in front of you (left picture).

Keeping your arms extended, bring them down to either side of your body and strike the tatami with the whole of each arm and palms of your hands at the same time. The angle between each arm and your body is about 40° (right picture).

Once you have struck the tatami immediately bring your arms back to the start position.

Step 2 – sitting
Sit with your feet together and legs straight.

Roll backwards bringing your chin onto your chest, rounding your back, bending your legs and drawing your knees into your chest.

Extend your legs and raise your hips as the roll nears its finish. At the end of this roll your shoulders are in contact with the tatami, your chin pulled down towards your chest and your body straight with your feet slightly forward from your head.

As your body comes back down reverse the movements so that you finish in the position that you started.

The whole movement from start to finish is done smoothly using the momentum of the roll to raise your hips. Practice the roll only to start with and then add in the arm movement to strike the tatami as in Step 1. This is done just as the shoulder blades touch the tatami letting your arms fall to the sides naturally with the rhythm of the roll. Moving your arms too early risks injury to your shoulders and too late may make your ukemi ineffective.

Step 3 – squatting
In this stage the roll is the same but the start position is altered. Start in a squatting position called sonkyo: balanced on your toes with your knees apart, torso upright and hands on your knees.

Bring your knees together and curl up. Roll backwards keeping your chin on your chest.

Extend your legs and raise your hips as the roll nears its finish. At the end of the roll your shoulders are in contact with the tatami, your chin pulled down towards your chest and your body straight with your feet slightly forward from your head.

As your body comes back down reverse the movements so that you finish in the position that you started. Use a hand to push yourself up into the sonkyo position if necessary.

Practise the roll only and then add in the arm movement to strike the tatami as in Step 2.

Step 4 – standing
The final stage is to start from a standing position.

Without moving your feet arch back as far as possible bringing your chin down on your chest. When you reach your limit step back, bring your feet together and immediately drop into a curled up squatting position. Continue the roll without stopping as in Step 3.

As your body comes back down at the end of this ukemi reverse the movements so that you bring yourself back into a squat then stand up and step forward into the position that you started. Use a hand to push yourself up into the squat if necessary.

Practise this first without striking the tatami with your hands. Start to use your arms once the roll is smooth and you have gained confidence.

From here you can practise ukemi by being thrown. Start slowly and gradually build up the speed and intensity as you gain ability and confidence.

YOKO UKEMI

This is used as a step towards learning the zenpō kaiten ukemi (forward rolling breakfall) and tobi ukemi ('flying' breakfall) as the finish position in both is the same.

Step 1 – supine

Lie on your back and turn half way on to your left side. The outside of your left leg, the left side of your body and your left arm (at about 40° from your body) all touch the tatami. Your arm is in contact with the tatami from your shoulder to palm of your hand. Your left leg is slightly bent and your right leg bent just enough so that you can comfortably place the sole of your foot on the tatami with your toes turned in slightly (picture right).

Lift up your legs and hips so your upper back is the only part of your body touching the tatami. Roll over to your right side and bring your legs down so that you finish on your right side in a mirror image of your start position. Your right arm and both feet make contact with the tatami at the same time.

Repeat this movement from one side to the other.

This position is used when finishing the zenpō kaiten ukemi and tobi ukemi so it is important to fall correctly to avoid injury. Avoid crossing your legs or bringing your feet down one on top of the other. When falling to the left for example, do not extend your right leg too much so that your heel hits the tatami rather than the sole of your foot. It is also important to ensure that the sole of your right foot is in contact with the tatami and your knee is pointing up. Turning your right leg with your knee and toes pointing to the left so that you land on the inside edge of your foot can lead to knee injury.

Step 2 – squatting (pictures opposite)
Start from the sonkyo position: balanced on your toes with your knees apart, torso upright and hands on your knees.

Extend your left leg to your right side by sliding your left foot across the tatami. At the same time take your left arm across to the right but remain facing forward.

Keep facing forward as you roll smoothly on to your left side and strike the tatami with your left arm.

Let your momentum lift your body and as it comes down strike the tatami with left arm and both feet at the same time to finish in the position described in Step 1.

It is important to keep facing to the front throughout so that you land on your side which distinguishes this from kōhō ukemi.

Repeat on the right side.

Step 3 – standing (pictures page 56)
Stand in mugamae. Hold the knot of your belt with your left hand and step forward with your left foot.

Slide your right foot across the tatami to your left side and extend your right arm also to the left. Put your weight on your left leg and keep the toes of your right foot touching the tatami. Lower yourself down on your left leg and roll smoothly to the right striking with your left arm at the end of the roll.

Let your momentum lift your body and as it comes down strike the tatami with your right arm and both feet at the same time to finish in the position described in Step 1.

Keep facing forward throughout this ukemi.

Repeat on the left side.

55

56

ZENPŌ KAITEN UKEMI

This ukemi is used when you are thrown forwards. The finish position is the same as that used in yoko ukemi so practise them first.

Step 1 – on one knee
From a standing position go down onto your left knee. Place your right hand blade on the tatami inside your right foot. Point your fingers back, elbow facing forward and keep your arm smoothly curved.

Place your left hand on the tatami with fingers facing forward immediately behind your right hand. Your left arm is also smoothly curved so that your arms and hands form a circle which is angled straight in front of you.

Turn your head to the side so that you are looking behind and push forward with your left leg. Try to avoid placing any weight on your hands, keep your arms from bending and roll smoothly along your right arm and diagonally down across your back from your right shoulder to left hip.

Finish the roll on the left side of your body as for the yoko ukemi with your left arm and both feet striking the tatami at the same time.

Repeat on the other side.

Step 2 – standing

From mugamae step forward with your right foot, bend forward and place your right hand blade on the tatami in front and to the inside of your right foot with the fingers facing back. Use the momentum of your step and a push with your left leg to roll forward as in Step 1.

Try to avoid placing any weight on your hand, keep your arm from bending and roll smoothly along your right arm and diagonally down across your back from your right shoulder to left hip.

Finish the roll on the left side of your body as for the yoko ukemi with your left arm and both feet striking the tatami simultaneously.

Repeat on the other side.

The aim is to fall safely and dissipate the energy from being thrown so you can finish this ukemi lying down. However, once you become proficient you should be able to use the momentum of your roll to stand up afterwards.

TOBI UKEMI

These are used in techniques such as kote gaeshi and sumi otoshi. The ukemi for kote gaeshi is practised first as it is more compact and easier to learn. In sumi otoshi your arm is extended so the ukemi is much larger and requires more confidence. You need to be proficient at forward rolling breakfalls before trying these.

If you are helping someone practise these ukemi or throwing someone in a technique that results in a tobi ukemi you have a particular responsibility for that person's safety. Firstly, you must never let go of his arm until he has completed the ukemi and landed safely on the tatami. Secondly, you must support him to allow him to complete his spin in the air. This generally means holding your hands at waist height or pulling them up to waist height just at the end of the ukemi so that you are supporting him while standing in a stable posture.

Kote gaeshi
Stand with your right foot forward. The person assisting you stands on your left facing to your right. Let the person throwing you take the normal kote gaeshi grip.

With your forearm in front of you swing your left leg up and at the same time throw your upper body down over your forearm. Keep facing in the same direction as you rotate over your arm.

Your partner supports you so that you do not drop. Once your body has turned over your forearm your arm will straighten and set you up for the final position which is the same as for the yoko ukemi and zenpō kaiten ukemi with your body, arm and legs landing at the same time.

When you are confident and proficient, progress to a basic application of kote gaeshi and then gradually increase the speed and power of the technique.

When kote gaeshi is applied at speed you should aim to turn your body towards your arm as much as possible before beginning this ukemi.

Sumo otoshi
Stand with your right foot forward. The person assisting you stands to your left with his left foot forward and facing you. He holds your wrist and lower part of your forearm with both hands.

He brings your arm to your right side so that it is extended, raises his hands and then drops them quickly with extended arms as he takes a deep step forward with his left leg. Step forward with your left foot as he moves and turn to your right to face in the opposite direction by pivoting on your right foot. Let your upper body bend forward and swing your left leg up as he drops his hands. Using this momentum, spin and fall in the same position as for kote gaeshi with your body, arm and legs landing at the same time.

The person throwing must support you by pulling his hands back into his body as you are spinning. He must also maintain his balance and can by step forward with his right foot if necessary.

Gradually increase the speed and power of the technique when you are proficient and have gained confidence.

When sumi otoshi is applied at speed you should aim to turn to face the opposite direction as much as possible before beginning this ukemi.

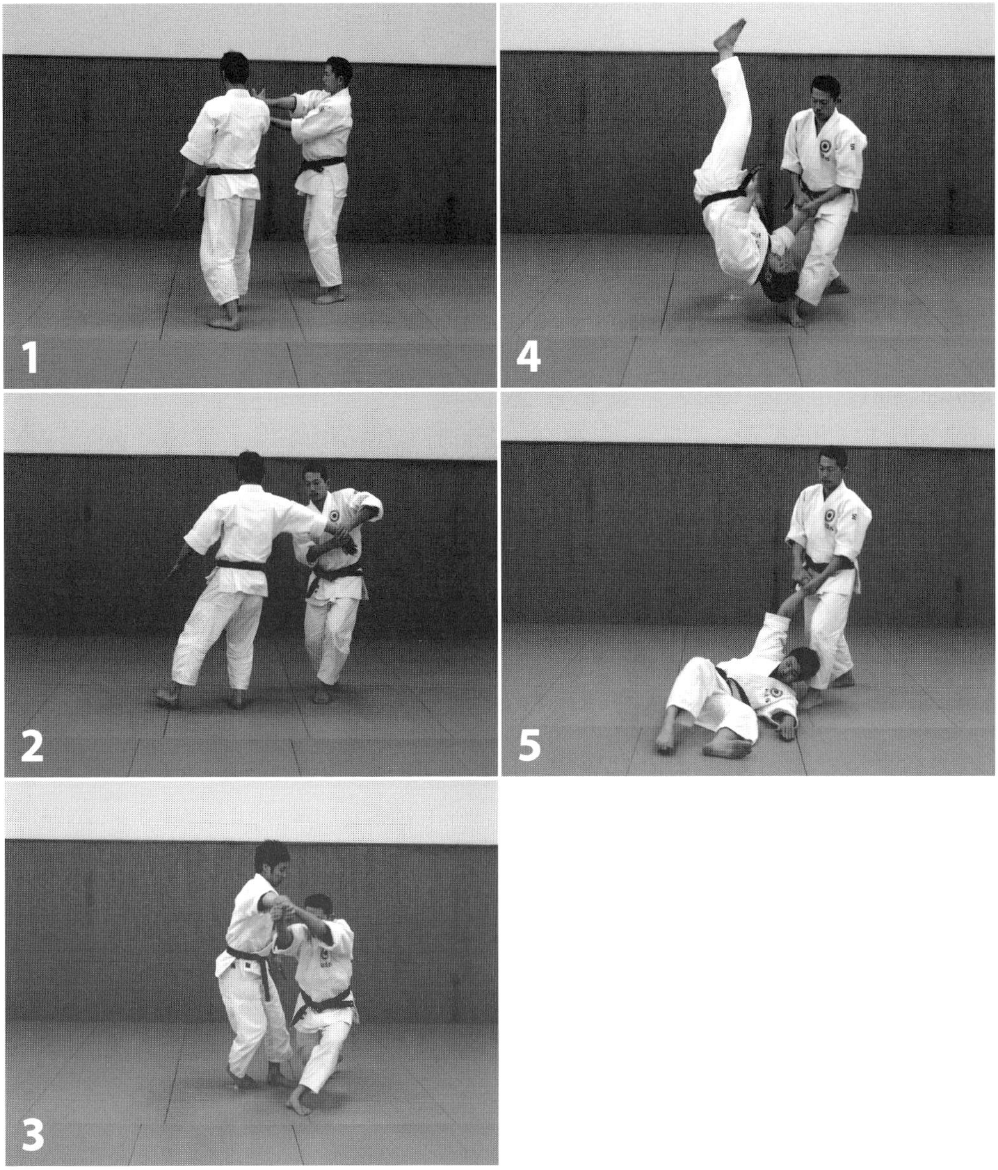
1
2
3
4
5

PART 2

TOSHU

Atemi waza and kansetsu waza comprise the technical content of aikido randori. They can be used by toshu either individually, in combinations or as counter techniques. They must conform to the principles of the basic technique, be applied safely and be consistent with the ideals of aikido. They must also be within the rules when used in competition.

There are 5 atemi waza and 12 kansetsu waza which are further divided into three groups: hiji waza (elbow techniques), tekubi waza (wrist techniques) and uki waza (floating techniques). The descriptions of the basic techniques in this book are numbered according to the order within this group of 17 techniques.

5 atemi waza
shōmen ate
aigamae ate
gyakugamae ate
gedan ate
ushiro ate

12 kansetsu waza
hiji waza
• oshi taoshi
• ude gaeshi
• hiki taoshi
• ude hineri
• waki gatame
tekubi waza
• kote hineri
• kote gaeshi
• tenkai kote hineri
• tenkai kote gaeshi
uki waza
• mae otoshi
• sumi otoshi
• hiki otoshi

ATEMI WAZA

The theory and practice of atemi waza come from old styles of jujutsu and can be seen in the koshiki no kata and itsutsu no kata of Kōdōkan judo for example. Tomiki referred to Daitō-ryū Aiki-jūjutsu among others in their creation. The corresponding principles in the koshiki no kata and sword strikes in kendo are noted in the table below.

Atemi waza	Koshiki no kata	Kendo
shōmen ate	tai	men
aigamae ate	shikoro dori	tsuki
gyakugamae ate	ko daore	men
gedan ate	uchi kudaki	dō
ushiro ate	ryoku hi	men

These techniques have a common principle. They are all applied by movement (idōryoku) in one direction through one point of contact. This is in contrast to judo where techniques are applied by forces in two directions at two points of contact.

This is apparent when considering a comparison from the point of view of kuzushi. When someone has their balance broken after being pulled forward for example, their immediate reaction is to step forward to regain balance. In judo if you place your foot so that your opponent cannot make that step he will not be able to regain his balance. The two points of contact working in different directions are the pull with your arms and the obstruction of his step with your foot. In aikido, rather than placing your foot, if you pull faster and further than he can move his leg then he will not be able to regain his balance. In this case your pull to break his balance is the single point of contact in a single direction.

Originally, the single point of contact in atemi waza was a physiological weak point. Hard strikes to these points would incapacitate a person but nowadays we think in terms of mechanical weak points and principles of breaking balance. The direction of application is the easiest direction mechanically in which to break balance and throw an opponent.

The hard strikes of the original techniques are replaced by the use of open hands. You must practise carefully to develop good control so you can place your hands or arms on your opponent, and then push or pull, rather than making a hard contact.

Atemi waza are most effective in randori if your opponent is tense as this tends to make him easier to topple. There will always be at least one atemi waza that you can use irrespective of the angle of your attack and his stance.

KIHON ATEMI WAZA

This book is focussed on randori so techniques are described along with their practical aspects and underlying principles without the formalities associated with practising a group of techniques as a whole. However, practice always begins and ends with a bow to the other person.

Start each technique as follows:

Both you and uke stand in migigamae (picture 1).

Bring your right hands low in the centre (picture 2) at the same time and take a tsugi ashi forward bringing your arms up to reach the position in picture 3. Your fingertips are on the line of sight between you and there is a small gap between your hand blades.

Each basic technique is described from this start position.

1. Shōmen ate

Raise your right arm straight up above your head keeping your hand blade on your centre line and your elbow down.

Move forward and to your right as you bring your hand blade down onto uke's wrist pushing his arm straight down to the level of your belt. At this point you are at an arm's length from him with your feet on a line 45° to your original position with your right foot pointing between his feet. His balance is broken slightly in this position but he keeps facing forward.

Place your left hand blade on the inside of his wrist and then move your right hand to the side of his jaw. The palm of your hand rests against his jaw with your elbow down so that the U shape between the thumb and forefinger is uppermost. This is the most efficient position for your arm when you push and also ensures your fingers are away from his eyes (picture right).

Push off with your left leg and slide your right foot between his feet pushing him back and down. Your feet become further apart as you push so your body will naturally lower. However, keep your hands in the same position relative to your body with your arms extended and use your whole body movement to push him down.

As soon as your right foot is placed bring your left foot up behind it to finish in a natural stance.

Coaching points

In kenjutsu it is critical you keep your sword in your centre and towards your opponent's centre to protect yourself. Simply letting it get pushed aside opens you up for attack. If it is forced aside while you are making an effort to keep it in your centre this will naturally disrupt your posture. This idea is behind the initial balance break in this technique with uke trying to keep his hand in his centre.

In all kata it is important that uke reacts correctly to your movements and does not fall too early so that you can practise each technique to the full extent. For the atemi waza this means uke must arch back as much as possible when a technique is applied before stepping back and falling.

67

2. Aigamae ate
Use your hand blade to lift uke's hand a little. Step forward with your left foot to his right side and place your left hand on the inside of his arm with your thumb up. At the same time turn your thumb down and grasp his wrist with your right hand so that the palm of your hand is on the inside of his wrist, then use both hands to roll his arm over so that his elbow is uppermost. As you end this movement bring your right foot to the left so that it is in line behind your left foot. You should be standing in a left stance parallel to your original line and with your hips angled forwards. Keep uke's arm at shoulder level and bring his balance onto his toes in a forward direction slightly to his left.

Release his arm. Uke straightens his body to regain an upright posture and turns his elbow down at the same time. As he does this keep your left hand blade on his elbow to pin it to his body and slide your right hand up his chest onto his chin.

Bring your right hand to your centre to break his balance. Keep facing forward and push off with your left foot moving forward and slightly to your right into his body to throw him.

Coaching points
This technique uses the idea of handō no kuzushi which is breaking balance by using a reaction to a preparatory movement in the opposite direction. In this case you draw him forward onto his toes then you break his balance backwards when he reacts and pulls back.

The throw is applied by body movement angled towards and through uke rather than by twisting your body. As you step forward with your right foot the right side of your body makes contact with the left side of uke. Keeping your arm extended and facing forward you push him off his feet by moving at an angle slightly to your right.

The picture to the right shows the position just before the final step to throw uke.

69

3. Gyakugamae ate

Step to the left with your left foot and then follow with your right foot so that you are at an angle of about 30° facing towards uke and with your right foot forward. As you step round drop your right hand in a fast clockwise circular movement and grasp his wrist without moving his hand.

Move your right foot forward slightly and drop your hand to pin uke's hand on top of his leg keeping your arm straight and maintaining an upright posture.

Bring your left arm straight up above your head on your centre line and down onto the top of his chest as you step in with your left leg to close the distance to him.

Keep your arms straight and turn your body so that you are facing in your original direction keeping your left arm in your centre to break his balance.

Push off with your right leg and move straight forward without turning your body. At the same time open your right hand.

Coaching point

There is no initial balance break when you make your first movement and catch uke's wrist. The underlying concept at this point is that as you make your initial quick movement to grab his wrist he reacts by tensing his body making him immobile for split second.

Keep your hand relaxed when you grasp his wrist. This is indicated by a crisp slapping sound at the point of contact.

In this basic technique your arm is placed across the top of his chest rather than using your hand on his temple. Be careful to avoid any pressure on his throat.

This technique is applied by breaking uke's balance and body movement across the tatami rather than by twisting your body.

The picture to the right shows the position just before the final movement to throw uke.

71

4. Gedan ate

Step to the left with your left foot and then follow with your right foot so that you are at an angle of about 30° facing towards uke and with your right foot forward. As you step round drop your right hand in a fast clockwise circular movement and grasp his wrist as for gyakugamae ate.

Raise your left arm to feint a high attack. Uke reacts with his left arm to block. Bring your left arm down and lift your right arm as you slide forward with your right foot. Both arms are straight and your right knee is bent considerably so that you can lower your body while keeping your torso upright. Your right heel is turned in and you are on the toes of your left foot to maintain balance. Do not let your left knee touch the tatami and keep your line of sight horizontal.

Release your grip on his wrist. Lift yourself up, step to his right with your left foot and place the inside of your left arm low across his body. At the same time bring your right hand down so that it is also in front of you. Your left leg is to the right of his body with your foot pointing forward.

Drive forward with your right leg pushing uke down and straight back. Your body will naturally lower as you do this. At the same time, turn your hips slightly to the left and draw your right foot up so that at the end of the movement you are facing your original direction in a natural posture.

Coaching points

The idea behind this technique is of bringing uke's attention up as a reaction to your feint and then immediately changing to a low attack.

In this basic technique the position of your left leg should be such that he is capable of stepping straight back with his right foot without tripping over your leg. This is a safety point to allow him the freedom to take a simple backward ukemi. It is particularly important when practising with beginners who must be allowed to fall at their own pace and without hindrance. The picture on the right shows the correct position just before the final throw. Tori's movement from here is straight, in the direction his toes are pointing, maintaining the freedom for uke to step back at any time.

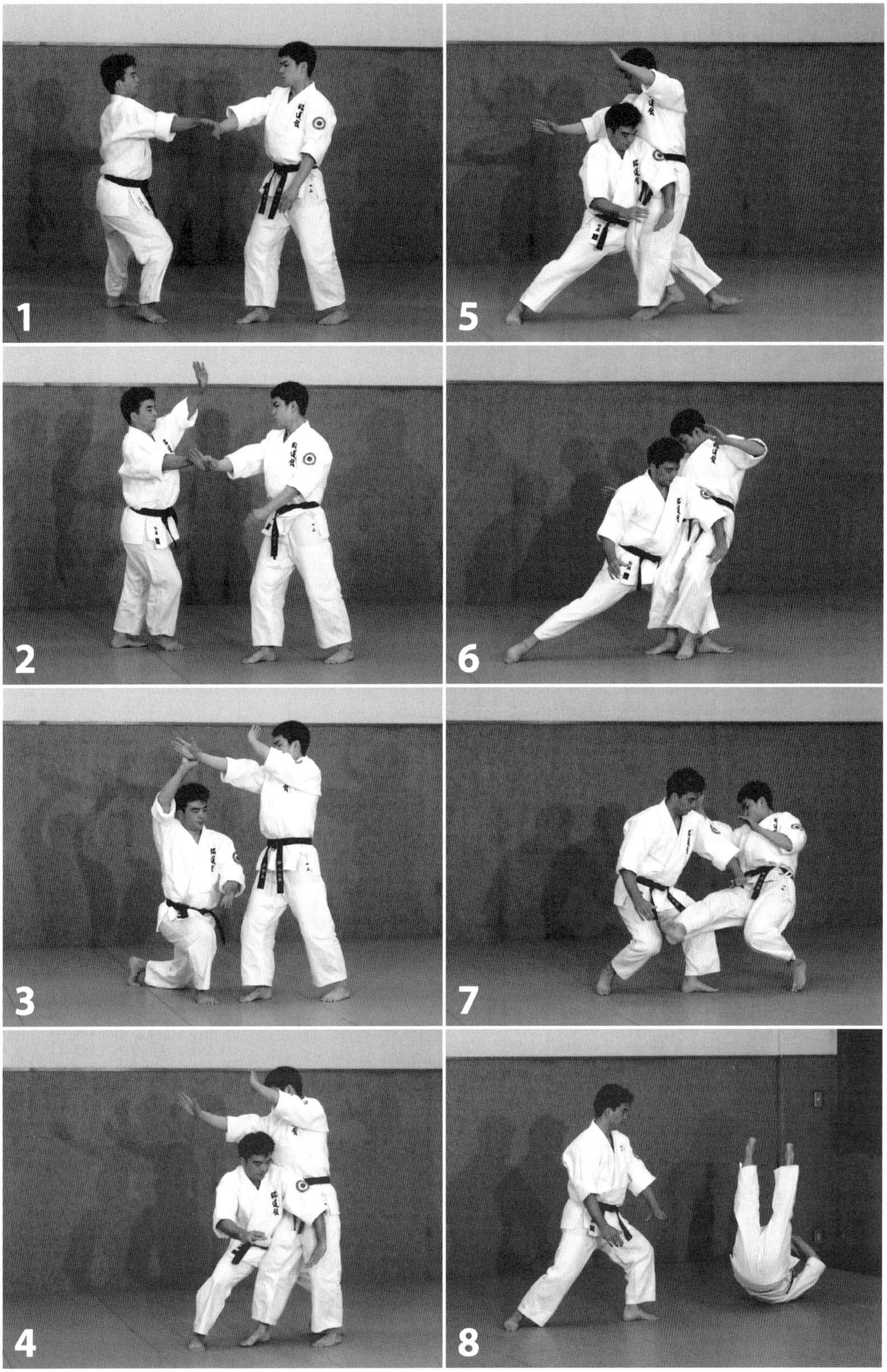
1
2
3
4
5
6
7
8

5. Ushiro ate

Move your right foot forward slightly and use your hand blade to lower uke's arm.

Grasp his wrist with your right hand, turn your left hand thumb down and place it on the inside of his elbow. Push his elbow into his body and then to your right as you twist your body to the right without stepping to the left. In this position your right heel is turned in and you are on the toes of your left foot. Both arms are extended pushing his forearm to his left and turning his body about 90° to expose his back.

Release your grip on his arm, make a fast tsugi ashi behind him passing as close to his back as possible and place your open hands just on the front of his shoulders. At the end of your movement you are standing behind his left shoulder.

Take two or three tsugi ashi movements back and to your left at 45° keeping your right foot forward. As you start to move pull your arms horizontally to your right keeping them at shoulder height applying the throw using the movement of your body. Uke takes a backward fall straight from the position in which he has been turned.

Coaching point

The position of your hands on uke's arm is shown below right. When you twist your body to turn him, extend your arms and push with both hands rather than pushing on his elbow and pulling his wrist.

The picture below right shows the open hands on uke's shoulders just before the final throw which is applied by body movement rather than a twist of your body or using the strength in your arms to pull him straight down.

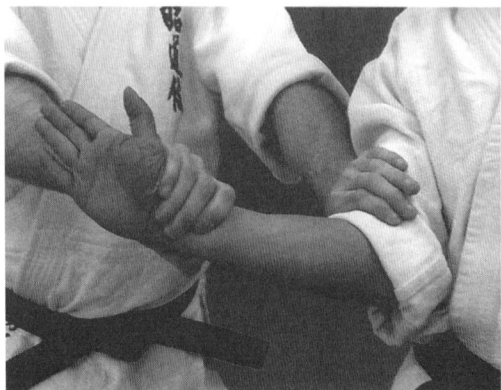

75

TANTŌ ATEMI WAZA

Against an opponent holding a knife the maai is greater than when he is unarmed as in the basic kata. The timing is also a little different. In the basic kata you both approach at the same time and meet with your hand blades facing each other. However, against a knife you come to the correct maai and wait for tantō to stab and close the distance to you.

In addition to these adjustments for all 17 techniques there are other differences between some basic applications and those used against a knife. The descriptions below (with uke holding the tantō in his right hand) highlight these differences.

Each technique starts with both of you standing in migigamae, you with your arms by your side and uke holding the tantō in his right hand on his centre line. He stabs from a distance where he can reach you with one movement.

Pictures for all 17 basic techniques against tantō tsuki can be found in the book 'Aikidō Kyōshitsu' translated into English under the title 'Aikido: Tradition and the Competitive Edge'.

Shōmen ate

The first movement of the basic technique involves avoidance away from the centre line between you and uke. This is also sufficient to avoid a straight stab so against a knife this technique is essentially the same as the basic form. As uke stabs, raise your hand from a low position on your centre line and continue as for the basic technique.

Aigamae ate

The basic technique and application against a knife are essentially the same in their movements but the timing is a little different. In the basic technique uke is static in front of you so you have time to manipulate his arm and move to the side. With the tantō uke is moving towards you rather than stationary and forces you to avoid his attack.

To get an effective twist on uke's arm you need to take a grip so that the palm of your hand is on the inside of his wrist. This is easier to do while you are in front of him but, against a tantō, you need to avoid the attack. So, there is a conflict in these two requirements which is resolved by precise timing of your body movement and use of your hands.

As uke stabs, raise your right hand on your centre line so that it comes up underneath his wrist. At the same time, start to step with your left foot as in the basic technique. Turn your thumb down and take a grip so that the palm of your hand is on the inside of his wrist as much as possible. As you do this, use your left hand on his elbow to roll his arm over and complete your footwork at the same time as you complete the turn on his arm.

Continue as for the basic technique.

Pictures 1-3 opposite show the actions of your right hand. The left hand is not shown. The bottom right picture is a view from the other side showing both arms. The left hand is on the inside of tantō's arm with the thumb up. Both hands turn in a clockwise direction together to roll tantō's arm over. This is the same hand movement as in the basic technique.

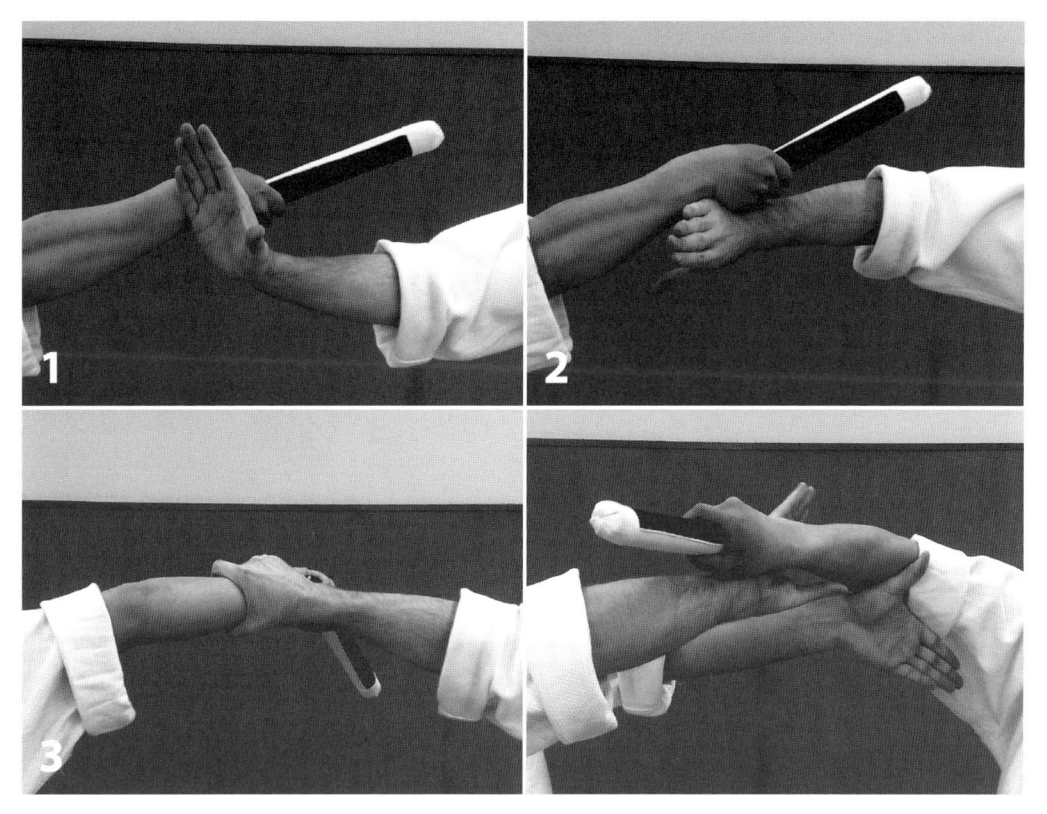

Gyakugamae ate and gedan ate
The first movement of these basic techniques are the same and involve an initial avoidance away from the centre line between you and uke. This is also sufficient to avoid a stab so against a knife this technique is essentially the same as the basic form. As uke stabs, raise your hand from a low position on your centre line and continue as for the basic technique.

Ushiro ate
In the basic technique the initial balance breaking movement is done while you remain in front of uke. This cannot be done against a stab because you are not avoiding the line of attack. You must avoid the knife by stepping forward and to the left at the same time as deflecting his arm.

Your hands work in a similar way to the basic technique although the direction of movement is different. In the basic technique uke's arm is pushed down and towards him before pushing it to his left to turn his body. This is not possible against a stab because you would be directly opposing the force of his arm. So, use your hands to redirect his stab away from you and turn his body as you avoid his attack (pictures overleaf).

Continue as in the basic technique.

DEVELOPING ATEMI WAZA SKILLS

The concept of tantō tsuki relates to a sword so the timing opportunities also come from kendo. A famous swordsman from the Edo period stated that there are three critical timing points. In aikido randori, from toshu's point of view, these are:

- okori o utsu – the instant that tantō makes his preparatory movement to stab
- tsukitaru o utsu – the instant that tantō's stab fails to reach or misses
- uketaru o utsu – this can be subdivided into two:
   - hikiokori o utsu – the instant tantō withdraws to make a second stab after the first one is ineffective, or
   - ōjitaru o utsu – the instant that tantō senses and reacts to toshu's attacking movement

In all cases there is a split second of time when tantō is immobile which is the instant that atemi waza can be effectively applied. The drills and exercises that follow are aimed at helping you to understand these timing opportunities and to make use of them to improve your atemi waza.

They start with the basic practice of hontai no tsukuri which teaches you how to move and the directions of attack but without any aspect of timing.

The next stage is shōki no tsukuri (shōki means a chance to win) which adds an element of timing to the previous drill. Uke jumps rhythmically so you can get a sense of the timing and move at the appropriate moment.

In shōki no tsukuri, uke decides on the speed of his jumps but you still decide when to move among the opportunities presented to you. To take away that choice, in other words to break the rhythm, we can develop this by allowing uke to decide when to move and making a single jump to which you have to respond.

This can be made more difficult by allowing uke to feint or jump to more than one position so you also have to decide which of the atemi waza to apply and which hand to use according to his stance.

An alternative route to practise atemi waza is against a shōmen uchi attack. This is split into four levels building up from avoiding the attack, closing the distance to uke, setting up the technique and then the final throw.

All atemi waza are applied using body movement with force applied in one direction through one point of contact.

The timing opportunities for atemi waza against tantō are also explained.

1. Hontai no tsukuri
This teaches you about correct distance, how to move and the directions of attack without concern for the timing involved. You need good control of your body and hands to quickly close the distance to uke and then stop your movement abruptly with your hand(s) placed on him rather than connecting with a hard contact. Your aim is to make one fast movement so that when you reach him you are balanced and have the potential to make a further movement to throw him.

There are two stages to this practice for each of the atemi waza. The first is setting up the technique (tsukuri) by moving to the point of throwing and stopping. The second is to move to the point of throwing, place your hand(s) and then complete the technique by throwing uke (kake) so that he takes a backward breakfall. The photographs that follow illustrate the complete technique in each case.

You must practise equally on left and right sides so you can exercise the same degree of control with both hands.

General coaching points
All of the atemi waza in this practice start from mugamae. Make sure that one foot is not slightly forward from the other.

Begin by standing at a distance from uke that is appropriate for your level. In general, this is the distance you can travel comfortably with one quick step to reach him.

Always look towards uke and maintain metsuke in your start position.

If you are applying a right-handed technique your right foot moves first. Do not take a small step with your left foot beforehand.

Do not lean forward to start your movement. Bend your knees and shift your weight onto your toes but keep your thighs and upper body vertical.

Control the movement of your arm so that when you reach uke you place your arm or hand (or hands as in ushiro ate) rather than make a hard contact. In shōmen ate for example, your slightly flexed arm acts like a spring and allows you to place your hand on his chin while moving at speed.

You can make this exercise more difficult by gradually increasing the distance to uke. Aim to increase your speed and range which gives you more control over maai.

i. Shōmen ate (pictures opposite)
1. Push off with your left leg and take a large step forward with your right foot, swinging your left arm forward and your right arm back to start your movement.

As you place your right foot onto the tatami, swing your right arm forward and your left arm back. Without stopping, slide your left foot up so that you finish in migigamae. Your right hand finishes a few centimetres in front of uke's chin with your elbow down and the U shape between your thumb and forefinger uppermost.

The timing is such that your hand stops in front of his chin at the same time as your body stops moving.

2. Go back to your start position. Repeat the movement described above and then, without stopping, place your hand on uke's chin and take a deep step forward with your right foot between uke's feet to push him back and down. Draw your left leg up to finish in a balanced posture.

ii. Aigamae ate (pictures on page 82)
1. To set up the correct start position, stand facing uke and then take one step to your left and slightly forward to maintain the original distance. Stand in mugamae. Uke stands with his feet together. Keep your body facing forward but turn your head to look towards him and maintain metsuke.

Your movement is the same as shōmen ate but the direction is at angle rather than straight ahead: push off with your left leg and take a large step forward with your right foot, swinging your left arm forward and your right arm back to start your movement.

Your right foot should come down onto the tatami just to the outside of his right foot. As you are placing your foot onto the tatami, swing your right arm forward and your left arm back. Without stopping, slide your left foot up so that you finish in migigamae. Your right hand finishes a few centimetres in front of uke's chin with your elbow down and the U shape between your thumb and forefinger uppermost.

The timing is such that your hand stops in front of his chin at the same time as your body stops moving.

2. Go back to your start position. Repeat the movement described above and then, without stopping, place your hand on uke's chin, bring his head into your centre and take a deep step forward with your right foot on the same line as your initial movement to push him back and down. Draw your left leg up to finish in a balanced posture.

81

82

83

84

85

iii. Gyakugamae ate (pictures on page 83)
1. To set up the correct start position, stand facing uke and then take one step to your right and slightly forward to maintain the original distance. Stand in mugamae. Uke stands with his feet together. Keep your body facing forward but turn your head to look towards him and maintain metsuke.

Turn on the balls of your feet to your left keeping your torso upright but flexing your knees and maintaining eye contact. As you do this, bring your right hand across to your left side.

Push off with your left leg and take a large step towards uke bringing your right arm over in a large vertical circle and turning back towards him as your arm comes down. Finish as close to him as possible with your arm across the top of his chest and your right foot just outside of his left foot. Without stopping, slide your left foot up so that you finish in migigamae. He leans back slightly to accommodate your arm which is in your centre.

The timing is such that you place your arm across his chest at the same time as your body stops moving.

2. Repeat this movement and then, without stopping, drive off with your left leg pushing uke back and down on the same line as your first movement.

Draw your left leg up to finish in a balanced posture.

iv. Gedan ate (pictures on page 84)
1. To set up the correct start position, stand facing uke and then take one step to your right and slightly forward to maintain the original distance. Stand in mugamae. Uke stands with his feet together. Keep your body facing forward but turn your head to look towards him and maintain metsuke.

Turn on the balls of your feet to your left keeping your torso upright but flexing your knees and maintaining eye contact. As you do this, bring your right hand across to your left side.

Keep your arm low and push off with your left foot taking a large step towards uke. As you move, start to turn your body back towards him and bring the inside of your arm low across his body. Finish as close to him as possible with your knees bent and your right foot just outside of his left foot but deeper behind him on the same line as your movement.

2. Repeat this movement and then, without stopping, drive off with your left leg and continue to turn to face uke as you push him back and down on the same line as your first movement.

Draw your left leg up to finish in a balanced posture.

v. Ushiro ate (pictures on page 85)
1. Face uke with both of you standing in mugamae. You both turn to the left so that you are facing in opposite directions but keep looking towards uke. This is the start position.

Push off with your left leg towards uke aiming to move as close to his back as possible. When your right foot comes down onto the tatami close to his right foot, draw your left leg up and turn to face the same direction as him.

Without stopping, continue moving until you are standing just to his left. As you move behind him bring your right hand up, following the line of his arm, onto his right shoulder and place your left hand onto his other shoulder.

2. Repeat this movement and then, without stopping, take two or three tsugi ashi movements at a 45° angle backwards and to the left using your body movement to throw uke. Draw your hands back to your right at shoulder height as you move.

2. Shōki no tsukuri
Your movements in shōki no tsukuri are the same as in hontai no tsukuri. The difference is that here you are adding an element of timing. Uke jumps up and down rhythmically with his feet together, feet apart, feet together and so on (pictures below) limiting the opportunities you have to move.

The aim is to move with the same speed and from the same distance as in hontai no tsukuri getting to the point of throwing at the instant uke's feet touch the tatami.

As in the previous drill, practice each technique twice: the first time as far as closing the distance to uke and the second time to include the throw. Practise left and right sides.

In shōmen ate, aim to reach uke just as he lands with his feet apart. For aigamae ate, gyakugamae ate and gedan ate aim to reach him when he lands with his feet together. For ushiro ate, because you are not moving between or beside his feet you can reach him when his feet touch the tatami either together or apart but normally it is when his feet are apart.

Coaching points
The movements are exactly the same as in the previous exercise, the difference is only in when to move.

Do not look at uke's feet, look at his eyes and use metsuke to see the whole of his body and judge when to move. Do not get into the habit of moving your body or nodding your head in time with his jumps. You should be motionless and then make one fast movement at the correct time.

Uke stops jumping as soon as you reach him so that you can judge the quality of your timing.

This drill can be adjusted to an individual's ability by changing the speed at which uke jumps and the distance from which you make your movement.

3. Shōki no tsukuri - extension 1
In hontai no tsukuri you are free to move whenever you like as the timing is not part of the drill. In shōki no tsukuri uke jumps up and down in one place giving you a chance to apply the technique every other jump. Although your opportunities to move are limited you are still able to choose when to move.

For this practice you are only presented with one opportunity to move because uke makes only a single jump from mugamae. In other words, the rhythm is broken and uke's single movement alone determines when you must move.

In this drill all atemi waza are applied from a start position where you are standing directly in front of uke in mugamae and at the correct distance. Aim to move quickly as soon as you see his movement. As before, always maintain eye contact and use peripheral vision to see his foot movement and the position of his feet. Close the distance quickly to get to the point of throwing that is, ideally, just as his feet touch the tatami. In practice though, unless you anticipate his movement, your reaction will be slower than his action so make your movement as early and as quickly as possible.

As above, practise these twice. The first time as far as setting up the technique (tsukuri) and the second time completing the technique (kake) to throw uke without stopping.

i. Shōmen ate
Uke jumps and lands with his feet apart. Move straight towards him as for shōmen ate in shōki no tsukuri.

ii. Aigamae ate
Uke jumps and lands with his right foot forward. Move as for shōmen ate in shōki no tsukuri but slightly to uke's right side so that your right foot is outside his right foot. Bring your right hand to your centre.

iii. Gyakugamae ate
Uke jumps and lands with his left foot forward. Move towards him as for gyakugamae ate in shōki no tsukuri slightly to uke's left side so that your right foot is outside his left foot. Bring your right hand to your centre.

iv. Gedan ate
Uke jumps and lands with his left foot forward. Move towards him as for gedan ate in shōki no tsukuri slightly to uke's left so that your right foot is outside his left foot. Bring your right arm low across his body.

v. Ushiro ate
Uke jumps and turns so that he is facing to his right with his feet apart. It is not possible to move deep to uke's right side with a single step so, as in hontai no tsukuri and shōki no tsukuri, take two steps to cover the distance stepping forward with your left foot first.

This drill can be made more difficult by uke randomly adding a feint before his jump to disrupt your timing and movement.

A common reaction to a feint is to start your movement, realise that it is only a feint and then stop. This leaves you momentarily immobile or even unbalanced if you have not managed to stop your movement quickly enough.

There are two responses to a feint. The first is to ignore it because it is not a threat. In this case, you remain balanced and ready to move. This is usually the aim during this exercise.

The alternative is to treat a feint as a suppressed attack. In other words, think of it as a genuine attack and respond accordingly.

This has direct applications in randori where often tantō will feint a stab to disrupt your balance or mobility and immediately follow up with a genuine stab. Either ignore the feint to maintain your position and maai or consider it as the start of a genuine stab and close the distance to apply a technique.

4. Shōki no tsukuri - extension 2
We can expand on the previous exercise by removing the expectation of which technique you will be applying. In this drill uke is allowed to jump into any of the four positions in the previous exercise as he chooses. Now you have to decide which technique to apply and then move as quickly as possible. Your movements are also the same as in the previous drill.

Practise first by restricting uke's jumps so that you only use your right hand to apply the atemi waza. Then restrict his jumps so that you only use your left hand. Practising this way forces you to use your less favoured hand.

Next, allow uke to jump into any position where you are allowed to use either hand to apply the most expedient atemi waza for his position.

Uke can then add a feint at random to make it more difficult.

5. Tsukuri from tai sabaki

An alternative path to developing atemi waza is to build the exercise against a shōmen uchi attack. This teaches how to apply atemi waza when uke withdraws in preparation for a second attack after you have avoided his initial attack. This is a separate timing opportunity to that used in shōki no tsukuri (which is related more to the point at which uke starts an attack) but the principle of catching the timing while uke is immobile is the same.

It is split into four stages:

i. tai sabaki
Avoid the shōmen uchi through body movement to nullify the attack. In terms of this practice, this is the time to get accustomed to the speed and distance of uke's movement.

ii. irimi
After you have avoided uke's attack he immediately moves straight back to prepare for a further attack. Move in and close the distance to him as he withdraws.

iii. tsukuri
Uke attacks and you avoid as above. Apply one of the atemi waza to the point of throwing as he withdraws.

iv. kake
As for tsukuri and then finish the technique to throw uke without stopping.

i. Tai sabaki

Stand in mugamae facing uke at the correct distance. Uke attacks using shōmen uchi. The right handed attack is shown overleaf (and is used in the descriptions for all stages of this drill).

Uke stands with his right foot forward and right hand held low in his centre (picture 1 overleaf).

He raises his hand on his centre line (picture 2 overleaf) and pushes forward with his left leg immediately cutting down with his hand blade to your forehead (picture 3 overleaf).

Uke controls his attack so that his hand stops just short of your forehead and he is standing in a balanced, stable posture. Even when you have avoided his attack he must retain this degree of control with his arm. The timing is such that his hand stops at the instant his right foot comes down onto the tatami.

Aim to avoid his attack by moving only at the last instant irrespective of whether he attacks slowly or quickly. The later you move the more difficult it is for him to change the direction of his attack. This point is relevant to randori where your aim is to move as late as possible so you retain the advantage and give tantō as little opportunity as possible to change the direction of his stab.

The directions of avoidance are to the sides and corners. Moving straight back is not included here because, although it is possible to avoid a stab in randori by moving straight back, you are not avoiding the line of attack and tantō is likely to stab again so at some stage you will have to move away from the this line.

These six movements are an application of the side and corner movements from unsoku. Unsoku is a basic solitary exercise so your stance after each movement is mugamae but this drill involves a partner so you have to adjust your footwork to ensure that your centre is angled towards him. In addition, working with a partner means that you must use metsuke to judge when and how to move.

When uke attacks (with his right hand in the examples that follow) move in one of the following six directions. They are usually practised in this order:

- Left
  Push off with your right leg and slide your left foot to your left immediately following with your right foot. Turn slightly to your right as you move so that your centre is towards uke and your feet are angled towards him as in migigamae. You should move directly to the left and not come forward from your start position.

- Right
  As above but move to the right.

- Front left corner
  Push off with your right leg and slide your left foot forward and to your left immediately following with your right foot. Turn to your right as you move so that your centre is towards uke. Your feet are angled towards him as in hidarigamae but further apart. Turn your shoulders enough to clear the attack but stay close to uke's arm.

- Front right corner
  As above but move to the right.

- Rear left corner
  Slide your right foot back and to your left immediately following with your left foot. Turn

Six directions of tai sabaki
1. Left, to the outside of the attack (top left picture)
2. Right, to the inside of the attack (top right picture)
3. Front left corner, to the outside of the attack (centre left picture)
4. Front right corner, to the inside of the attack (centre right picture)
5. Rear left corner, to the outside of the attack (bottom left picture)
6. Rear right corner, to the inside of the attack (bottom right picture)

to your right as you move so that your centre is towards uke. Your feet are angled towards him as in hidarigamae but further apart. Your body naturally turns a little as you sweep your right foot back.

- Rear right corner
  As above but move to the right.

Each attack and avoidance must be a quick, sharp movement. After each one, return to your start positions and pause before practising the next movement. Practise these movements and those in the following stages against left-handed and right-handed attacks.

ii. Irimi

The next stage builds on the previous movements. After uke has made his attack and you have avoided he immediately withdraws straight back and lowers his arm in order to make a further attack. As he withdraws move in towards his centre and close the distance to him.

Uke makes two distinct moves in his attack and withdrawal, and is static momentarily while changing direction. In contrast, your aim is to avoid and enter (irimi) in one continuous movement without stopping. Do this by not letting your weight settle after your initial avoidance.

Finish your entering movement at the same time as uke finishes moving back, matching his movement in terms of speed, distance and timing. This can be viewed as an application of the principle of non-resistance.

Your entering movement prevents uke's second attack and is also connected to the movements required to apply atemi waza and kansetsu waza. With uke's fast attack and retreat this is a good way to improve the speed and depth of your body movement and your timing.

These movements are illustrated opposite and overleaf from just after the avoidance of the initial attack as described above. They are usually practised in the order illustrated.

- Left (pictures on opposite page top row)
  Move to your left side to avoid his attack and, without stopping, move your right foot and right shoulder in towards uke's centre as he withdraws. Follow up with your left foot and turn into hanmi to ensure that your upper arm touches him. Keep your right foot moving after your initial avoidance and move it immediately towards him as he goes back.

- Right (pictures on opposite page second row)
  Move to you right side to avoid his attack and, without stopping, move your left foot and left shoulder in towards uke's centre as he withdraws. Follow up with your right foot and turn into hanmi to ensure that your upper arm touches him. Keep your left foot moving after your initial avoidance and move it immediately towards him as he goes back.

95

- Front left corner (pictures on page 95 third row)
  Step forward deeply and slightly to the left of the attack turning your shoulders and keeping close to uke's arm. Without stopping, step forward deeply with your right foot as he withdraws turning into hanmi and finishing back to back with him.

The front left movement is different from the others in that for every other movement, after avoiding the attack, the nearest foot (and shoulder) to uke is the one that you move towards him. It is not incorrect in this case to move your left foot and shoulder towards him as this can be used in randori to close distance effectively. However, for this drill you are aiming to incorporate all five atemi waza so moving in with your right side in this case ensures that ushiro ate can be used (see the next stage).

- Front right corner (pictures on page 95 bottom row)
  Move to your front right corner to avoid the attack by stepping with your right foot first and then left foot. Push off with your left foot as soon as you place it on the tatami and move your right foot and right shoulder in towards uke's centre as he withdraws. Follow up with your left foot and turn into hanmi to ensure that your upper arm touches him.

- Rear left corner (pictures top tow)
  Sweep your right foot back and to the left following it with your left foot to avoid the

attack. Push off with your right foot as soon as you place it on the tatami and move your left foot and left shoulder in towards uke's centre as he withdraws. Follow up with your right foot and turn into hanmi to ensure that your upper arm touches him.

- Rear right corner (pictures on opposite page second row)
  Sweep your left foot back and to the right following it with your right foot to avoid the attack. Push off with your left foot as soon as you place it on the tatami and move your right foot and right shoulder in towards uke's centre as he withdraws. Follow up with your left foot and turn into hanmi to ensure that your upper arm touches him.

Do not move back too far in your initial avoidance for the two rear corner movements as this creates too great a distance to cover when uke withdraws.

iii. Tsukuri

Your footwork for tsukuri is the same as for irimi, the difference is in the use of your hands. In irimi you move towards uke and turn one shoulder towards him; in the tsukuri practice instead of turning your nearest shoulder towards him you use the nearest arm to prepare to apply one of the five atemi waza. The nearest hand and foot to uke indicate the least distance to travel and therefore the fastest application of a technique.

When uke finishes moving back his weight is coming down onto the tatami and for a short time he is immobile. This is when you should also be finishing your movement taking advantage of this timing opportunity to break his balance in preparation for a technique.

You should make your avoidance and entering movement to set up the technique a single continuous movement as much as possible. Control your forward movement so that you match uke's movement back and reach the point of applying the technique when his feet come to rest. You must also control the placement of your hand or arm on uke's body so that there is no hard contact.

It should be noted that for the all avoidance to the right (from a right handed shōmen uchi) shōmen ate is always used. You are positioned in front of uke each time and the technique is the same whether applied with the left or right hand. This leaves three further tai sabaki movements and four remaining techniques to include all five atemi waza into this practice. Therefore, the rear left corner tai sabaki is repeated finishing with gedan ate.

These movements are shown from just after the avoidance of the initial attack as described above.

- Left – aigamae ate (pictures on page 99 top row)
  After your avoidance, move towards uke as he withdraws and bring your right hand straight up to his chin. This requires uke to lower his hand quickly when he moves back to avoid a contact between your arm coming up and his arm coming down.

- Right – shōmen ate (pictures on opposite page second row)
  After your avoidance, move towards uke as he withdraws and bring your left hand straight up to his chin.

- Front left corner – ushiro ate (pictures on opposite page third row)
  After you have moved behind uke so you are back to back, turn to your right and place your right hand on his left shoulder. Move back slightly to break his balance. You are aiming to pull him so that he falls to your right side.

- Front right corner – shōmen ate (pictures on opposite page bottom row)
  After your avoidance, move towards uke as he withdraws and bring your right hand straight up to his chin.

- Rear left corner – gyakugamae ate (pictures on page 100 top row)
  After your avoidance, move towards uke as he withdraws and bring your left hand straight up to his left temple. Turn your hand so that you are placing the soft part of the palm below your little finger onto his temple.

- Rear right corner – shōmen ate (pictures on page 100 middle row)
  After your avoidance, move towards uke as he withdraws and bring your right hand straight up to his chin.

- Rear left corner – gedan ate (pictures on page 100 bottom row)
  After your avoidance, move towards uke as he withdraws and bring your left arm low across his body.

You should also practise these against an uke who is attacking with his left hand.

iv. Kake
The final stage continues from the tsukuri above to finish with the final application of the throw. Once you have completed the tsukuri continue to apply the technique without stopping using your body movement to throw him. There are no pictures to illustrate this.

Kake is an opportunity for uke to practise ukemi. You can adjust the speed and intensity of your throws according to the ability of your partner.

Also practise these against someone who is attacking with his left hand.

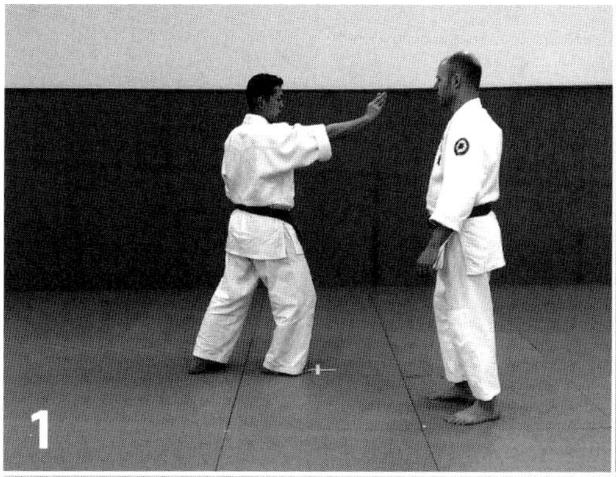
1
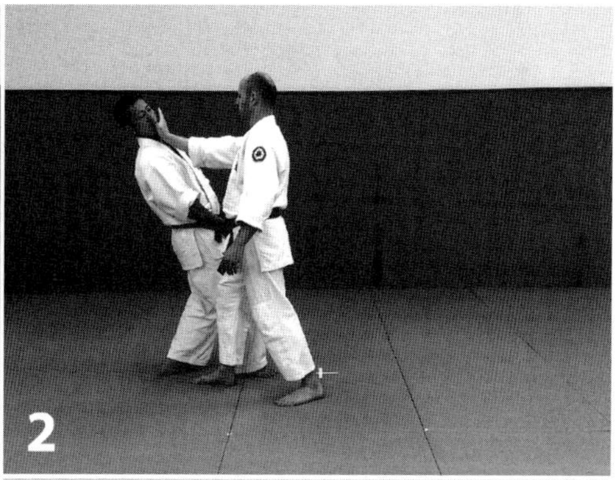
2
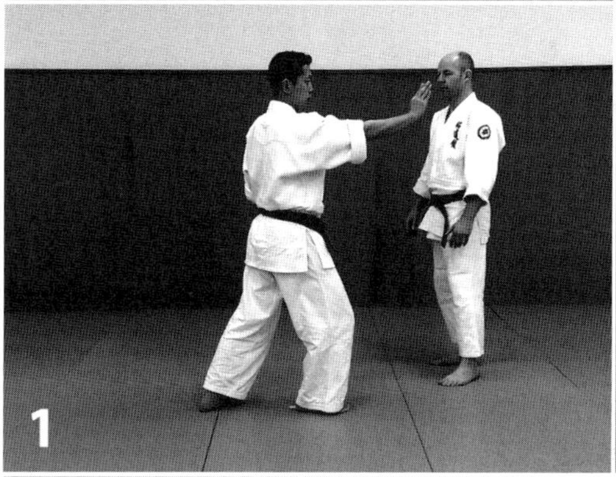
1
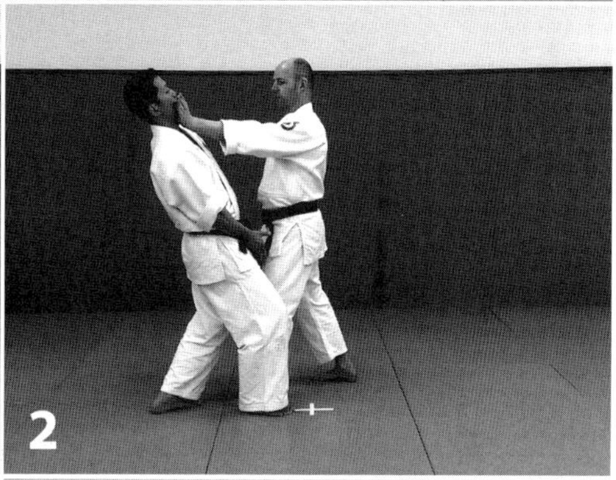
2
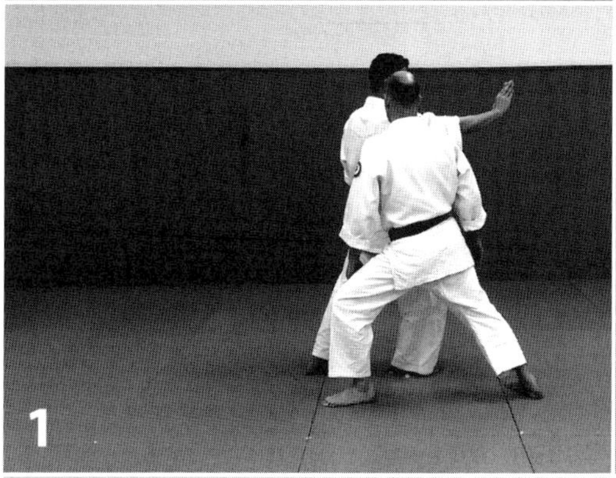
1
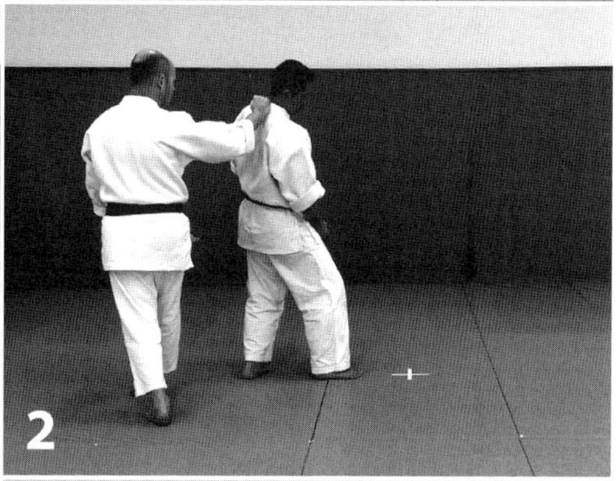
2
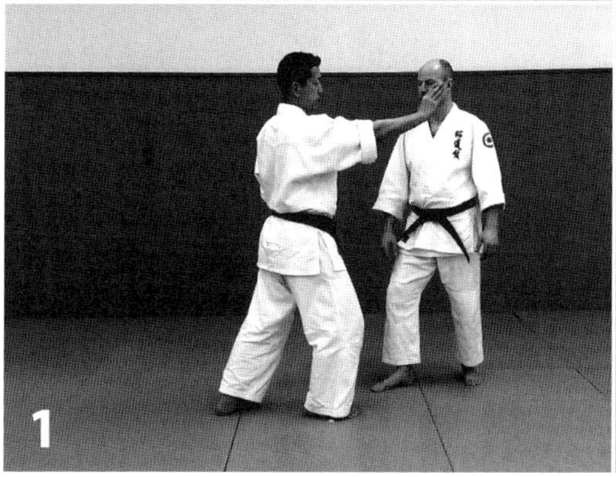
1
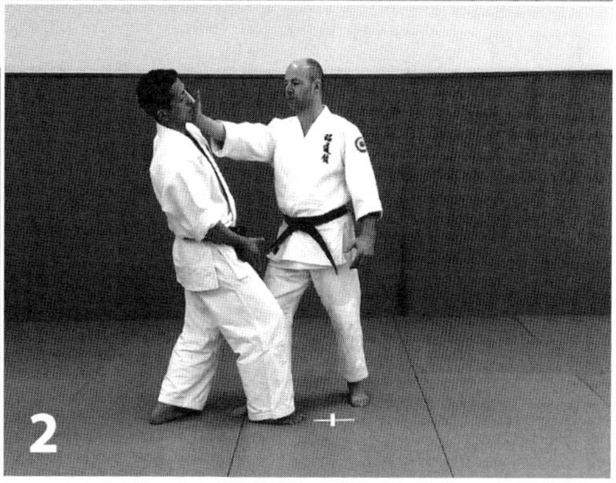
2

Atemi waza - tsukuri from tai sabaki
Left side followed by aigamae ate (page 99 top row)
Right side followed by shōmen ate (page 99 second row)
Front left corner followed by ushiro ate (page 99 third row)
Front right corner followed by shōmen ate (page 99 bottom row)
Rear left corner followed by gyakugamae ate (top row)
Rear right corner followed by shōmen ate (middle row)
Rear left corner followed by gedan ate (bottom row)

TIMING OPPORTUNITIES AGAINST TANTŌ TSUKI

The five atemi waza are described for each of the timing opportunities introduced earlier.

Practise every technique twice. The first time is as far as tsukuri, moving to the point of throwing where tantō's balance is broken and then stopping. The second time, complete the technique by throwing tantō without stopping. The pictures show the techniques as far as tsukuri. Remember to practise left and right sides.

Okori o utsu

To make an effective stab tantō must flex his legs before moving forward. This preparatory movement only lasts for a short time and can be very subtle if he is already poised to strike. Added to this the fact that you are separated from him and have some distance to cover, it is very difficult to take advantage of this timing opportunity. However, seeing his habitual, telltale movements just before his stab can help to give you more time. His feint or movement forward a little to gain an advantage over the maai also give you the same opportunity to attack.

This timing opportunity is the same as the shōki no tsukuri – extension 1 exercise. Uke stays in one place and you move towards him reaching him at the instant he finishes his preparatory movement. The difference is that in this drill uke is holding a tantō so your movement to reach him cannot be straight towards him. You must move off of the line of his intended attack even if he does not actually make the stab.

Tantō can emphasise his movement to assist in this practice. He can either stand in mugamae and then move to his preparatory position with one foot forward (previous page top row) or he can stand ready with one foot forward and sink his weight (previous page bottom row). The second option is a quicker, less obvious movement so makes this exercise more difficult.

i. Shōmen ate
In shōki no tsukuri, uke's feet are side by side whereas here tantō is standing with one foot forward. This alters the line of his weakest direction. In this case, the weakest line is to his rear right corner and your feet should be lined up in that direction.

A more important difference arises with your direction of movement. In shōki no tsukuri you move straight towards uke which is the quickest direction in which to move. This is not possible here because you have to avoid the intended line of attack of the tantō. Move slightly to tantō's left away from the line of attack as you close the distance to him and finish facing to his rear right corner as in the basic shōmen ate.

ii. Aigamae ate
Move in a straight line slightly to tantō's right side so that your right foot is outside his right foot and your body is away from the line of attack.

iii. Gyakugamae ate
Move slightly to tantō's right side so that your left foot is outside his right foot and your body is away from the line of attack. Use your left arm across his chest or take the soft part of the palm your left hand below your little finger to his temple.

iv. Gedan ate
Move slightly to tantō's right side so that your left foot is outside his right foot and your body is away from the line of attack. This is a difficult technique to achieve with this timing because of the distance you have to move to get to the final position with your arm across his body.

v. Ushiro ate
You have no time to make two steps to move deep behind tantō. Therefore, you have to make a single step just to his right side away from the line of attack and use your left hand on his left shoulder. The aim is to make him fall to your left side.

Tsukitaru o utsu
Tantō's foot comes down onto the tatami at the same time as his arm reaches full extension. At that instant he is committing his weight to one place and although he is balanced he is immobile and therefore vulnerable to an attack. This is the moment you are aiming to apply your technique.

Clearly, because tantō is making his stab you have to move off of the line of attack and control his stab with one hand while the other hand applies the technique. It is important to use both hands as it is difficult to apply a technique without using tegatana to control his stab.

Okori o utsu

Shōmen ate (right)
Aigamae ate (page 104 left column)
Gyakugamae ate (page 104 right column)
Gedan ate (page 105 left column)
Ushiro ate (page 105 right column)

103

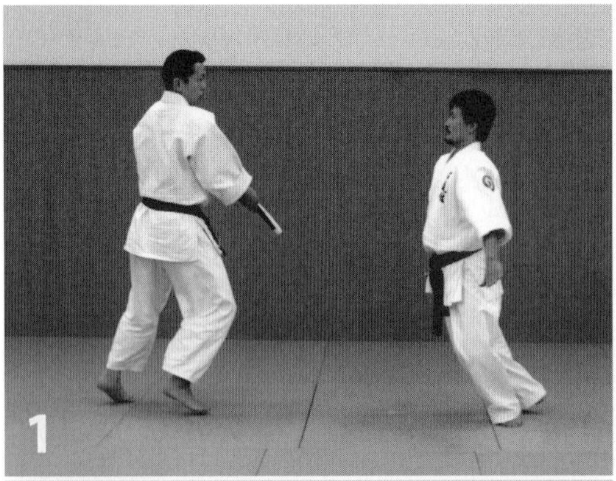
1
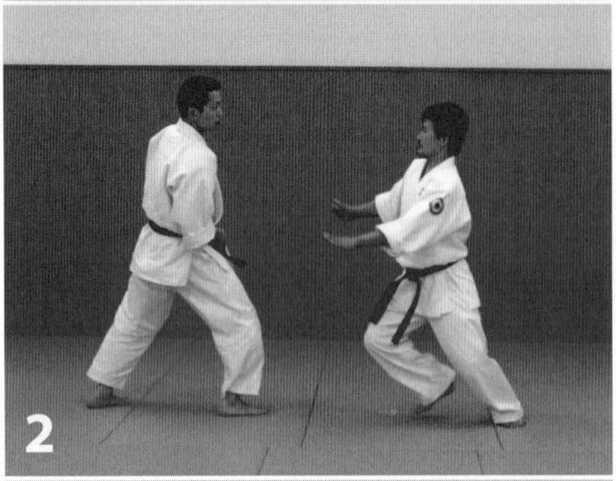
2
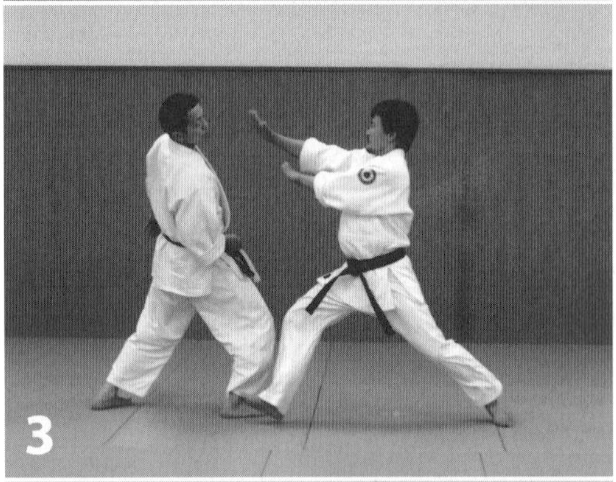
3
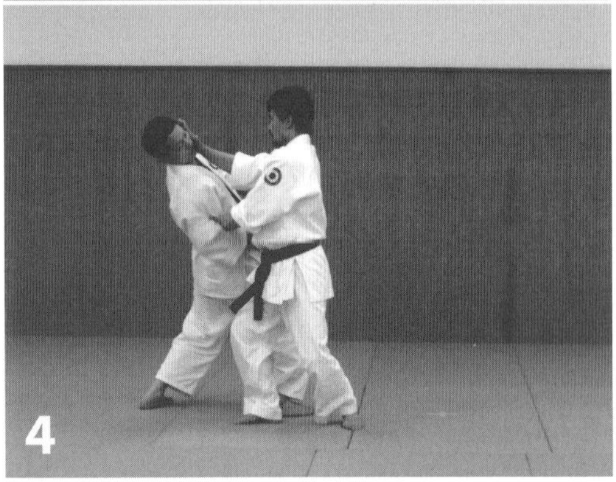
4
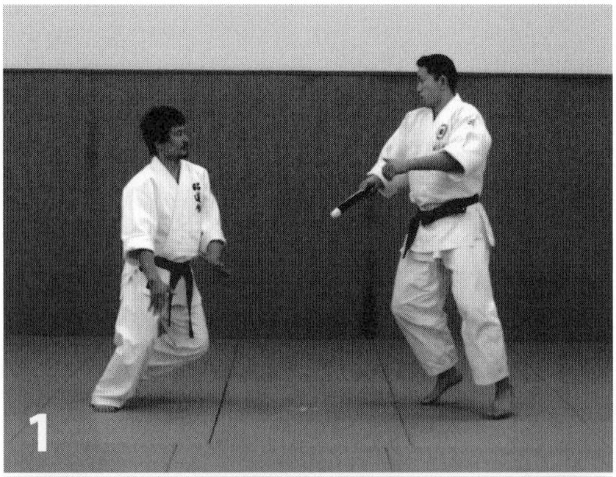
1
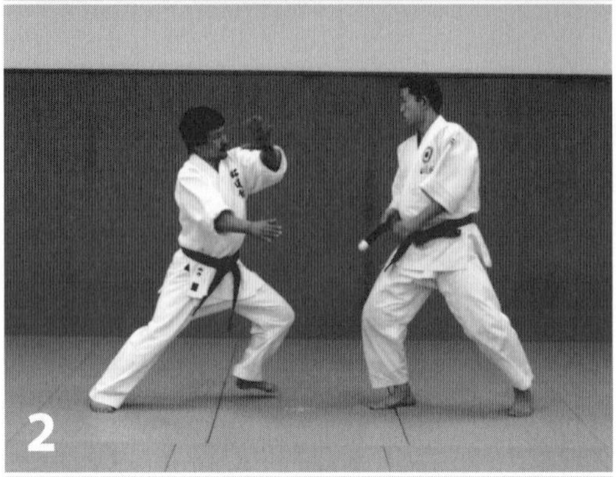
2
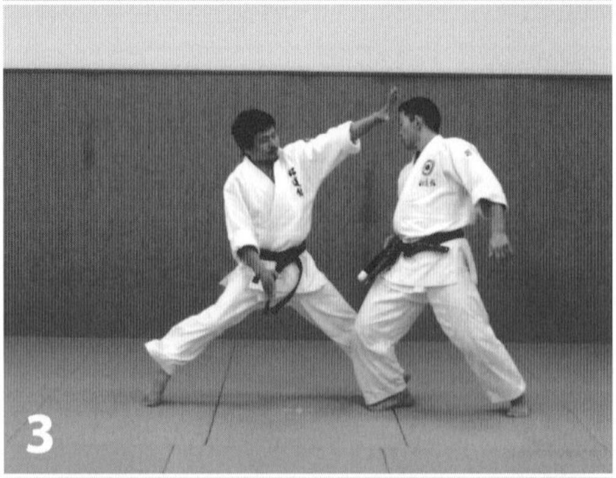
3
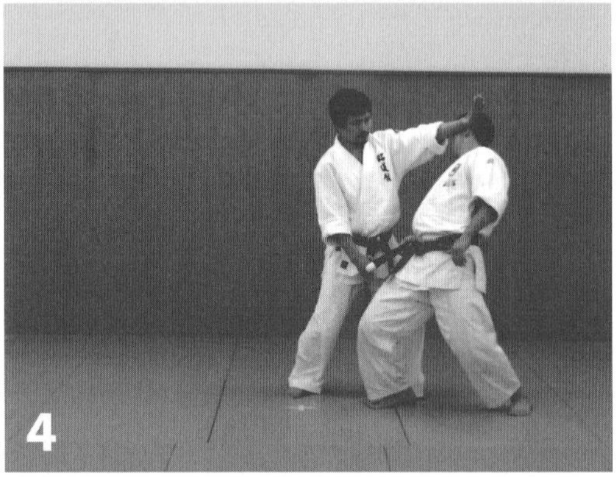
4

105

The depth of your forward movement is less than in okori o utsu as tantō is moving towards you. This is the easiest and most commonly exploited timing opportunity for atemi waza because stabbing you is one of tantō's aims. He closes the distance so you have less distance to travel and you have more time. It is perhaps also the timing chance that most people are aware of and more likely to defend against by not fully committing themselves with the stab.

This can be practised by tantō starting in a ready position and then making a single tsugi ashi movement towards you to make a straight stab (pictures above).

i. Shōmen ate
As tantō attacks, move forward and to the right avoiding the line of attack. Move your right hand directly to his jaw and use your left arm between your body and his arm in a clockwise sweeping movement similar to that in kesa uchi (pictures 3 and 4) from tegatana dōsa.

ii. Aigamae ate
Move straight to tantō's right side so that your left foot is outside his right foot and you are avoiding his line of attack. Use the tegatana of your left hand to control his arm and place your right hand on his chin. You can have either foot forward at the point of contact with uke.

iii. Gyakugamae ate
Move forward and to the left as tantō stabs. Bring your left hand directly to his temple and use your right arm between your body and his arm in an anti-clockwise sweeping movement similar to that in kesa uchi (pictures 3 and 4) from tegatana dōsa.

iv. Gedan ate
This is a difficult technique to apply because, although the distance you have to move is less than in okori o utsu, you have to get underneath the stab. This is made easier if tantō tends to stab high but it still requires a good sense of timing.

As his stabs turn to your right and move forward deeply bringing your left arm over and down to set up your position just before your throw. Keep your torso upright as much as possible and bend your legs.

Tsukitaru o utsu

Shōmen ate (right)
Aigamae ate (page 108 left column)
Gyakugamae ate (page 108 right column)
Gedan ate (page 109 left column)
Ushiro ate (page 109 right column)

108

109

v. Ushiro ate

As tantō stabs move forward and to the left using your right arm between your body and his arm in an anti-clockwise, sweeping movement similar to that in kesa uchi (pictures 2 and 3) from tegatana dōsa. Aim to move deeply so that you can get behind him. As you complete this movement bring your left hand onto his left shoulder and your right hand up under his armpit. The aim is to throw him to your right side.

In this basic practice it is important that tantō makes a straight stab. After you have moved he must continue to stab to the position where you were originally standing.

Hikiokori o utsu

After tantō's ineffective stab, usually after you have avoided it (picture 1 below), his next move is to withdraw to make a second attack (picture 2 below). Move at the same time as he moves back and close the distance to him. When he finishes moving and his weight settles on his back foot he is momentarily immobile. This is the instant that you reach him and get to the point of applying your technique.

Picture 1 below shows toshu using tegatana when avoiding the initial attack. In this basic practice tantō stabs straight to where you are standing initially, even after you have moved, so you should be able to avoid the tantō with or without using tegatana. However, it should be noted that in situations when tantō intends to stab you it is very difficult to avoid his attack purely by using body movement.

This timing opportunity is the same as that used in the atemi waza tsukuri practice from tai sabaki. In terms of difficulty, this is easier than the okori o utsu timing but more difficult than the tsukitaru o utsu timing.

i. Shōmen ate

Move to your right as tantō attacks. At the end of your avoidance your weight will be on your right foot. Keep your left foot moving, stepping towards him as he withdraws and bringing your left hand up to his chin.

Hikiokori o utsu

Shōmen ate (right)
Aigamae ate (page 112 left column)
Gyakugamae ate (page 112 right column)
Gedan ate (page 113 left column)
Ushiro ate (page 113 right column)

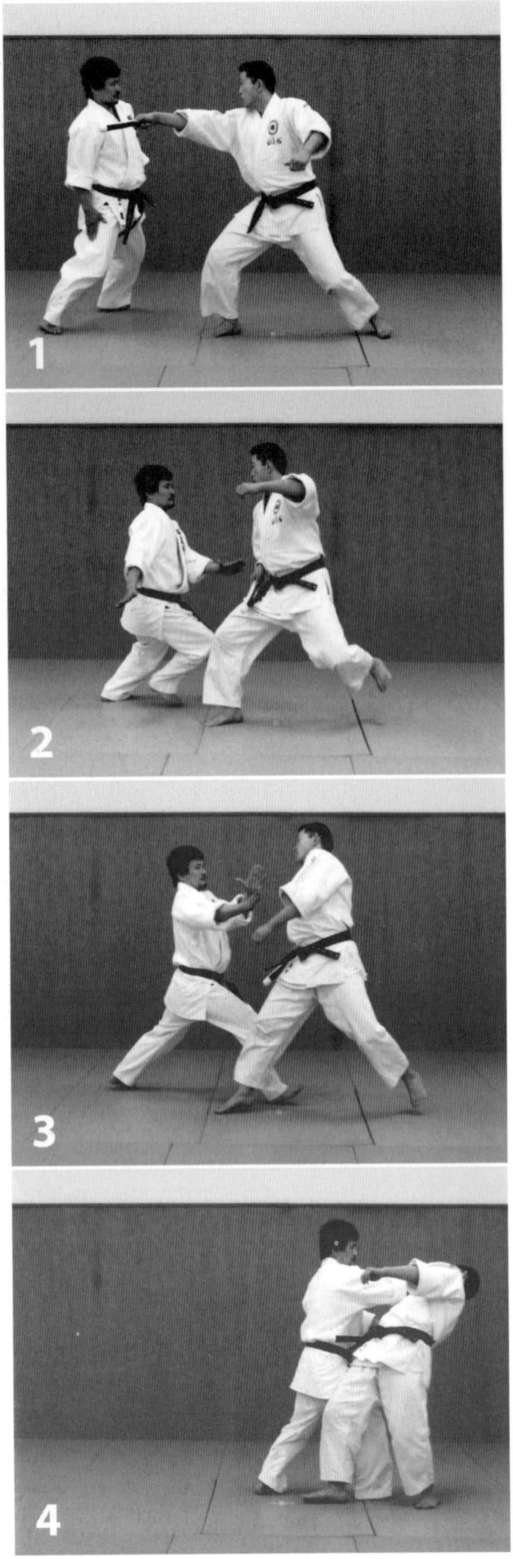
1
2
3
4

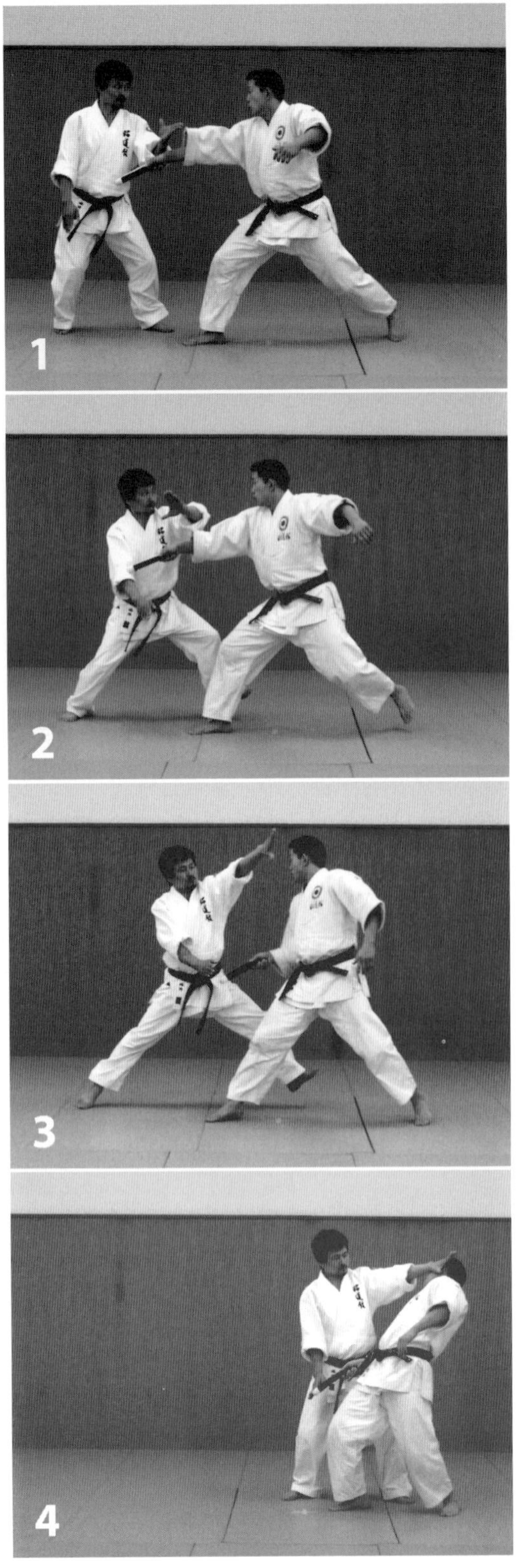
1
2
3
4

113

ii. Aigamae ate
Move to the left as tantō attacks. As he withdraws move towards him taking your right hand to his jaw and slide your left hand blade to the inside of his elbow to control his arm.

iii. Gyakugamae ate
Move forward and to your left using your left hand blade to control tantō's attack. Move towards him taking your left hand to his left temple ready to apply gyakugamae ate as he withdraws.

iv. Gedan ate
Move forward and to your left using your left hand to control tantō's attack. Move towards him taking your left arm low across his body as he withdraws.

v. Ushiro ate
Move forward and to your left using your left hand blade to control tantō's attack. Move to his right side as he withdraws keeping close to him and placing your left hand onto his left shoulder. The aim is to throw tantō to your left side.

Ōjitaru o utsu
This timing chance is created by you rather than by tantō. It starts from either a genuine atemi waza or a feint from you and can be considered as a combination of one atemi waza leading into another.

As tantō moves away in defence follow him with an atemi waza suitable for his position and stance. In general, to achieve a fast transition between the techniques, apply the first technique with one hand and the second technique with the other. Two examples are given below.

To practise this, start at the correct distance from tantō in migigamae or hidarigamae. Move towards him to apply one of the atemi waza. As he steps to avoid your attack, make a smooth change into another atemi waza.

i. Gyakugamae ate to aigamae ate (pictures on opposite page left column)
Start with your left foot forward. Move to attack tantō using gyakugamae ate with your left hand. As he makes a tsugi ashi movement back to avoid your attack step forward with your right foot and apply aigamae ate with your right hand.

ii. Gyakugamae ate to gyakugamae ate (pictures on opposite page right column)
Start with your left foot forward. Move to attack tantō using gyakugamae ate with your left hand. As he steps back to avoid your attack step forward with your right foot and apply gyakugamae ate with your right hand.

115

KANSETSU WAZA

Kansetsu waza are joint techniques applied specifically to the wrist and elbow joints. There is of course a close physiological relationship between the wrist and elbow that has a deep effect on the efficiency of techniques. Pay attention to the position of the elbow as well as the wrist when applying wrist techniques and also consider the wrist when applying elbow techniques. Think about transmitting your power through your opponent's wrist to his elbow, shoulder and body. Kansetsu waza are intended to prevent the opponent from moving rather than to be overly painful so practise with this in mind to develop the required level of control. The key is to have good body movement combined with the ability to adapt to the opponent's movements.

As with the atemi waza, kansetsu waza are applied with movement and applying a force in one direction through one point of contact. Instead of applications that damage joints we think in terms of balance breaking principles and mechanical weak points. Break an opponent's balance by attacking his wrist or elbow and then taking advantage of his weakened position or immobility to apply a technique. In judo, kansetsu waza include groundwork whereas in aikido randori they are applied only while standing (although placing one knee on the tatami is allowed).

Kansetsu waza are split into three subgroups:
- hiji waza (elbow techniques)
- tekubi waza (wrist techniques)
- uki waza (floating techniques)

In randori, kansetsu waza are most effective when used against an opponent whose body is not stiff.

KIHON HIJI WAZA

Tomiki carefully selected the hiji waza (and tekubi waza) from old styles of jujutsu and with reference to Daitō-ryū Aiki-jūjutsu. They can be seen in judo randori and the koshiki no kata in Kōdōkan judo for example.

There are six hiji waza divided into two groups of three. These are shown below with the corresponding koshiki no kata technique.

Group	Technique	Koshiki no kata
oshi taoshi	oshi taoshi	mizu guruma
oshi taoshi	ude gaeshi	mizu guruma
oshi taoshi	waki gatame	mizu guruma
hiki taoshi	hiki taoshi	mizu nagare
hiki taoshi	ude hineri	hiki otoshi
hiki taoshi	waki gatame	mizu nagare

There are two versions of waki gatame. The first one, in the oshi taoshi group, is included in the basic kata of 17 techniques and is described below. The second one is applied after a reaction from uke during hiki taoshi. Either can be used in randori as well as any other variations and combinations with other techniques.

6. Oshi taoshi (pictures page 119)
Step to your left with your left foot and follow with your right foot so that you are about 30° from your original line. Keep your right foot forward, your right hand in your centre and facing uke.

With your hands held together grasp his forearm a little above his wrist. Your right hand holds firmly and your left hand is loose. Keep your arms straight and take a small tsugi ashi back. At the same time, twist his arm using your right hand to raise his elbow and slide your left hand down around his arm as much as possible.

Change your grip so that you hold with your left hand and your right hand is loose. Without pausing from the last movement make a tsugi ashi forward on the same 30° angle from your original line. As you move, slide your right hand around his arm so that the palm of your hand is on the inside of his wrist. At the end of this movement his arm is raised towards his face.

Slide your left hand to the inside of his elbow. Keep your left arm straight and push towards his ear stepping with your left foot in the direction you are facing. Just as your left foot passes by his left foot start to move slightly to your left behind him but remain facing the same way. Aim to push him forward and down in a large movement rather than straight down.

Once he has fallen to his hands and knees make a tsugi ashi movement to close any distance between your left leg and his armpit.

Step up with your right foot and step back and away from his body with your left foot. Place his arm on top of your leg just above the knee with your thumb on the outside of your leg. The angle between your leg and his arm is 90°, the angle between his arm and his body is much greater than 90°. Your right leg is bent and your left leg is straight. Your open left hand rests gently on his elbow.

Coaching points
Uke must not give up and fall too early. He must remain facing towards you until he has no choice but to turn and fall.

In the finish position your right hand is placed outside of your leg to help prevent him pulling his arm back. Your other hand is resting on his elbow to prevent him standing. His arm is raised towards his head and you are positioned so that your back leg is away from his body preventing him from bringing his leg behind you.

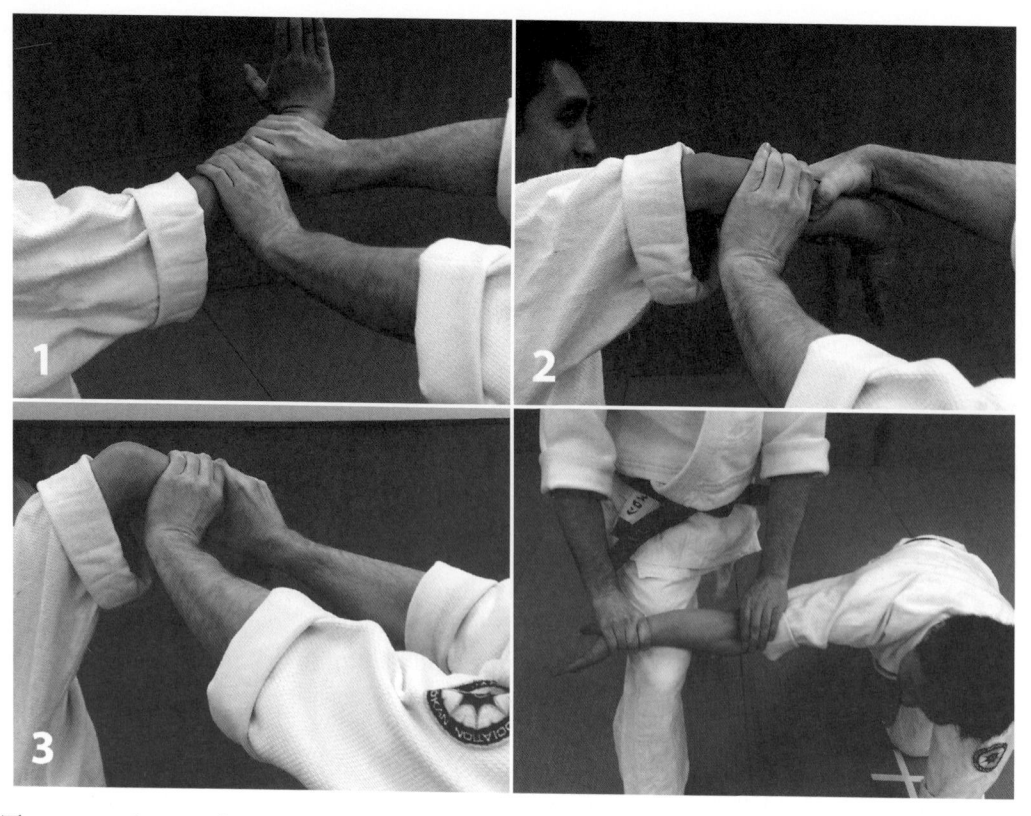

The manipulation of your hands on uke's arm is shown above. Grasp his forearm just above the elbow with both hands held close together (picture 1).

Use your right hand to rotate uke's arm so that his elbow is raised. As you do this, slide your left hand around his arm in the direction of your thumb (picture 2).

Hold his arm with your left hand and slide your right hand around his arm in the direction of your thumb as you push his arm up (picture 3).

The finish position is shown in the bottom right picture. Uke is on his knees supporting himself with one arm while the other is extended and raised towards his head so that it is well away from his body. Hold his wrist and place his arm just above your knee with your thumb on the outside of your leg. Your left hand is placed lightly on his elbow. Your right leg is bent and your left leg is straight. The angle between your centre line and his arm is 90° so that your left leg is away from his legs.

7. Ude gaeshi (pictures page 121)
Step to your left with your left foot and follow with your right foot so that you are about 30° from your original line. Keep your right foot forward, your right hand in your centre and facing uke.

119

With both hands held together grasp uke's forearm a little above the wrist. Keep your arms straight and take a small tsugi ashi movement back. At the same time turn slightly to the left and draw his elbow up and away from his body.

Uke reacts by dropping his elbow. As he does, turn your body slightly back to the right to face him, open your left hand with your thumb down and slide it over his arm as far as your wrist. Bring your right hand over to fold his arm over the top of your left arm and bring your left tegatana into the space between his arm and your forearm.

Continue this large movement taking his arm over his shoulder and down the centre of his back. At the same time take a deep step forward with your left foot to his right side following up with your right foot to maintain your balance with your hands in your centre and at shoulder height. In this position uke should be arching backwards and unable to push against you.

Without stopping make a further tsugi ashi movement and open your right hand to release uke so that he can fall. Keep your hands at shoulder height to finish.

Coaching points
Uke must not fall too quickly. He arches back as much as possible and falls only when you release your grip on his arm.

It is important to direct his arm down the centre of his back rather than away from his body so that you break his balance but significantly reduce the risk of injury to his shoulder. The technique effectively ends when you have taken his arm behind him and his is arching back. He should not be able to stand upright from this position.

The picture below left shows the position after uke has reacted and dipped his elbow. Open your left hand and slide it on top of his arm as far as your wrist.

The picture below right shows the position just before the throw. Keep your arms at chest height and direct uke's arm as much as possible down the centre of his back so that he is arching back.

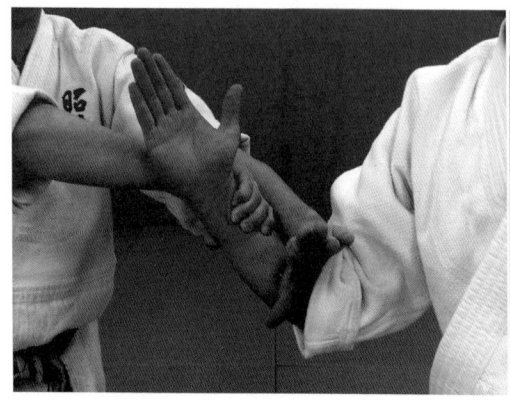

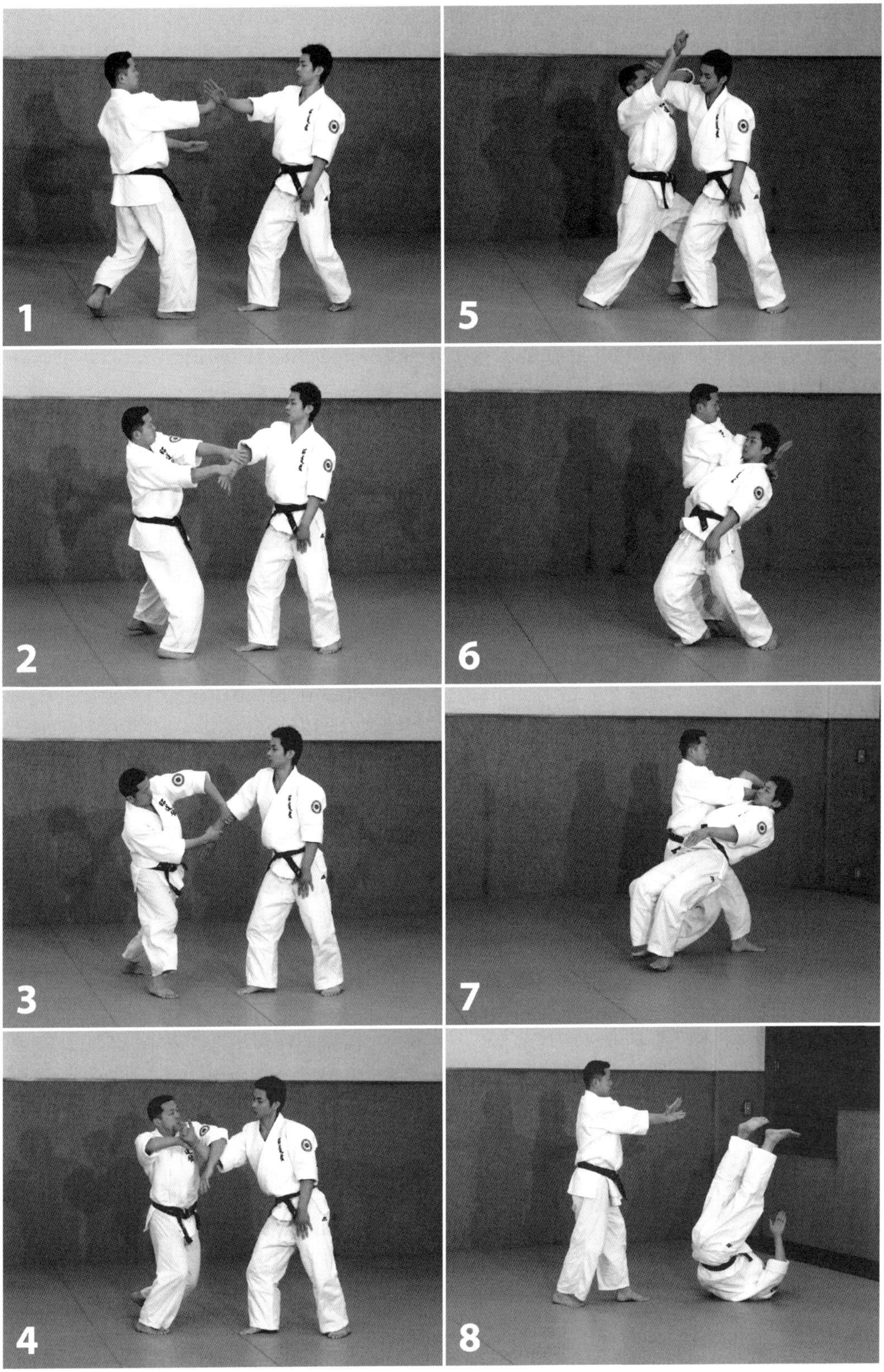
1
2
3
4
5
6
7
8

8. Hiki taoshi

Move your right foot forward slightly and raise uke's hand a little with your tegatana. Bring your left hand palm up underneath his arm and grasp his wrist with both hands.

Make a tsugi ashi movement straight back and bring your arms down low by taking them in a large clockwise circular movement. In this position his balance is broken enough so that he touches the tatami with his left hand. The movement of your hands finishes so that they are to the left of your body resulting in his elbow being in your centre.

Let go with your right hand, turn it thumb down and place it on his elbow. Push down as you make two or three tsugi ashi straight back until he is lying face down. Extend and hold his arm above his head and close to your right leg. Your right leg is bent and left leg straight.

Coaching points

Relative to you, the initial direction of the pull on uke's arm is to your right, 90° to the centre line between you and uke. This keeps his arm extended and affects his balance immediately by turning his shoulders. This not only affects his posture as soon as you move but is much safer. Moving his arm towards him not only has no immediate effect on his posture it also means that when you pull his arm down it snaps straight which can lead to a whiplash injury if this is done at speed.

The initial grip on uke's arm with the left hand reaching underneath as far as possible and the right hand on top is shown below left. The picture below right shows the position of your hands after the initial pull down. Your hands are a little to your left so that his elbow is in your centre.

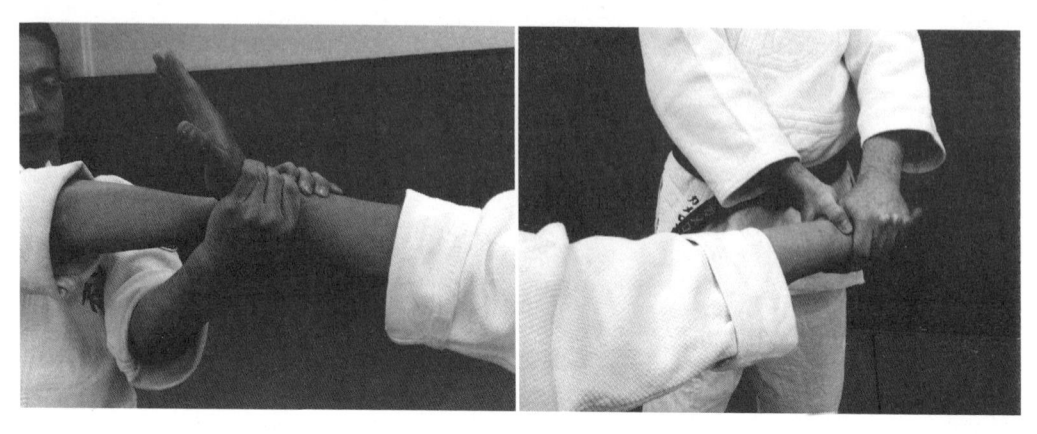

9. Ude hineri (pictures page 125)

Move your right foot forward slightly and raise uke's hand a little with your tegatana. Bring your left hand palm up underneath his arm and grasp his wrist with both hands.

Make a tsugi ashi movement straight back and bring your arms down low by taking them in a large clockwise circular movement.

123

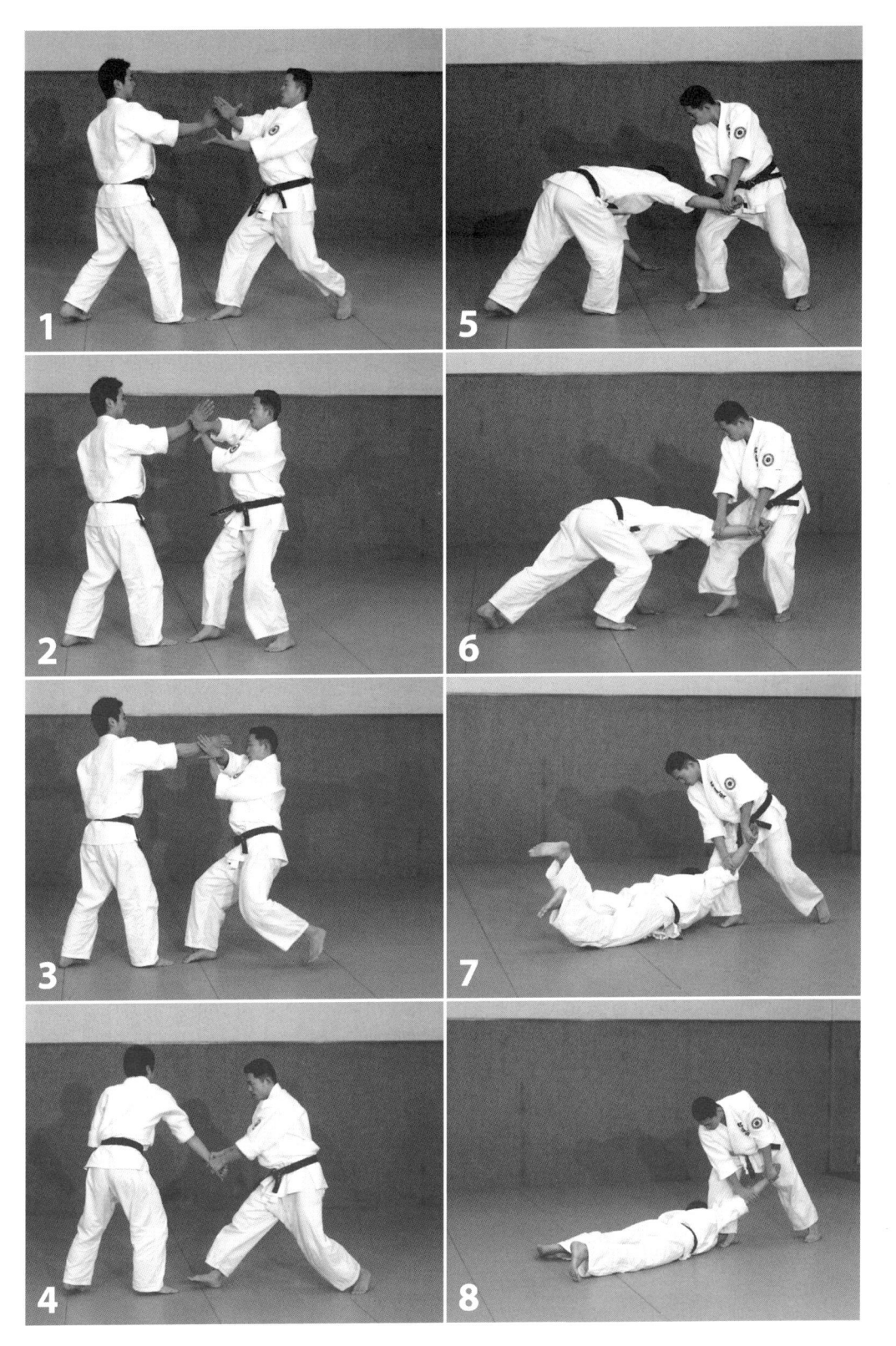

Uke responds to prevent his balance from being broken by stepping back with his left leg and straightening it. He keeps his right leg bent significantly and head down low towards you.

Let go of his wrist with your right hand and step forward with your left foot placing the thumb of your left hand on the back of your hip keeping your elbow close to you. Turn your right hand thumb down as you step in and place the base of your thumb on the top of his arm preventing him from standing upright (picture bottom left).

Push your left hand straight down keeping it close to you. As your hand reaches its lowest point start to turn to your right to face in the opposite direction and continue the push on his arm bringing it up and across his back. Your left hand stays in your centre as you turn and keep his hand about 20-30cm away from his back. Use your right hand to control his elbow but do not entangle your arm around his arm (picture bottom right).

Uke steps forward with his left foot as you reach the end of your turn and does a forward rolling fall with his left hand. Finish with your hands in your centre (picture below right).

Coaching points
Uke's movement is simply to stop your pull and he should remain balanced and not with his weight on his back foot which would cause him to fall backwards if you let go of his arm. Keep the tension in his arm as you step towards him.

As you turn to throw uke, if his hand is too close to his back or too far away from it, you will not affect his posture but you can easily cause injury to his arm or shoulder. Keeping his hand 20-30cm away from his back affects his posture by dropping his left shoulder and turning his body without causing any pain.

The position after you have stepped towards uke (picture below left).
Your arms as you turn your body to throw uke (picture below right).
The finish position (picture above right).

125

10. Waki gatame

Make a tsugi ashi movement forward and just to uke's left lifting his hand with your tegatana. As soon as you start this movement bring your left hand underneath his wrist with your elbow down. Keeping moving in the same direction and continue lifting his extended arm. Take a grip with your left hand when it is possible to grasp with the palm of your hand on the inside of his wrist.

When you have moved far enough, so that he is stretched and the toes of his right foot are just about to lose contact with the tatami, move your body up towards his arm and place his wrist in the inside of your right elbow with you left hand just to the outside of your arm.

Bring his arm down to your chest and continue for two or three more tsugi ashi movements in the same direction before stopping.

Your right arm is bent with your thumb pointing towards you so that it squeezes uke's wrist more effectively. His arm should be in contact with your chest with your left hand to the outside of your arm.

In the finish position uke has his left foot forward and arm extended and well above his shoulder line. He is bent over with so that his arm, shoulders and head are at the same level. Stand with your right foot forward in a natural posture with your shoulders level.

Coaching points

The further you reach around his wrist when you take the initial grip the more effective the twist on his arm. The aim is to finish with his elbow uppermost when his arm is extended.

There is no pressure on his elbow in any way at any time during this technique. When done properly this technique does not cause any pain. The aim is to extend his arm, lock it close to your body and use body movement to control him.

In the final position, the thumb of your right hand is turned towards you as this holds his arm more securely.

The top right picture shows the initial movement with the left hand.

The picture bottom right shows the final position.

127

The picture on the right shows the alternative application of waki gatame which is equally valid in randori. The principles are the same as above but you are on the other side of his arm with your arm positions swapped.

This application occurs when uke reacts against hiki taoshi. Let go of his arm with your right hand, turn your thumb down and grasp his wrist again in a reverse grip.

Quickly move to the inside of his arm and take the final arm position as shown. Take two or three tsugi ashi movements back and slightly to your right to finish.

TANTŌ HIJI WAZA

Each technique starts with both of you standing in migigamae, you with your arms by your side and tantō holding the knife in his right hand in his centre. He stabs from a distance where he can reach you with one movement.

Oshi taoshi and ude gaeshi

When uke stabs, your avoidance to the left for both of these techniques is the same as in the basic technique. Bring your right tegatana onto uke's wrist as you avoid and immediately follow it with your left shōtei. Grasp his arm and then proceed as for the basic techniques.

Hiki taoshi and ude hineri

In the basic form of these techniques you do not move from the centre line as you take your grip on tantō's arm. You cannot do this against a stab as you must avoid the line of the attack. So, as he stabs, move to your left just enough to avoid the knife by stepping with your left foot and then bringing your right foot across so that you remin in migigamae.

Turn a little to your right as you move and grasp his arm. Pull down as in the basic technique but move back and slightly to the right by pushing back with your right leg so that you are in front of tantō on the original centre line between you. Proceed as for the basic techniques.

Waki gatame

With the position of your body and the force of a stab it is not possible to move tantō's arm in the same direction as in the basic technique.

Against a knife your first movement is to avoid it by moving just to your left and turning so that you are at an angle of about 30° from line of attack keeping your right foot forward. As you do this, bring your right tegatana on to his wrist followed immediately by your left hand grasping his wrist from underneath (picture right). This is made easier by bending your knees.

Extend your legs and left arm to start breaking his balance. As you do this, turn to your right, roll his arm over to turn his elbow up and use your body movement to move him. The direction of movement from his perspective is forward and just to his left which is in effect redirecting the line of his stab. Continue and finish as for the basic technique.

KIHON TEKUBI WAZA

As a whole there are eight possible wrist techniques within aikido. If we consider holding someone's right hand it can be twisted in two directions:

- turning the thumb down (clockwise from your point of view)
  This breaks his balance forward and is called kote hineri
- turning the palm up (anti-clockwise from your point of view)
  This breaks his balance backward and is called kote gaeshi

Both of these twists can be applied with your left hand and right hand so that amounts to four distinct applications. In addition, your grip in each of these four applications can be a regular grip (junte) or a reverse grip (gyakute).

A regular grip is when you grasp uke's wrist with your forefinger nearer to his elbow and your little finger nearer to his hand. A reverse grip is the opposite.

The result is eight different applications summarised below with the corresponding koshiki no kata principle from judo:

Group	Grip	Koshiki no kata
kote hineri	aigamae junte dori*	mizu guruma mizu nagare hiki otoshi
	aigamae gyakute dori	
	gyakugamae junte dori*	
	gyakugamae gyakute dori	
kote gaeshi	aigamae junte dori*	
	aigamae gyakute dori	
	gyakugamae junte dori	
	gyakugamae gyakute dori*	

Of these eight techniques, four are not included in randori because they are difficult to apply or the risk of injury is too high. The four remaining ones included in the 17 randori techniques are marked by asterisks in the table above and are named as follows:

- kote hineri – aigamae junte kote hineri in the table
- kote gaeshi – gyakugamae gyakute dori kote gaeshi in the table
- tenkai kote hineri – gyakugamae junte dori kote hineri in the table. This technique involves a body turn
- tenkai kote gaeshi – aigamae junte dori kote gaeshi in the table. This technique involves a body turn

11. Kote hineri

Step to your left with your left foot and follow with your right foot so that you are about 30° from your original line. Keep your right foot forward, your right hand in your centre and face uke.

Grasp his wrist with your left hand and his hand blade with your right hand. Take a small tsugi ashi back keeping your arms straight. As you move back, twist his arm with your right hand to raise his elbow and slide your left hand around his wrist. Continue turning his wrist as you take a tsugi ashi forward staying on the same angle away from the original centre line and taking his arm towards his face.

Slide the palm of your left hand to the inside of his elbow. Keep your arms straight and push towards his ear stepping straight through with your left foot. Just as your left foot passes by his left foot start to move slightly to your left behind him. Make a few tsugi ashi movements with your left foot forward as you push him down until his is lying face down on the tatami.

Push his elbow above his head as far as it goes before meeting some resistance. Hold his arm there, step up with your right foot so that your knee is behind your right hand and then step back with your left foot so that you are about 30° from his body. The back of your hand is on the front of your knee and the back of your forearm is on top of your thigh.

Place your left hand in the small of your back and push his hand forward until he taps on the tatami to finish.

Coaching points

As in oshi taoshi, bring uke's arm up and towards his head using straight arms and body movement. Grasp his hand blade rather than his fingers for safety reasons and maintain the twist on his wrist throughout the technique.

After he is lying on the tatami you push his arm above his head as far as it goes so that only a small movement is required in the finish position to get him to submit.

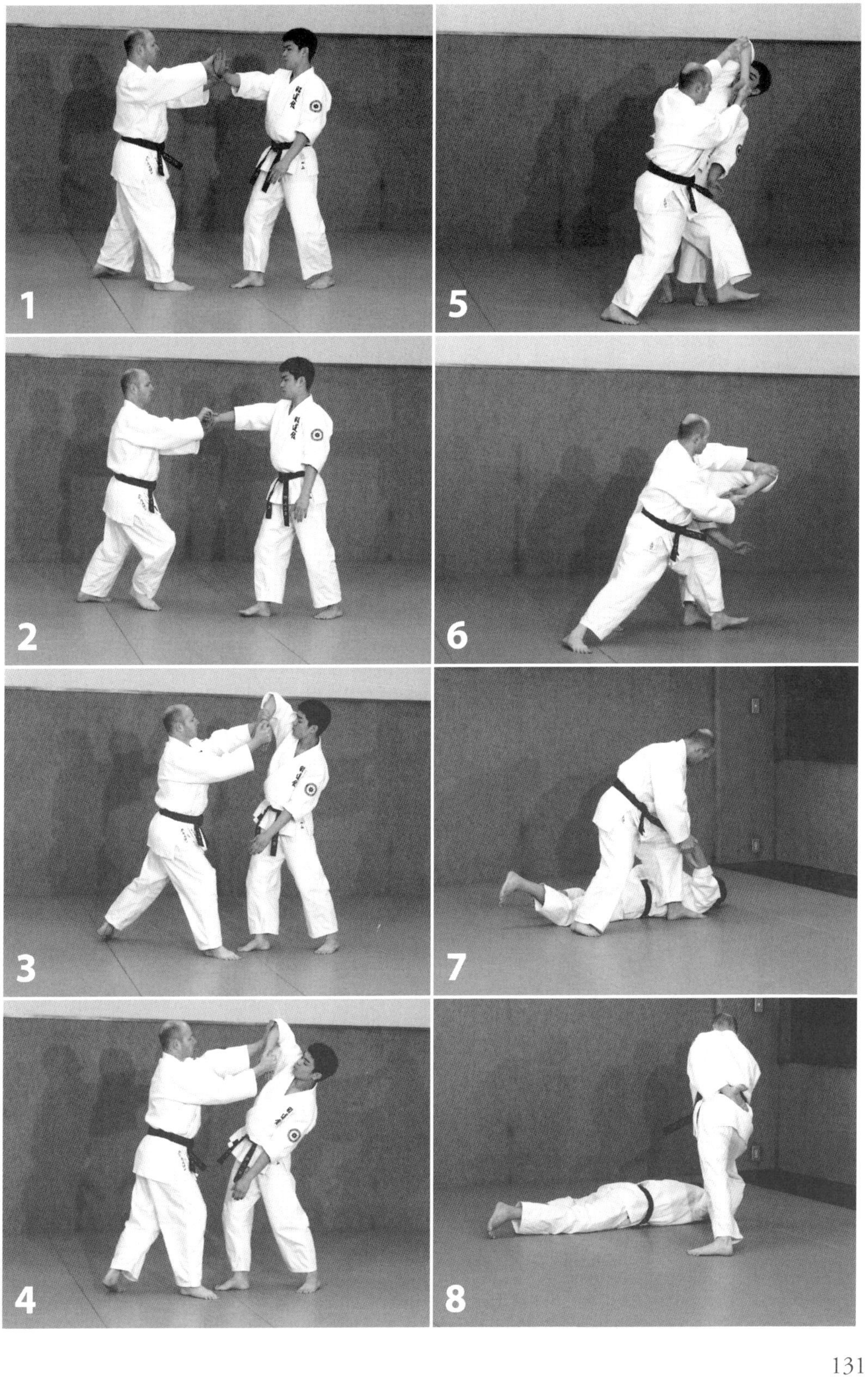
1
5
2
6
3
7
4
8

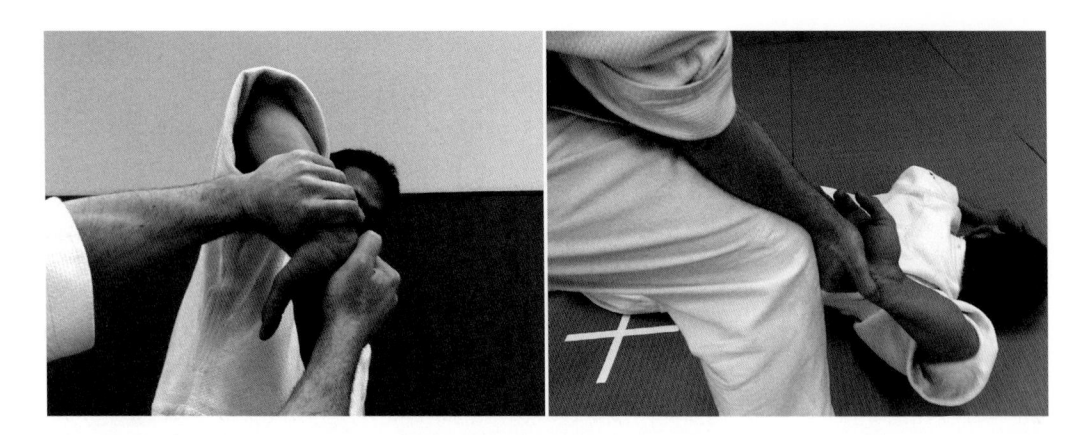

The picture above left shows the grips on the wrist and hand blade just before you slide your left hand to his elbow. The picture above right shows the finish position with the back of your hand on the front of your knee and the back of your forearm on top of your thigh. Your arm is in contact with your leg from your knuckles to your elbow. The grip in this position is unchanged from your initial grip (picture above left).

12. Kote gaeshi

Step to your left with your left foot and follow with your right foot so that you are about 30° from your original line. Keep your right foot forward, your right hand in your centre and face uke.

Grasp his wrist with your left hand and his hand blade with your right hand. Take a small tsugi ashi back keeping your arms straight. At the same time turn slightly to the left and draw his elbow up and away from his body.

He reacts to this movement by dipping his elbow. Turn to the right as he does this and immediately break his balance by moving to his front left corner driving his arm down low towards the inside of your right knee keeping your arms close to you in your centre and holding his arm with both hands.

Slide your left hand round his wrist so that your thumb is on the back of his hand on the knuckle of his ring finger and you are holding his hand around the base of his thumb. Then change the grip with your right hand so that your right thumb is crossed over your left thumb and you are holding his hand with both hands.

Pivot on your right foot sweeping your left leg behind and twist his wrist by turning his arm in an anti-clockwise direction. Finish the sweep with your left leg so that you are facing to uke's right. Apply this technique with his arm bent so that you push his hand to his right. Uke takes a tobi ukemi.

Continue your turn after he has fallen. Place your right foot just beneath his shoulder with the

133

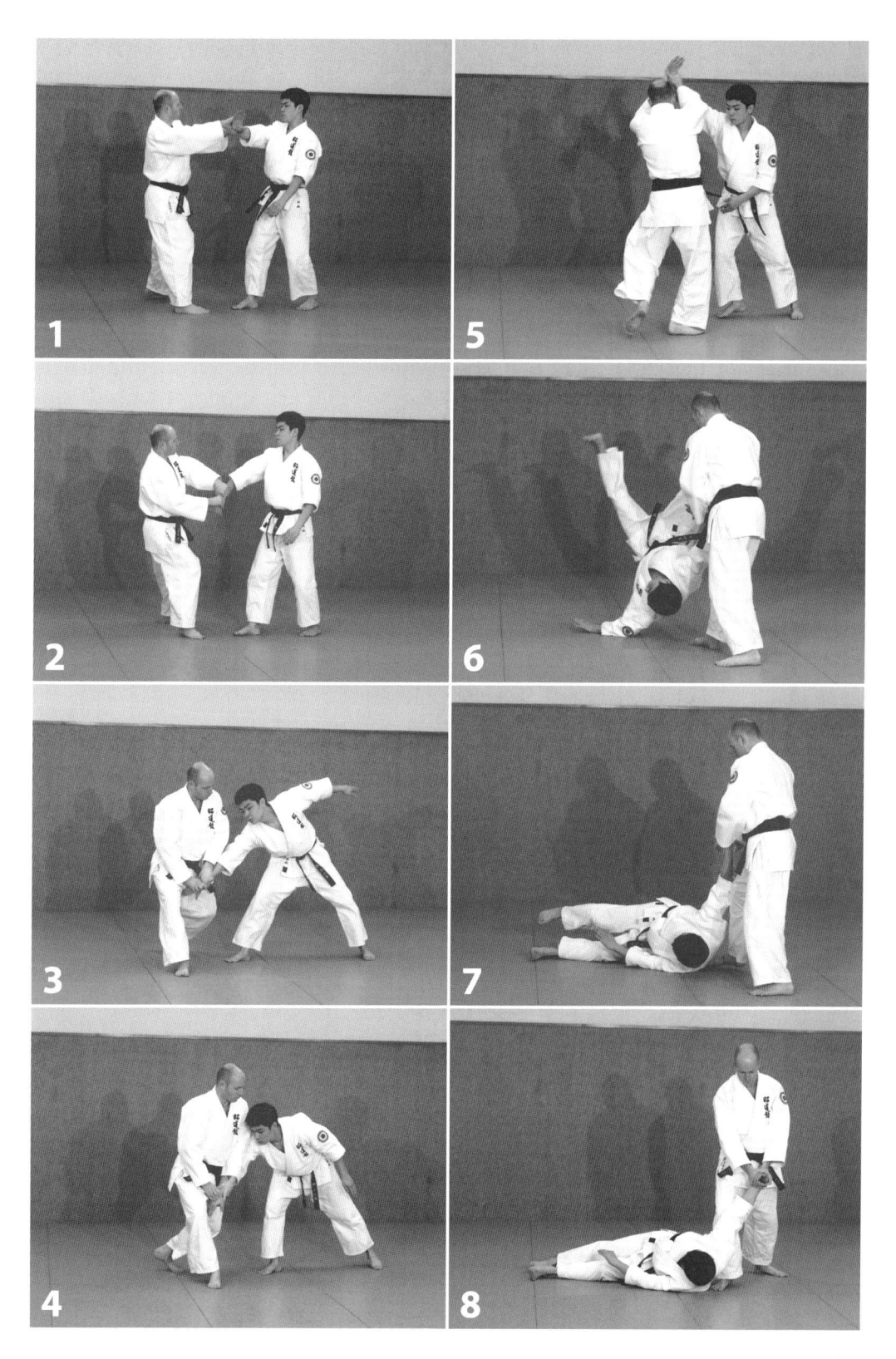

line of your feet at about 30° to his body. Your front leg is bent and your rear leg is straight. Hold your hands in your centre with your knee inside his bent arm. Do not twist or apply any pressure to his arm.

Coaching points
Do not wait for uke to react by dipping his elbow. If he does not react then immediately take his arm down low to break his balance and continue with the rest of the technique.

Hold his arm with both hands when you break his balance to ensure that it is effective and that your grip does not break.

Applying kote gaeshi with his arm bent means that the rotation of his arm is restricted to his forearm. If his arm is straight then this allows rotation in the shoulder which is not as effective.

The finish does not involve a twist on his arm. Hold your hands in your centre with his arm relaxed.

Pictures 1-3 below show the change of grip on uke's wrist. Picture 1 is just after the balance break, picture 2 shows the change of grip with the left hand and picture 3 shows the final hand position after you have changed the grip with your right hand. This grip stays unchanged for the rest of the technique. The picture bottom right shows the finish position.

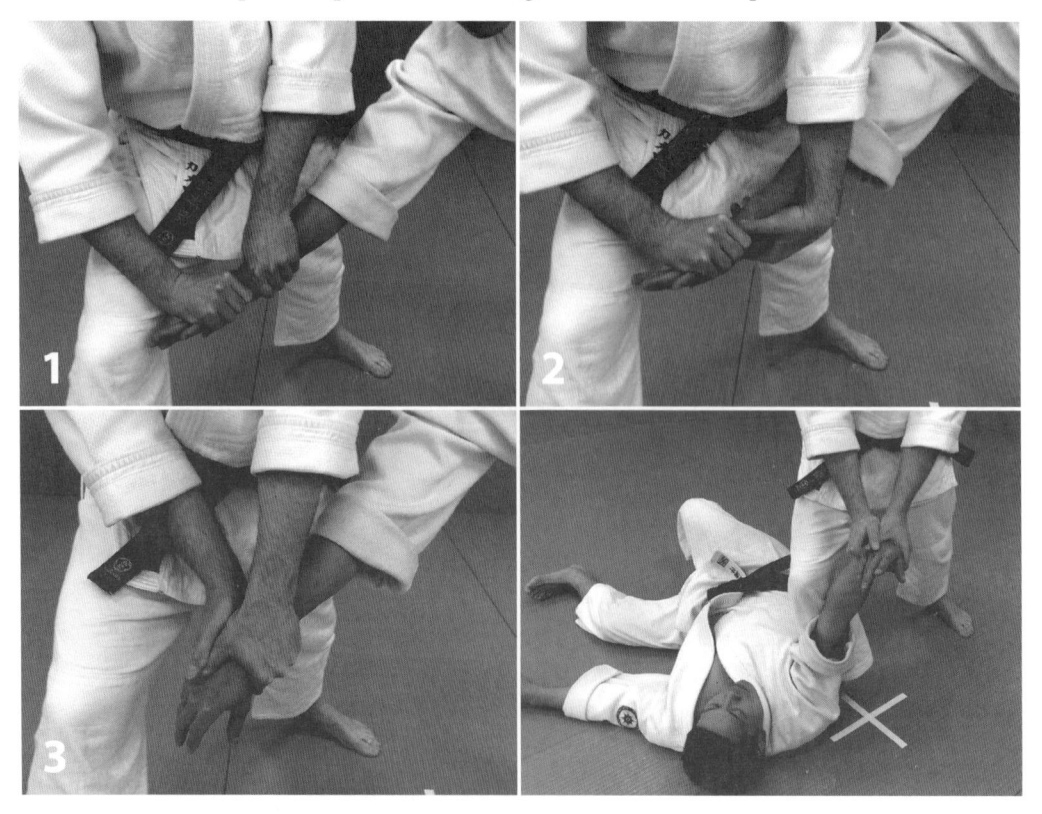

13. Tenkai kote hineri (pictures page 137)
Step forward with your left foot and use your tegatana to push uke's hand straight down.

Grasp his wrist with your left hand but keep your right hand open. Step forward with your right foot so that your shoulder touches the front of his shoulder.

Lift your hands on your centre line above your head and turn to your left to face the opposite direction. Bring your hands down to about shoulder level in your centre. Keep your left foot forward and turn slightly to your left to break his balance by twisting his wrist with your left hand assisted by the hand blade of right hand. Maintain a natural posture and keep your hands in your centre.

Step forward with your right foot taking his arm down in front of you with your left arm extended to break his balance forward. Sweep your left leg back so that you are facing in the opposite direction bringing his arm with you and place your right hand on his elbow with your thumb pointing towards you.

Keep his arm extended above his head, maintain the twist on his wrist, apply pressure to his elbow and make two or three tsugi ashi movements back until he is lying flat on the tatami.

Finish with your right foot forward. Your right leg is bent and left leg is straight. Maintain the twist on his wrist and keep your hand on his elbow holding his arm extended above his head and on the inside of your right leg.

Coaching points
Do not lift your left hand to grasp uke's wrist. Keep your left hand low and use your right hand to drop his arm.

The picture below left shows your hands just before you turn. Grip his hand with your left hand and keep your right hand open to allow you to close the distance to him so that your shoulder touches his shoulder.

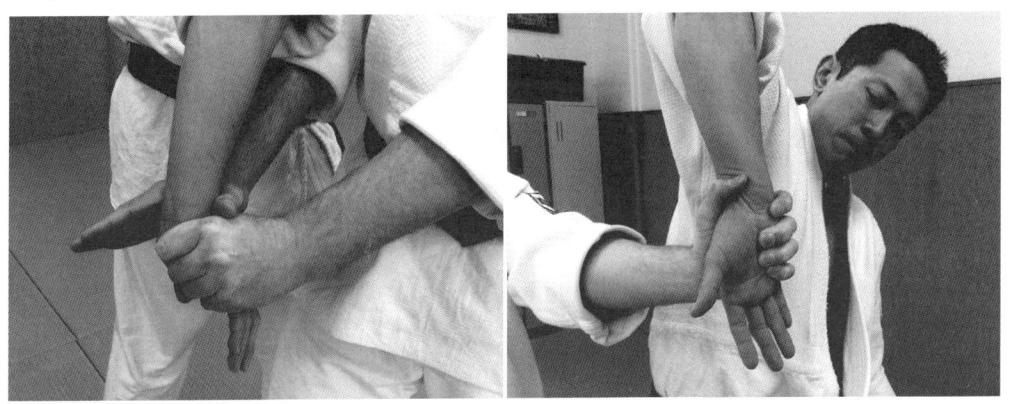

The picture below right shows your left hand after you have turned. The right hand is not shown but assists in the wrist twist by using your tegatana on the palm of his hand. The twist is mainly applied with the left hand. Grip so that there is no space between the palm of your left hand and the back of his hand and push the base of your thumb forward. His arm and fingers are pointing straight down. If uke is flexible you may need to turn more to break his balance. If you need to do this keep your hands in your centre and turn your whole body moving your feet to maintain a good posture.

You may use your right hand on his elbow to bend him forward but normally you should be able to do this with just your left hand as you step forward.

The picture on the right shows the final position. There is no pressure applied to his elbow but the twist on his wrist is maintained until the end.

14. Tenkai kote gaeshi (pictures page 139)
Move forward and to the right off of the centre line and at the same time bring your left hand over the top of your right arm to grasp uke's wrist.

Bring your arms down to your centre. Grasp with your right hand and open your left hand. Keep your arms extended and step forward with your left foot. In this position, just before you turn, there is no gap between your left arm and his right arm.

Lift your arms on your centre line above your head and turn to the right to face in the opposite direction taking hold with both hands as you turn. Bring your arms down to about chest level so that his arm is brought behind him and down the centre of his back to break his balance.

Keep your arms in your centre and face forward as you make a tsugi ashi forward and slightly to the right into his body. Let go as he does a backward fall and finish with your hands in your centre.

Coaching points
The top left picture on page 138 shows your arm position just before your turn. Grip his wrist with your right hand and keep your left hand open to allow you to close the distance to him so that there is no space between your left arm and his right arm.

Keep uke's arm directed down his back rather than bringing it to his side. This is an effective method of breaking his balance without causing injury (picture page 138 top right).

137

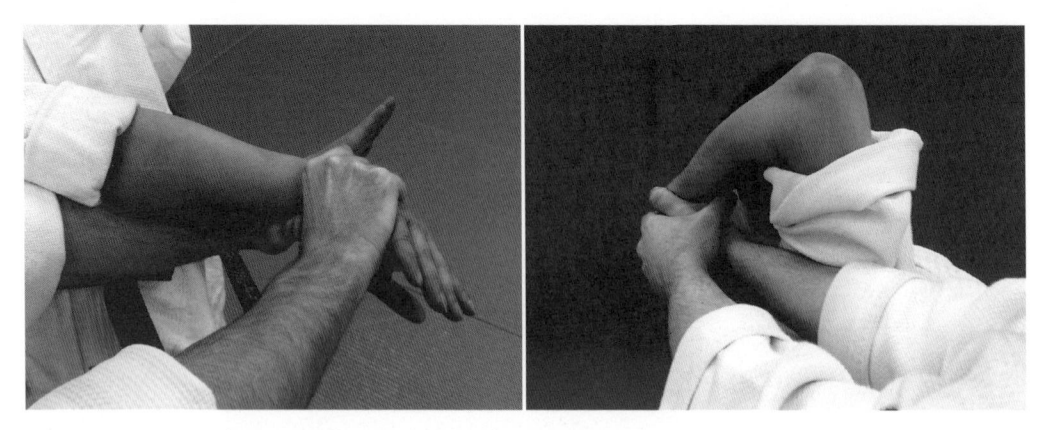

The outside of your leg makes contact with his body as you move to throw him. Your step forward which is slightly to the right pushes him off of his feet by moving through where he is standing. The throw is with movement in one direction rather than by twisting your body.

TANTŌ TEKUBI WAZA

Each technique starts with both of you standing in migigamae, you with your arms by your side and tantō holding the knife in his right hand in his centre. He stabs from a distance where he can reach you with one movement.

Kote hineri and kote gaeshi

Your avoidance to the left as uke stabs for both of these techniques is the same as in the basic technique. Bring your right tegatana onto uke's wrist as you avoid immediately followed by your left shōtei (picture below left). Grasp his wrist with your left hand and his hand blade with your right hand. Proceed as for the basic techniques (picture below right).

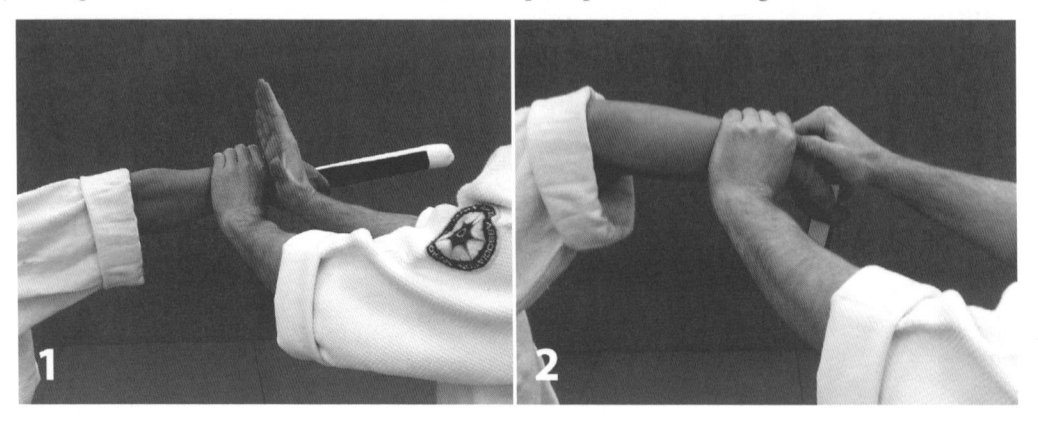

Tenkai kote hineri

The basic technique involves a movement to drop uke's hand while you remain in front of him. This is not possible against a knife so, as he stabs, avoid forward and to your left bringing your open hands down his forearm to grasp his wrist with both hands.

139

Without stopping, step forward with your right foot so that your shoulder touches the front of his shoulder.

Lift his arm on your centre line and turn under it. As you turn under his arm release your grip on his arm just enough so that his wrist can rotate freely in your hands.

Once you have turned underneath his arm and are facing in the opposite direction step back with your left foot and pull his arm down low and make several tsugi ashi movements back. He turns to face you as you do this and ends up lying flat on the tatami. Finish as for the basic technique.

The whole technique is done quickly and smoothly without stopping (pictures below).

Tenkai kote gaeshi
The avoidance in the basic technique and against a stab are slightly different. In the basic technique your right hand is already up next to uke's right hand and your bring you left hand over as you avoid. Against a stab bring your hands together and down his forearm to grasp his wrist with both hands as you avoid his attack. Bring his arm to your centre and continue as for the basic technique.

KIHON UKI WAZA

Tomiki wanted to include techniques that encapsulate the principle of non-resistance with 'softness prevailing over strength'. Uki waza (floating techniques) in aikido are related to kūki nage (air throws) in judo that require no close physical contact and which are applied through precise timing. He added three uki waza that are shown in the table below alongside the corresponding techniques in judo.

Uki waza in aikido	Technique in judo
mae otoshi	tai otoshi
sumi otoshi	sumi otoshi
hiki otoshi	uki otoshi

In Tomiki's book Aikido Nyūmon (Introduction to Aikido) published in 1958 there were only 15 techniques listed in the basic kata. These included 3 atemi waza, 4 hiji waza and 8 tekubi waza. There was no mention of the uki waza at that time.

Five years later they were mentioned in his 1963 publication Shin Aikido Tekisuto (New Aikido Textbook). Hideo Ōba, Tomiki's best student at that time and instructor at Waseda Aikido Club, wrote a letter in July 1961 addressed to the club members. He stated that a kata of 17 techniques had been created by Tomiki. So, we can see that the basic randori kata we know today was completed around this time.

With the help of members of the university clubs doing practical research he excluded techniques that were difficult to apply, introduced new techniques (gedan ate, ushiro ate and waki gatame) and the uki waza which have principles from the nage no kata in judo.

The importance of idōryoku and its extensive use in techniques has already been mentioned and is particularly obvious in sumi otoshi. To develop idōryoku for uki waza, use the tsukuri practices for atemi waza. The use of your legs and hips in turning one way and then the other, flexing and extending the knees to create a fast, powerful movement are all in this practice and connected to the uki waza as follows:

- shōmen ate and aigamae ate – the upright torso with relaxed shoulders, sinking your weight and using a rapid arm swing are related to the balance breaking movements in mae otoshi.
- gyakugamae ate, gedan ate – these are applied by sinking your weight, twisting your hips one way and using a fast swing of your arms while turning back. The movement of your hips is used in sumi otoshi and hiki otoshi. Your arm swing is used in sumi otoshi.
- ushiro ate – the rapid movement while turning your upper body is used in the balance break for mae otoshi and the throws in sumi otoshi and hiki otoshi.

15. Mae otoshi
Move forward and to the right off of the centre line and at the same time bring your left hand over the top of your right arm to grasp uke's wrist.

Bring your arms down to your centre. Grasp with your right hand, open your left hand and slide it up to his elbow. Keep your arms extended and bring him onto his toes.

Slide your left arm forward under his arm and lift it up keeping him on his toes as you take a big step forward with your left leg. Once your arm reaches its highest point turn your thumb down and complete your step. To apply a little more pressure on his arm at the end, turn into hanmi as you finish your movement.

He takes left hand forward rolling fall.

The position of your hands after your initial avoidance and bringing your hands to your centre (picture right).

The position of your arms before turning your left thumb down, turning your left shoulder forward to throw uke (picture below left).

The hanmi position at the end of the technique (picture below right).

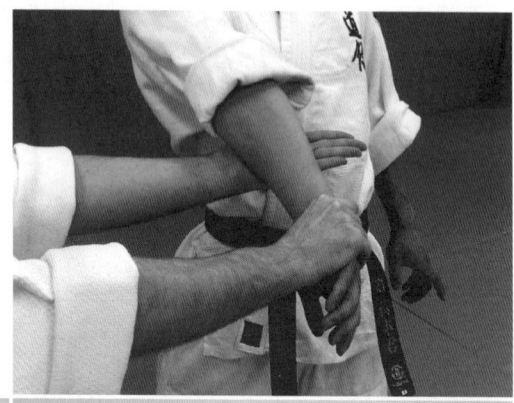

Coaching points
Uke's balance is broken by raising him onto his toes which is the best time to throw him.

Be careful to avoid excessive pressure on his elbow. Do not pull back with your right hand or slide your shoulder underneath his arm.

143

16. Sumi otoshi
Step forward and slightly to the left with your left foot and bring your right foot to the left as well so that your feet are on a line parallel to the original centre line between you and uke. As you do this, turn to the right and take hold of his wrist with both hands, your right hand nearer to his elbow than your left hand (picture below).

Pull him forward slightly and then turn your hips so that you are facing your original direction. Keep your arms extended as you turn and bring your hands down and around so that they are always in your centre. Keep his arm extended so that he cannot regain his balance which is pulled onto the outside edge of his foot during this movement.

As you finish turning your hips lift your arms up to about eye level and draw your right foot right up behind your left foot.

Take a deep step forward and to your right behind him while dropping your arms forward and down. He turns so that he can take a tobi ukemi. Pull back so that you are supporting him as he falls. Bring you right foot up to keep your balance and do not let go of his arm.

Coaching points
Uke's balance is broken by pulling his hand forward to bring his weight onto his toes. Then his arm is taken in a wide arc to his side to bring his weight onto the outside edge of his foot. This wide movement is continued by taking his arm deep behind him to throw him. You must keep his arm extended throughout the technique so that you do not give uke his balance back at any time.

17. Hiki otoshi (pictures page 147)
This technique starts with a tsugi ashi forward by uke. As he does this take a tsugi ashi back to maintain the distance between you, bring your left hand over the top of your right arm and grasp so that your palm is on the inside of his wrist. Start to move your right hand onto the inside of his elbow.

Without stopping, make a big tsugi ashi movement back and slightly to your right. Pull your left hand to your hip as you move back and rotate your hand anti-clockwise. Your right hand rests on the inside of his elbow and does not assist in the application. Keep facing forward and do not let go with your left hand.

145

Turn to face him after he has taken his tobi ukemi. Step up to him with your right foot so that your feet are together and place the palm of your right hand under his elbow. Step back with your left foot to finish with your left leg straight and your right leg bent. There is no pressure applied to his elbow.

Coaching points
This technique is applied through body movement and the pull (and twist) on uke's arm with your left hand only. Your right hand rests on the inside of his elbow but plays no part in the application in this basic form of hiki otoshi.

Your movement to throw him is back and slightly to your right so that you move off of the line between you as this is the direction that he is pulled and will fall.

His momentum as he falls will pull your left hand away from your hip. Let this happen but maintain a strong posture and support him by not letting your hand drop.

His movement and ukemi occur in a straight line so once he has fallen and you turn to face the opposite direction your feet should be parallel to the original line between you.

The grip on his arm (picture right).

The pull and twist on his arm to bring your hand to your hip (picture below left).

The finish position (picture below right).

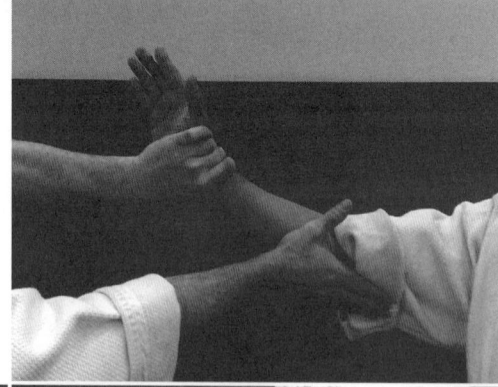

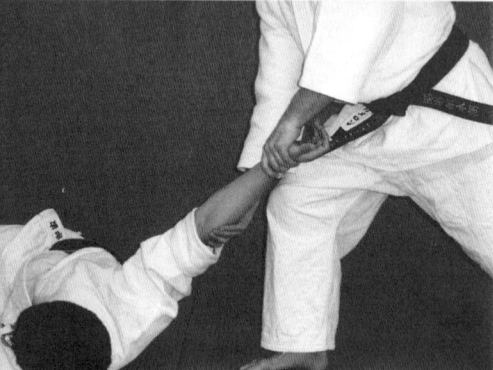

147

TANTŌ UKI WAZA

Each technique starts with both of you standing in migigamae, you with your arms by your side and tantō holding the knife in his right hand. He stabs from a distance where he can reach you with one movement.

Mae otoshi
Avoid forward and to the right as uke stabs, bringing your open hands down his forearm to grasp his wrist with both hands. Bring your hands down to your centre, open your left hand and continue as for the basic technique.

Sumi otoshi
The initial movement in the basic technique is sufficient to avoid tantō's stab. At the same time, bring your open hands down his forearm to grasp his wrist with both hands. Continue as for the basic technique.

Hiki otoshi
As tantō stabs take a tsugi ashi back to avoid the knife. At the same time bring your left hand up underneath his arm to grasp his wrist and place your right hand on the inside of his elbow (picture right). Continue as for the basic technique.

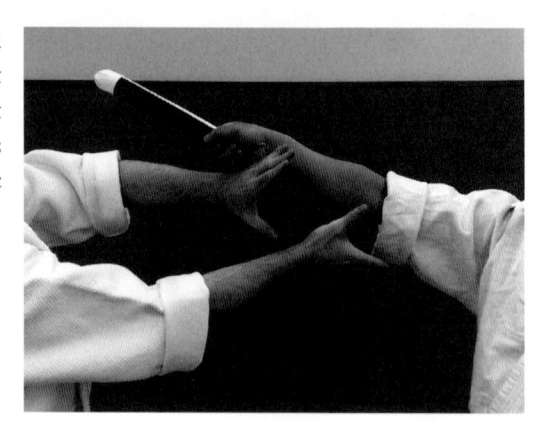

DEVELOPING KANSETSU WAZA SKILLS

The possibilities of holding and twisting someone's wrist were described in the tekubi waza section. If we consider the whole arm the two directions of movement are:

- Turning his arm so that his elbow is raised and turned away from his body. This is called ude hineri and breaks his balance up and forward.
- Turning his arm so that his elbow is lowered and turned into his body. This is called ude gaeshi and breaks his balance down and backward.

As a step towards setting up a technique you control an opponent's arm in either of these two directions. The first lifts his arm to eye level (jōdan) and the second lowers it to knee level (gedan). Together these form the basis for a tsukuri practice system for kansetsu waza explained below and summarised in the table on page 150.

From left to right the table shows how tsukuri practice in kansetsu waza is developed from basic movements towards randori applications in a structured way to speed learning and understanding. Each practice introduces skills and concepts that help with the next level or with final application so it is important to be competent before proceeding to the next stage.

Although these are tsukuri practices each one has a technique that naturally fits onto the end of it. As with the atemi waza it is usual to practise tsukuri only then to practise the tsukuri and continue without stopping into a technique.

The first two columns are described above and split the table into two according to the position of your opponent's arm. The different stages of practice are summarized in the third, fourth and fifth columns with the relevant points in each highlighted below. The final column indicates some techniques that are possible in randori using the tsukuri noted in the fifth column.

Third column: tegatana no tsukuri
These form the basic structure with the tsukuri applied using tegatana. They teach correct body movement and positioning, and use of the hand blade in your centre.

- Start with uke grasping your wrist with either hand, aigamae or gyakugamae
- After each grip you take his arm high or low
- Result is a total of four possible applications
- Tsukuri are applied with the hand that is grasped, held open and using tegatana

Fourth column: nigiri gaeshi no tsukuri
These use the same movements as for tegatana no tsukuri but after uke grasps your wrist you move and finish by grasping his wrist. These grips are an important step towards the hiji mochi no tsukuri.

- Start with uke grasping your wrist with either hand, aigamae or gyakugamae
- After each grip you can take his arm high or low
- Tsukuri are applied with the hand that uke grasps but with you grasping his wrist either with a regular grip (junte) or reverse grip (gyakute)
- Result is a total of eight possible applications

Fifth column: hiji mochi no tsukuri
The single handed grasps on uke's wrists when paired up as indicated by the arrows in the table are used against a stab. Both hands always have the same regular grip or reverse grip.

- Start with uke stabbing rather than grasping
- You grasp his wrist with both hands either in a regular or reverse grip
- Take his arm high or low
- Result is a total of four possible applications

The rest of this section describes these practices in this order followed by timing opportunities for kansetsu waza against tantō tsuki.

	when gripped			when gripping	examples of techniques possible in randori
	tegatana no tsukuri	nigiri gaeshi no tsukuri		hiji mochi no tsukuri	
kuzushi - ude hineri (breaking the balance by turning the elbow up) tsukuri - jōdan (eye level)	aigamae	junte	↑		oshi taoshi ude gaeshi hiki taoshi ude hineri waki gatame
		gyakute	↗ junte dori		
	gyakugamae	junte	↖ gyakute dori		waki gatame kote gaeshi
		gyakute	↑		
kuzushi - ude gaeshi (breaking the balance by turning the elbow down) tsukuri - gedan (knee level)	aigamae	junte	↑	junte dori	tenkai kote hineri tenkai kote gaeshi
		gyakute	↗		
	gyakugamae	junte	↖	gyakute dori	kote hineri kote gaeshi
		gyakute	↑		

150

1. Tegatana no tsukuri

Tegatana no tsukuri are based on the third to sixth movements of the go no sen no kuzushi and are practised with uke holding a knife. His attack is a grasp to your wrist and then a step to make the stab.

The pictures below show the attacks used for the jōdan tsukuri. In both cases the knife is held so that a downward strike to the shoulder is possible. The pictures in the left column show the aigamae grip, the pictures in the right column show the gyakugamae grip. It is usual to practise against the aigamae grip first and then the gyakugamae grip. Uke must swap the tantō from one hand to the other as required.

151

The pictures below show the attacks for the gedan tsukuri. In both cases the knife is held so that a straight stab to the body is possible. The pictures in the left column show the aigamae grip, the pictures in the right column show the gyakugamae grip.

These are drills rather than real methods of self defence. Uke's attacks are artificial in that they are predetermined with restrictions in his actions. They are used for timing your movements and making you move to the correct positions.

Each of these is done in two stages as with the tsukuri practices for atemi waza. The first time is as far as the tsukuri and the second time is with the tsukuri and kake (throw or pin).

i. Jōdan - aigamae (pictures page 155)

This is almost identical to the third balance break from the go no sen no kuzushi. The difference is in uke's intent and the direction of movement after you have moved behind him.

1. Turn your thumb down the instant before uke grasps your wrist. Turn your hand in the opposite direction by bringing your elbow down so that your thumb is uppermost as he steps to make his stab. Keep your arm extended in front of you in your centre as you turn your elbow down and slide forward with your right foot so that it is about level with his right foot.

Step forward with your left foot keeping your right arm extended in front of you. When your hand gets past his body direct it to his centre behind him and up towards his head as you start to turn to face in the opposite direction. Keep your hand in your centre as you turn.

Finish with your hand at eye level, your fingers extended and together, and your hand blade facing away from you in your centre. You are behind him with your right foot forward facing towards your original position.

From here, for this exercise, tantō's objective is to step around in front of your arm to stab you in the shoulder as he originally intended. Take a tsugi ashi forward and slightly to the right to cut off his step in front of you. When he steps again make a further tsugi ashi. Repeat this several times before stopping. He releases his grip and you lower your hands.

2. Repeat the movement as above but, after a few tsugi ashi and without stopping, place your left hand on his elbow and step across in front of him with your left foot pushing his elbow down to apply oshi taoshi. Wrap the fingers of your right hand around his wrist as you push down and grasp it when you move to your finish position which is as for the basic technique. The whole movement including the technique is shown on page 155.

Coaching points

Uke makes two distinct movements during his attack: first grasping your wrist and then stepping forward to stab. You move behind him as he stabs and raise his arm behind him. He retains a degree of balance by turning slightly towards you and letting his arm bend while maintaining an upright posture. He steps forward from this position with the intent of stabbing to his original target rather than remaining stationary and pulling back on your arm. In practice he does not make a further stab but attempts to step around in front of you.

His steps forward while applying no pressure on your arm encourage you to move. He steps while you tsugi ashi to cut off his movement by moving forward and slightly to the right on the arc of a large circle. He travels in the same direction but on a slightly larger arc as he is outside of you. Therefore, it is possible for you to only tsugi ashi while he runs forward and still prevent him from getting around in front of you.

You can test the quality and speed of your movement starting from your position behind him after he has stabbed. When you are both ready, he attempts to run around your arm (without pulling back on it) as you tsugi ashi to prevent him from getting in front of you.

Uke offers no resistance throughout this practice except when testing your position and posture. Step and turn behind him as he stabs and then stop. From this position he does not move his feet and pushes back against your arm. If you have moved deep enough behind him, turned completely and have your hand blade in your centre then you should be able to resist him.

The position of your open hand after your turn is shown below left. Your hand in your centre after your turn is shown below right.

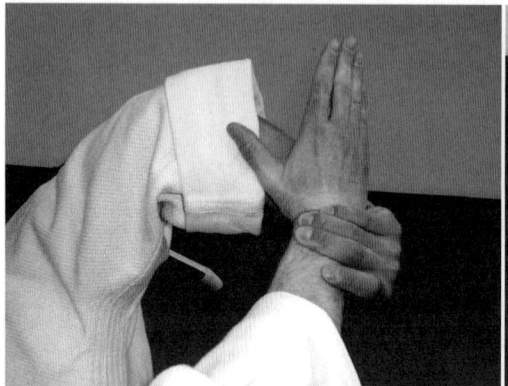

ii. Jōdan - gyakugamae (pictures page 157)
This is almost identical to the fourth balance break from the go no sen no kuzushi. The difference is in uke's intent and the direction of movement after you have moved behind him.

1. Turn your palm up the instant before he grasps your wrist. Turn your hand in the opposite direction so that your thumb is uppermost as he steps to make his stab. Keep your arm extended in front of you in your centre as you turn your hand and at the same time slide forward with your right foot so that it is about level with his left foot.

Slide your right foot forward again keeping your right arm extended in front of you. When your hand gets past his body direct it to his centre line behind him and up towards his head as you start to turn to face in the opposite direction. Keep your hand in your centre as you turn.

Finish with your hand at eye level with your palm facing way from you, your thumb slightly pointing down and your left foot forward.

From here, for this exercise, his objective is to step around in front of your arm to stab you in the shoulder as he originally intended. As he steps take a tsugi ashi forward and slightly to the left to cut off his step in front of you. When he steps again make a further tsugi ashi. Repeat this several times before stopping. He releases his grip and you lower your hands.

2. Repeat the movement as above but, after a few tsugi ashi and without stopping, place your left hand on his elbow and step across in front of him with your left foot pushing his elbow down to apply hiki taoshi. Keep your right hand open until you have pushed his arm down and

155

you have swept your right foot back to face him. At this point his wrist will be under the palm of your hand and it is only now that you grasp his wrist. Finish as for the basic technique. The whole movement including the technique is shown on the page opposite.

Coaching points
You can check your position, posture and movement as in the previous exercise.

The position of your hand after you have turned behind uke is shown in the picture to the right.

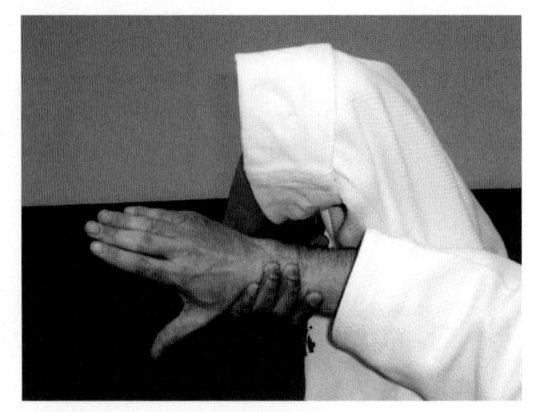

iii. Gedan - aigamae (pictures page 159)
This is based on the fifth balance break from the go no sen no kuzushi but there are some clear differences in the action of your hand and your movement.

1. Turn your palm up the instant before he grasps your wrist. Step forward with your left foot to his right as he steps to make his stab. Turn to face in the opposite direction and step with your right foot away from him bringing your tegatana directly to the inside of your right knee.

As in the jōdan practices, his aim is to move around your arm and stab to his original target rather than pulling your arm back and turning in one place. Take a tsugi ashi to your right and slightly forward to cut off his step in front of you. When he steps again, repeat your tsugi ashi and continue for several steps before stopping. He releases his grip to finish.

2. Repeat the movement as above but, after a few tsugi ashi and without stopping, bring your left hand underneath his wrist with your thumb on top and fingers underneath. At the same time, bring your right hand over the top of his wrist and grasp it. Step across in front of him with your left foot and apply tenkai kote gaeshi as for the basic technique. The whole movement including the technique is shown opposite on page 159.

Coaching points
In the go no sen no kuzushi you turn your hand over after it is grasped and use the heel of your hand on top of uke's wrist. In the tegatana no tsukuri do not turn your hand over his wrist but take your tegatana directly to the inside of your knee as you move to his side.

After you move to his side you are positioned far enough away from him so that his balance is

157

broken and he is unable to pull your hand away from the inside of your knee. You can test your position and posture by stopping after this movement and allowing him, without moving his feet, to try to pull your hand away from your knee.

You can also check the quality of your movement. After you have moved to his side and stopped, when you are ready, he can try to run around in front of your arm as quickly as possible (without pulling back on your arm). As he steps forward tsugi ashi to your right and slightly forward to cut off his movement so that he has to take another step and so on. The result is a race with uke running along the arc of a large circle and you making tsugi ashi movements inside on a smaller arc until you reach the edge of the tatami.

Aim to keep your hand blade pinned to the inside of your knee as you move. You must bend your legs and keep your torso upright and turned towards your hand.

Your body position after your turn is shown below left and your hands just before raising them to start the throw are shown below right.

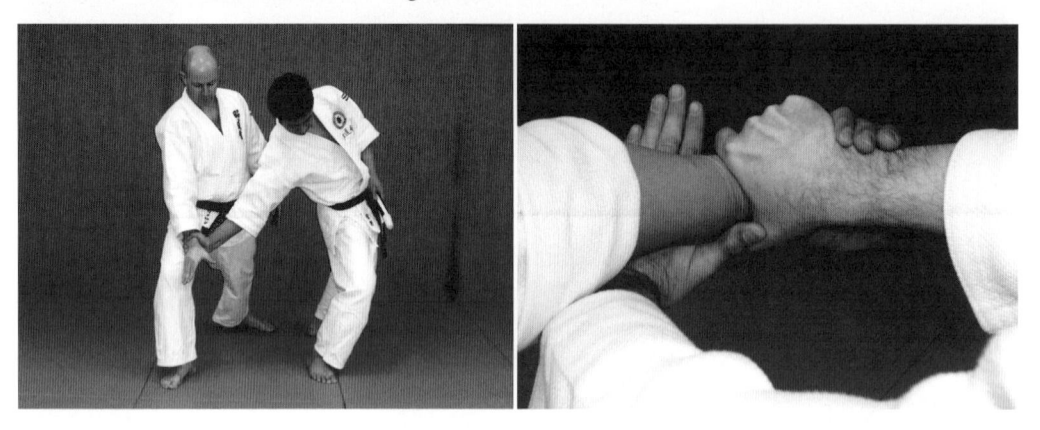

iv. Gedan - gyakugamae (pictures page 161)
This is based on the sixth balance break from the go no sen no kuzushi but there are some clear differences in the action of your hand and your movement.

1. Turn your thumb down the instant before he grasps your wrist. Step forward with your right foot to his left side as he steps to make his stab. Turn to face in the opposite direction and step with your left foot away from him bringing your tegatana directly to the inside of your left knee.

As above, his object is to move around your arm and stab to his original target rather than pulling your arm back and turning in one place. Take a tsugi ashi with your left foot forward and slightly to your left to cut off his step in front of you. When he steps again, repeat your tsugi ashi and continue for several steps before stopping. He releases his grip to finish.

159

2. Repeat the movement as above but finish by applying kote gaeshi without stopping. After a few tsugi ashi movements raise your right hand and dip your elbow to expose his hand. Bring your left hand over your arm and, with thumb uppermost, take a grip on his wrist so that your thumb is on the inside of his wrist and your fingers are along the back of his hand. As you do this turn your right hand away to break his grip then grasp with your right hand too so that your thumb is on the back of his hand and your fingers are on his palm.

Break his balance by making a tsugi ashi movement with your left foot and taking his hand down low in front of him. Sweep your right foot back and apply kote gaeshi without changing the grip on his hand. The whole movement including the technique is shown opposite.

The grip change is shown in pictures 1-3 below and the final grip with both hands is shown below right.

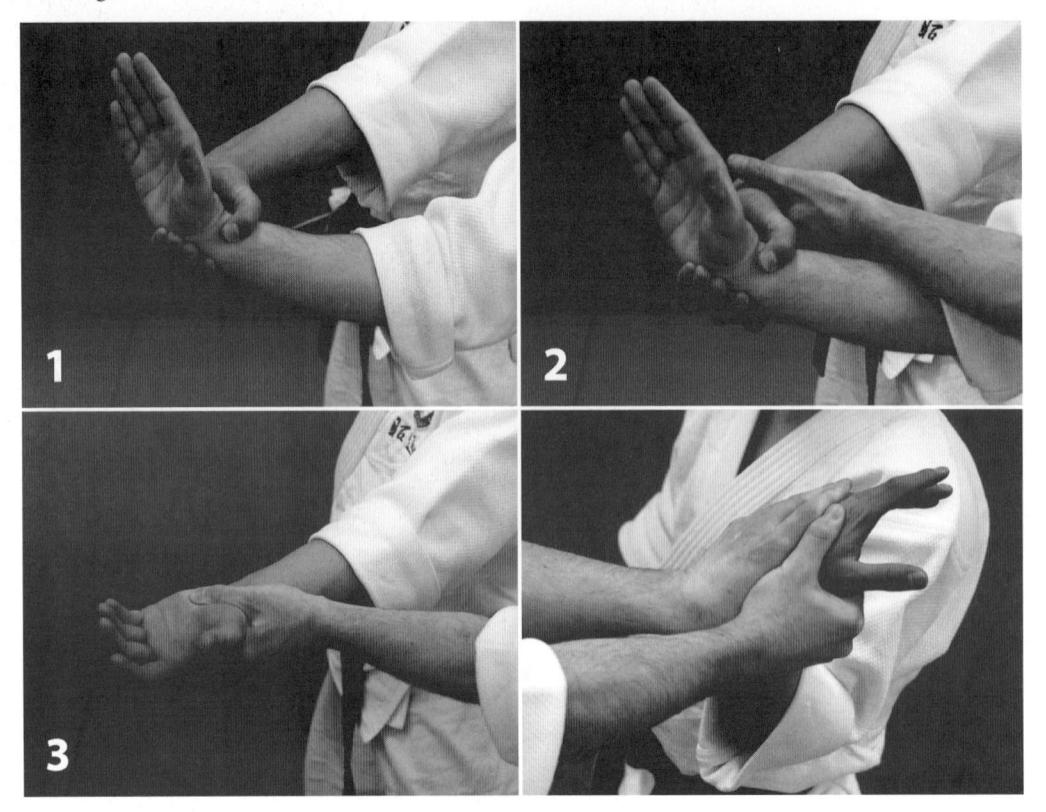

Coaching points

You can check your position, posture and movement as in the previous practice. In this case move forward and slightly to your left keeping your left foot forward.

As in the previous practice aim to keep your hand blade pinned to the inside of your knee as you move. Bend your legs and keep your torso upright and turned towards your hand.

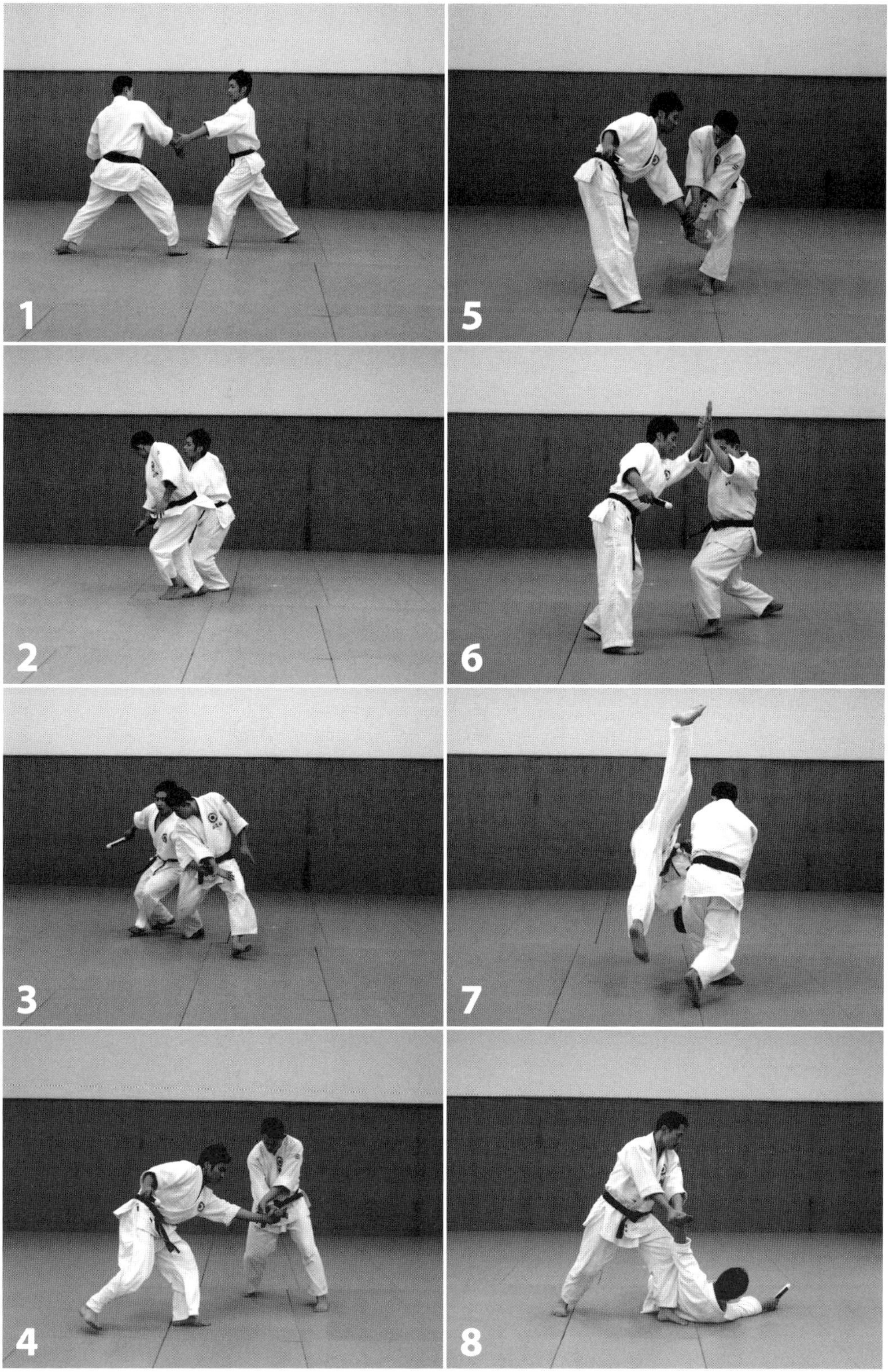

Your body position after your turn is shown in the picture to the right.

2. Nigiri gaeshi no tsukuri

These use the same body movements as described in the tegatana no tsukuri above but the use of the hands is different. In each case, instead of using an open hand you take a grip on uke's wrist. Nigiri gaeshi means 'return a grip' indicating that he first grasps your wrist and you use that hand to then grasp his wrist. For each of the four movements of the tegatana no tsukuri there are two grips: junte (regular) and gyakute (reverse) resulting in eight possibilities.

As with the tegatana no tsukuri, each one is practised twice: the first time as far as the tsukuri and the second time as far as completing the technique.

i. Jōdan - aigamae junte dori

Your movements are the same as the aigamae tegatana jōdan no tsukuri (page 153). The difference is that as you complete your turn grasp uke's wrist in a regular grip when it comes into the palm of your hand (picture right).

The whole movement including the tsukuri and application of oshi taoshi (the same as in the aigamae tegatana jōdan no tsukuri) is shown opposite.

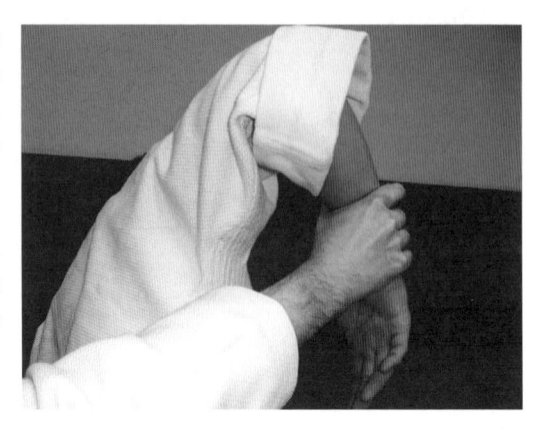

ii. Jōdan - aigamae gyakute dori (pictures page 165)

Your movements are the same as the aigamae tegatana jōdan no tsukuri (page 153). The difference is that at the instant he grasps your hand turn it anti-clockwise so that your fingers are on top of his wrist and thumb underneath. This bends his wrist which puts him at a disadvantage (picture page 164 top left).

163

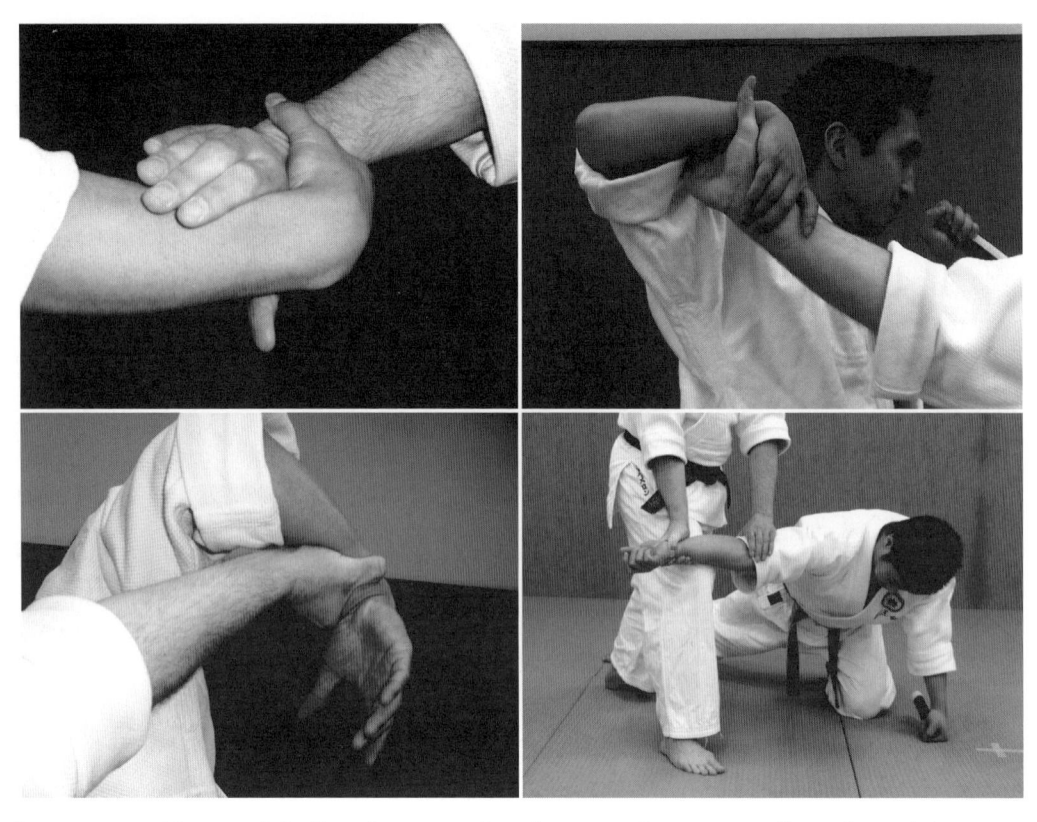

As you step with your right foot, keep your hand open and turn your elbow down (picture top right). Keep turning your hand as you step with your left foot and turn to face the opposite direction. As you complete your turn grasp his wrist in a reverse grip (picture second row left).

The whole movement including the tsukuri and application of oshi taoshi is shown opposite. Oshi taoshi is the same as in the aigamae tegatana jōdan no tsukuri except the reverse grip on the wrist which you maintain to the end of the technique (picture second row right).

iii. Jōdan - gyakugamae junte dori (pictures page 167)
Your movements are the same as the gyakugamae tegatana jōdan no tsukuri (page 154). The difference is that as you complete your turn grasp uke's wrist in a junte (normal) grip when it comes into the palm of your hand.

The whole movement including the tsukuri and application of hiki taoshi (the same as in the gyakugamae tegatana jōdan no tsukuri) is shown on page 167.

Do not take hold or uke's wrist too early. Wait until you have raised his arm and you are turning to face in the opposite direction. His wrist will naturally come into the palm of your hand as you turn and it is only then that you should grasp his wrist.

165

The grip on uke's wrist after you have turned is shown in the picture on the right.

iv. Jōdan - gyakugamae gyakute dori (pictures page 169)

Your movements are the same as the gyakugamae tegatana jōdan no tsukuri (page 154). The difference is that at as he grasps your hand draw it into your centre and turn your hand blade down (picture below left top row). Immediately move your hand back in the opposite direction with your thumb on top of his wrist and your fingers underneath (picture below right top row).

Step forward with your right foot as you do this and continue turning your open hand in an anti-clockwise direction (picture below left bottom row).
Keep turning your hand as you step again with your right foot and turn to face the opposite

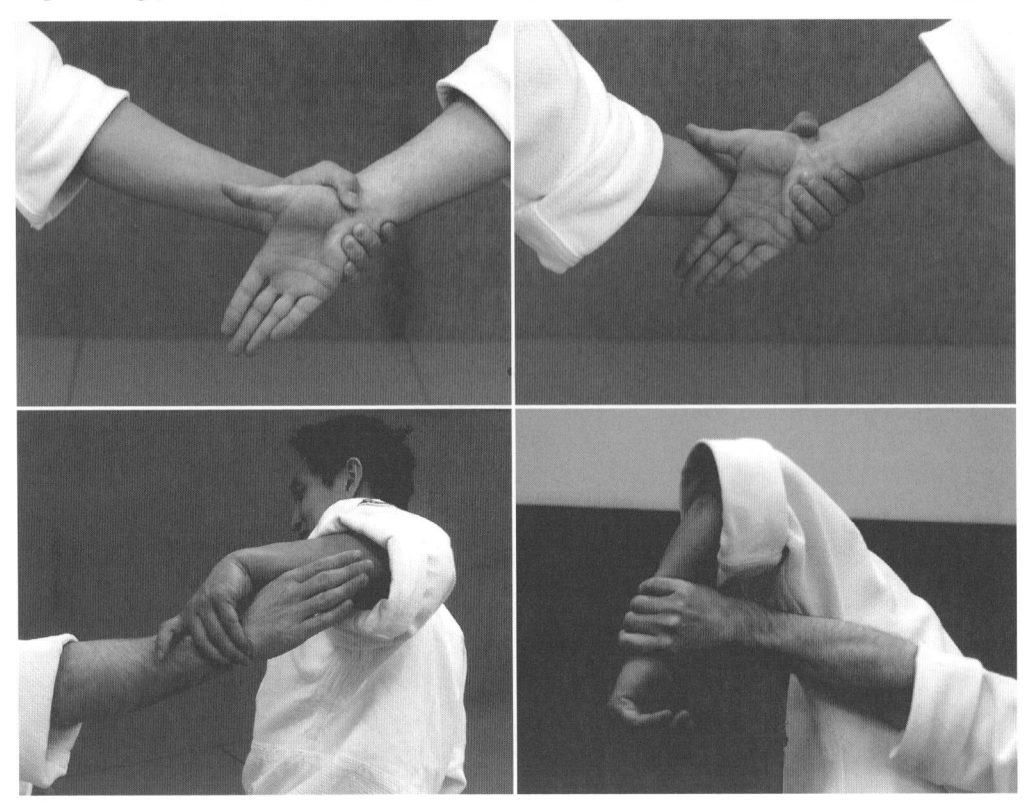

167

direction. As you complete your turn grasp uke's wrist in a reverse grip (picture page 166 bottom row right).

When you apply hiki taoshi place your left hand on uke's elbow and change the grip with your right hand to a normal grip (junte). Push down while stepping forward with your left foot. Continue to apply hiki taoshi as in the gyakugamae tegatana jōdan no tsukuri.

The whole movement including the tsukuri and technique are shown opposite.

The picture to the right shows your hand on uke's elbow just before swapping your right hand to a normal grip and proceeding with the application of hiki taoshi.

v. Gedan - aigamae junte dori (pictures page 171)
Your body movements are the same as the aigamae tegatana gedan no tsukuri (page 156). The difference is in your hand movements.

As in the basic aigamae tegatana gedan no kuzushi practice, immediately before uke grasps your wrist turn your palm up. Step forward with your left foot as you turn your hand over so that your palm is above the inside of his wrist and take hold of it in a regular grip. Bring it down to the inside of your knee as you step to the side (picture below) and continue as in the aigamae tegatana gedan no tsukuri.

The whole movement including the tsukuri and technique are shown on page 171.

169

vi. Gedan - aigamae gyakute dori (pictures page 173)
Your body movements are the same as the aigamae tegatana gedan no tsukuri (page 156). The difference is in your hand movements.

As in the basic aigamae tegatana gedan no kuzushi practice, immediately before uke grasps your wrist turn your hand palm up. In this case, turn your hand as much as possible (picture 1) without affecting your posture.

As you step forward with your left foot bring your hand over the top of his arm (picture 2) and place the back of your hand against the outside of his wrist so that your thumb is above his arm and your fingers below it.

Slide your hand down towards his wrist to break his grip and take a reverse grip on his hand (picture 3). In doing this, there is short amount of time where neither of you have a grip on the other person's wrist. To achieve this grip you must step to his right side and turn to face in the same direction as him.

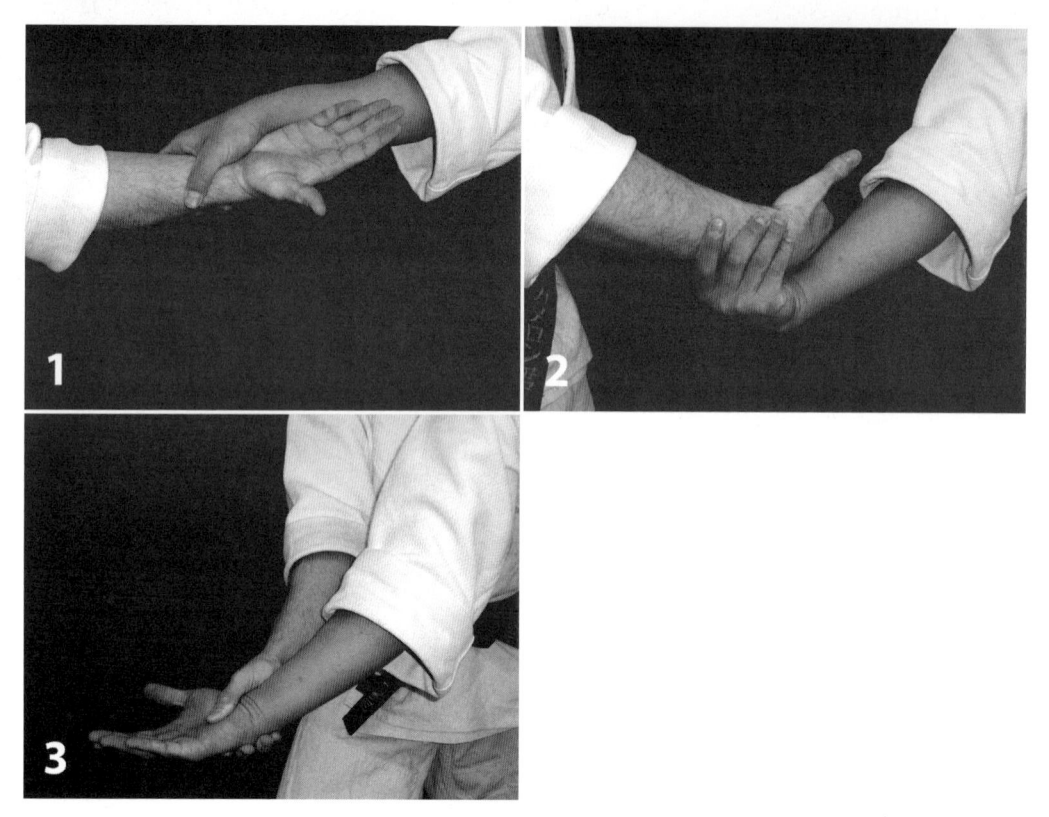

Bring your hand to the inside of your right knee and continue as for the aigamae gedan no kuzushi practice as far as to the point of starting to apply the final technique which is kote gaeshi. When you are ready to throw him take a reverse grip with your left hand so that your fingers are on the palm of his hand and thumb on the back of it (picture page 172 top left).

171

Break his balance by making a tsugi ashi movement with your right foot and taking his hand down low in front of him. Sweep your left foot back and apply kote gaeshi without changing the grip on his hand (picture below right).

The whole movement including the technique is shown opposite.

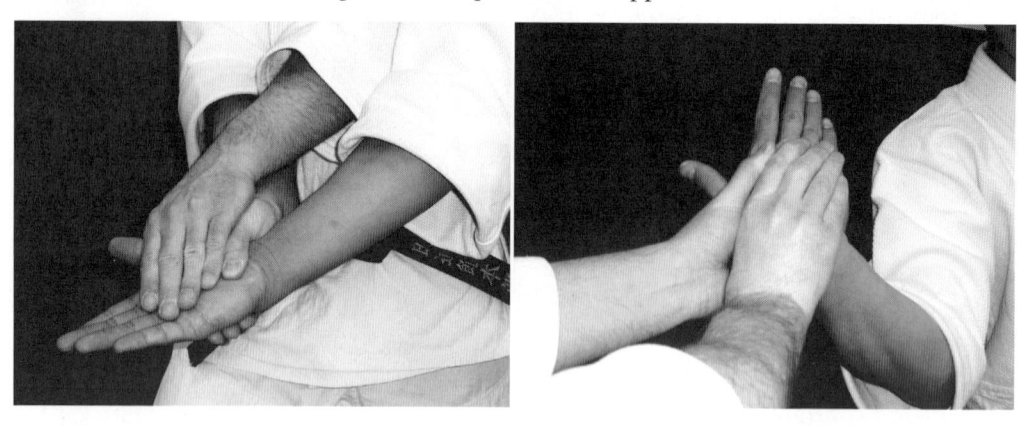

vii. Gedan - gyakugamae junte dori (pictures page 175)

Your body movements are the same as the gyakugamae tegatana gedan no tsukuri (page 158). The difference is in your hand movements.

As in the basic gyakugamae tegatana gedan no kuzushi practice, immediately before uke grasps your wrist turn your thumb down.

As you step forward with your right foot turn your elbow down to turn your hand so that your palm is above the inside of uke's wrist and take hold of it. Bring your hand down to the inside of your left knee as you step to the side (picture below) and continue as in the gyakugamae tegatana gedan no tsukuri.

At the end of your tsukuri apply tenkai kote gaeshi by grasping uke's wrist with your left hand and opening your right hand. Step across in front of him with your right foot and apply tenkai kote gaeshi as in the gyakugamae tegatana gedan no tsukuri.

The whole movement including the tsukuri and technique are shown on page 175.

173

viii. Gedan - gyakugamae gyakute dori (pictures page 177)
Your body movements are the same as the gyakugamae tegatana gedan no tsukuri (page 158). The difference is in your hand movements.

As in the basic gyakugamae tegatana gedan no kuzushi practice, immediately before uke grasps your wrist turn your hand thumb down. In this case, turn your hand as much as possible (picture 1) without affecting your posture.

As you step forward with your right foot turn your hand in the opposite direction bringing it over his arm. Slip your thumb under the outside of his arm and keep your fingers on top (picture 2).

Slide your hand down towards his wrist to break his grip and take a reverse grip on his hand (picture 3). In doing this, there is short amount of time where neither of you have a grip on the other person's wrist. To achieve this grip you must step to his left side and turn to face in the same direction as him.

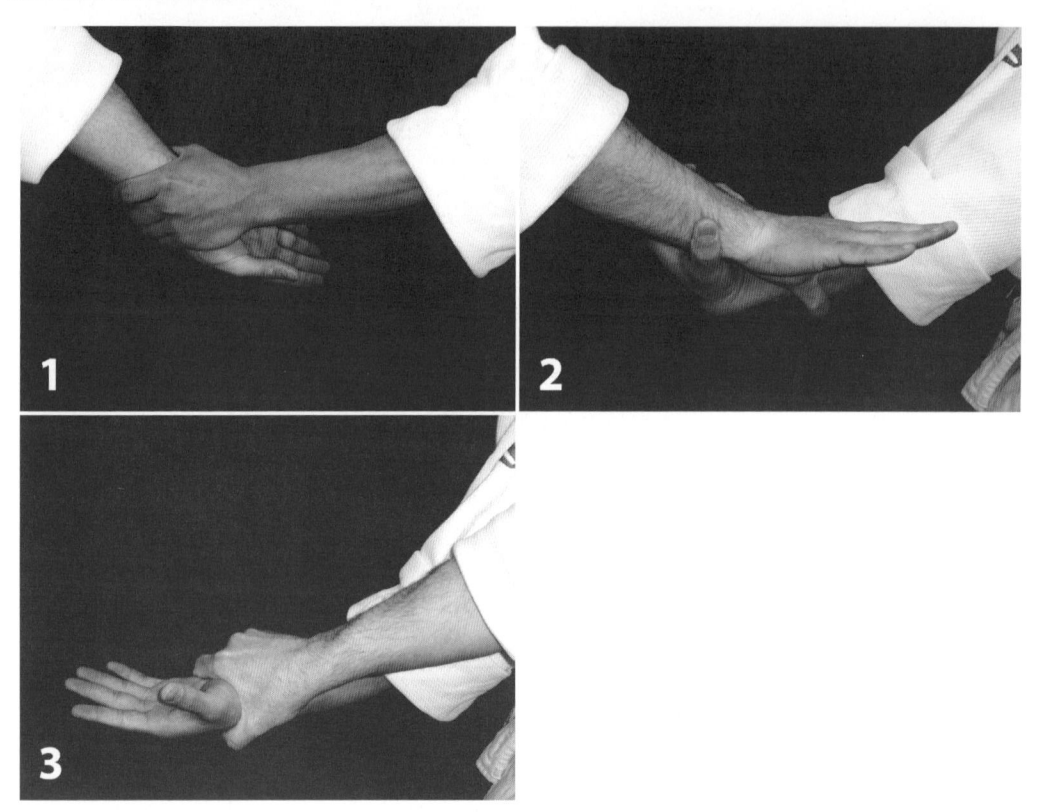

Bring your hand to the inside of your left knee and continue as for the gyakugamae gedan no kuzushi practice as far as to the point of starting to apply the final technique which is kote gaeshi. When you are ready to throw him take a reverse grip with your left hand so that your thumbs are crossed on the knuckle of his ring finger just as in the basic technique.

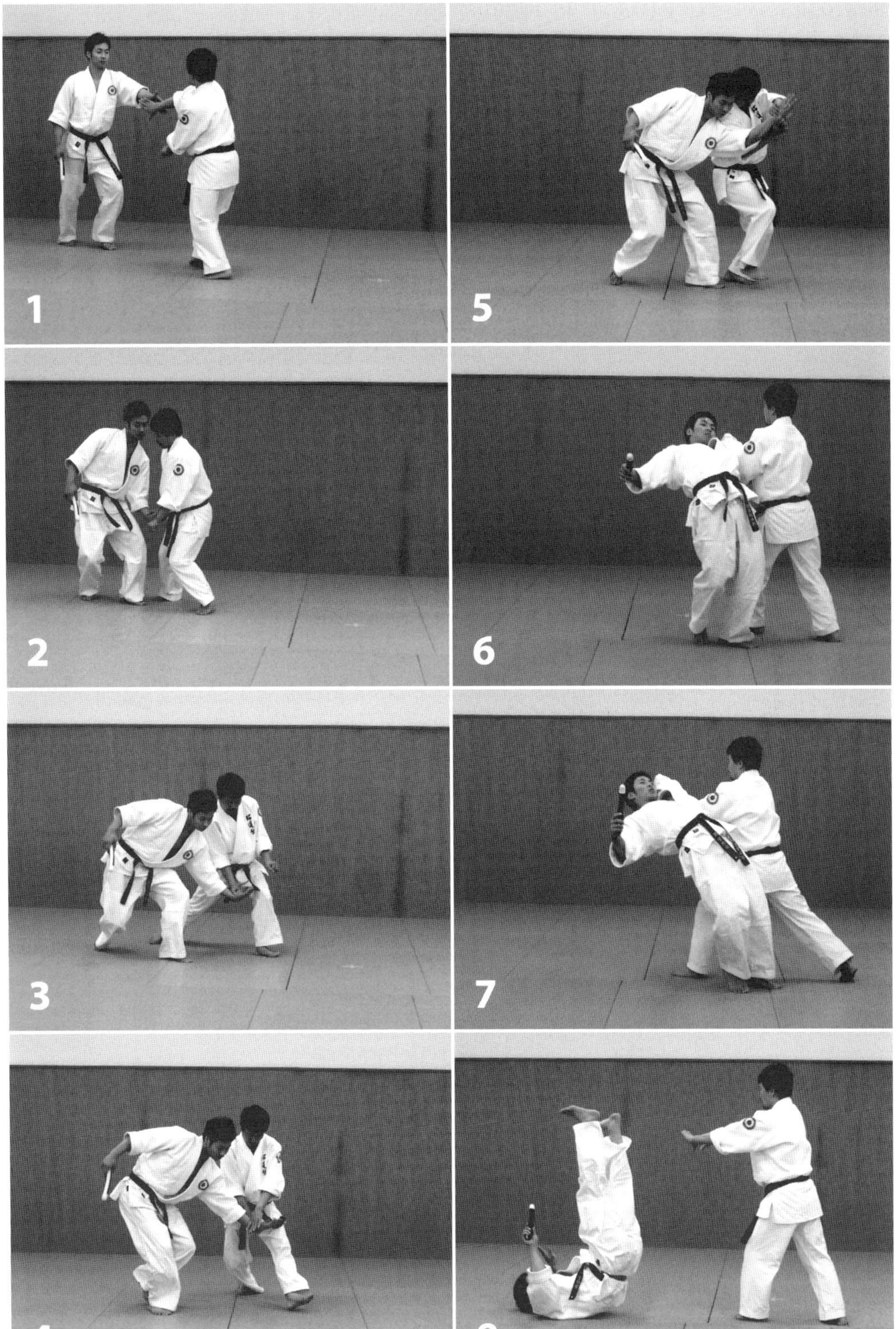
1
2
3
4
5
6
7
8

Break uke's balance by making a tsugi ashi movement with your left foot and taking his hand down low in front of him. Sweep your right foot back and apply kote gaeshi.

The whole movement including the technique is shown opposite.

The grip used here is different from that used on page 172. In both cases the right hand is the one that is taking the main grip and the left hand is used as support. You must not let the hand position used on page 172 slip into the hand position used here.

3. Hiji mochi no tsukuri
Some of the individual grips used in nigiri gaeshi no tsukuri are awkward and do not appear to be strong. However, these eight grips are used as four pairs (see the table on page 150) to good effect in hiji mochi no tsukuri. They are used against a stab where uke has no intention of grasping.

There are two directions to avoid a tantō tsuki: to the outside of tantō's arm or to the inside. For each of these two avoidances you can grasp his wrist with both hands either in a regular grip (junte) or reverse grip (gyakute). The basic grips are described below followed by the hiji mochi no tsukuri practices.

Your position, stance and direction you are facing may alter when these grasps are incorporated into your techniques. However, for this basic practice finish your movement with your feet positioned so that your centre is towards your opponent.

For each grip, aim to bring your hands down tantō's arm from his elbow to his wrist rather than grabbing directly to his wrist. Your hands stay in your centre during this movement so turn your hips slightly as your hands move down his arm. Picture 1 below shows an example of your hands preparing to grasp, starting near his elbow and then sliding down his forearm to grasp at his wrist (picture 2). Using your hands in this way fits in with the way that you use tegatana in terms of sword principles and it also gives you a much better chance of grasping his wrist than trying to catch it directly.

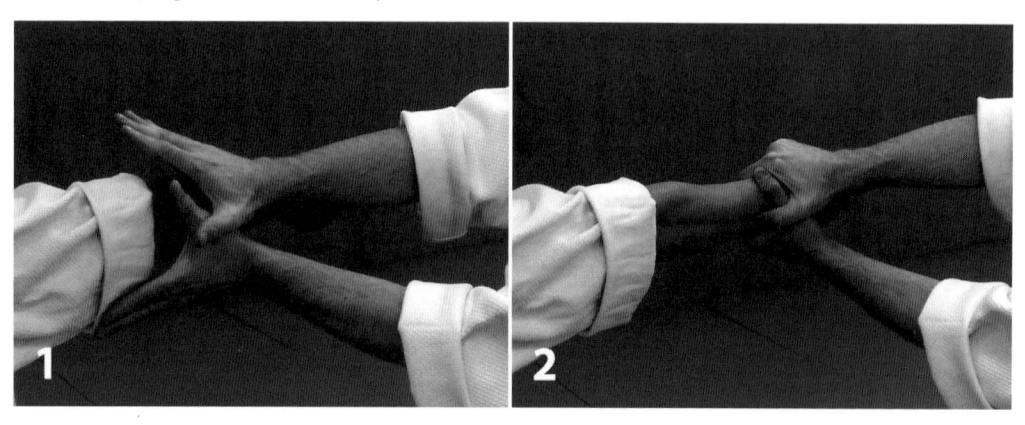

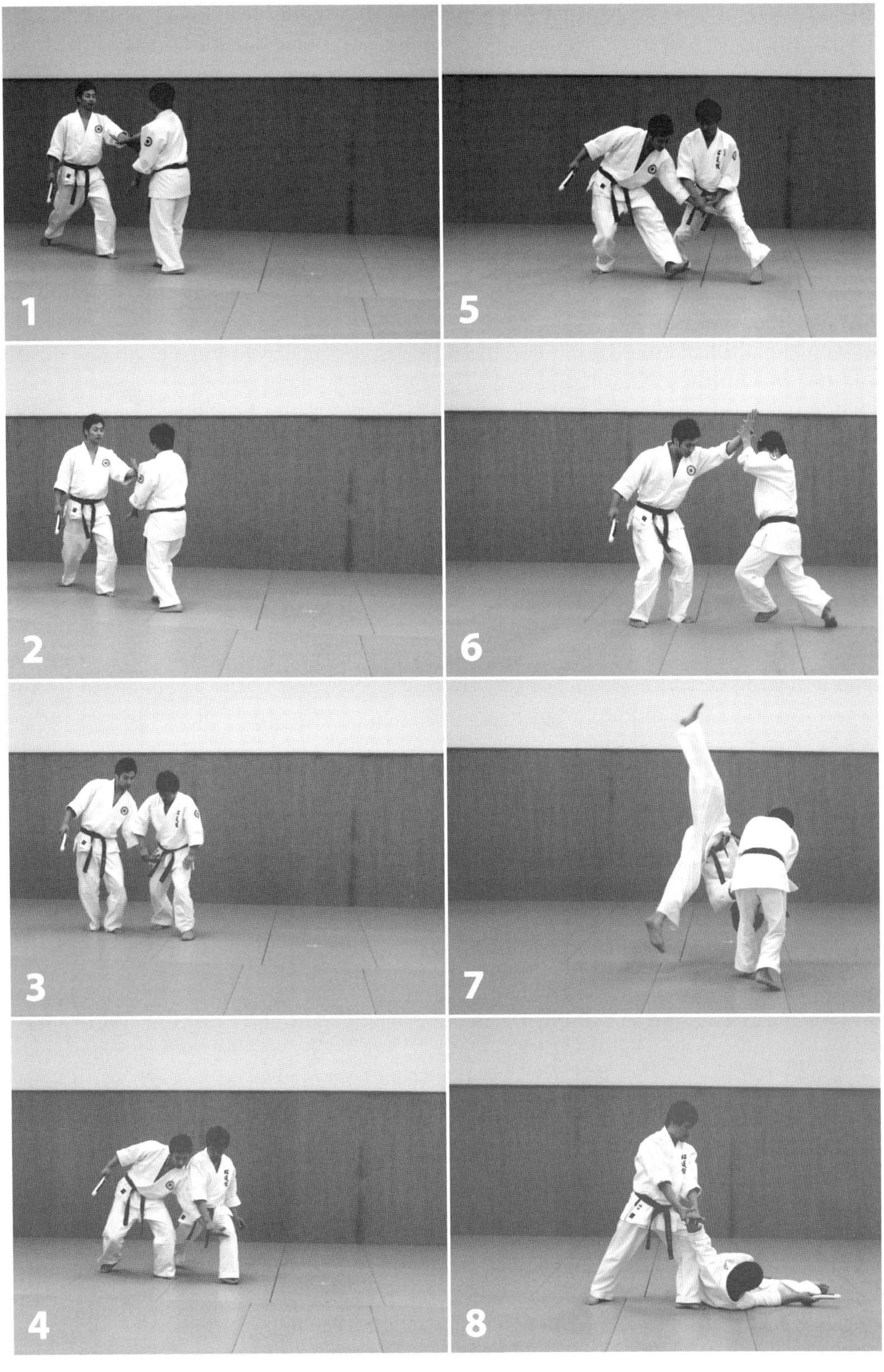
1
5
2
6
3
7
4
8

It is possible to stand in mugamae and move to the inside or outside of tantō's arm as he stabs. This gives him no indication of which direction you will move but it is much harder to do. Usually, in these practices, as in randori, toshu adopts a stance with one foot forward, either migigamae or hidarigamae.

In each case you move your whole body away from the line of attack as you grasp his arm with both hands.

i. Junte - outside of tantō's arm
Stand in hidarigamae and move forward and to your left, outside of the line of attack (picture top row left). Your thumbs point towards him in the junte grip (picture top row right).

ii. Junte - inside of tantō's arm
Stand in migigamae and move forward and to your right, inside of the line of attack (picture second row left). Your thumbs point towards him in the junte grip (picture second row right).

iii. Gyakute - outside of tantō's arm
Stand in hidarigamae and move forward and to your left, outside of the line of attack (picture third row left). Your thumbs point in the same direction as the knife in the gyakute grip (picture third row right).

iv. Gyakute - inside of tantō's arm
Stand in migigamae and move forward and to your right, inside of the line of attack (picture bottom row left). Your thumbs point in the same direction as the knife in the gyakute grip (picture bottom row right).

These are the four basic double-handed grips. In terms of kuzushi and tsukuri they are classified according to the whether you take your hands high or low (jōdan or gedan) and the grip (junte or gyakute) in the hiji mochi no tsukuri that follow which are usually practised in the order described.

The grasps on the arm or the movements to get to them may differ slightly from the basic form above in that your hands may not always be on the wrist as shown on the opposite page. However, if you look close at the orientation of the hands you will see that they correspond.

Each of the hiji mochi no tsukuri are practised twice, tsukuri only and then tsukuri with a technique to finish, as with the previous tsukuri practices.

It is important when you start practising this that tantō stabs straight and does not follow you as you avoid his attack. This allows you to practise the correct form and gives you the opportunity to judge how effectively and precisely you avoid his stab. Tantō can increase the speed of his attack, can include a feint and follow your body movement as you become more proficient. These all increase the difficulty but it is important that tantō stops after his stab and you also stop after your movement to judge your avoidance and grip.

179

i. Jōdan - junte

1. Stand in hidarigamae. Move forward and to the left off of the line of attack and control his stab with your left hand blade on his arm. Grasp his wrist with your right hand, slide your left hand to the inside of his elbow and close the distance to him with your left foot forward taking his arm close to his body (picture top right).

Push mainly on his wrist using the leverage gained to push his arm behind him towards his centre line (picture second right) moving forward at the same time.

Once his arm is behind him you need to get behind his arm to push it forward. Step deeper behind him with your left foot and slide your left hand around his forearm. Bend your knees deeply and turn to face in the opposite direction lifting his arm so that your fingers are under his upper arm and your shōtei (heel of the hand) is on his forearm. Keep your right hand on the other side of his arm (picture third right). Aim to move yourself around his arm and then push it up rather than staying stationary and pulling his arm up.

Use the shōtei of your left hand to push his elbow up and in front of you taking several tsugi ashi movements forward leading with your right foot before stopping. Keep close to him with you hips low and arms straight so that you can push up to bring him onto his toes using the movement of your whole body.

2. Repeat the tsukuri as above and apply oshi taoshi by pushing down on his arm and stepping with your left leg. Finish as for the basic technique but maintain the orientation of your left hand on his arm (picture bottom right).

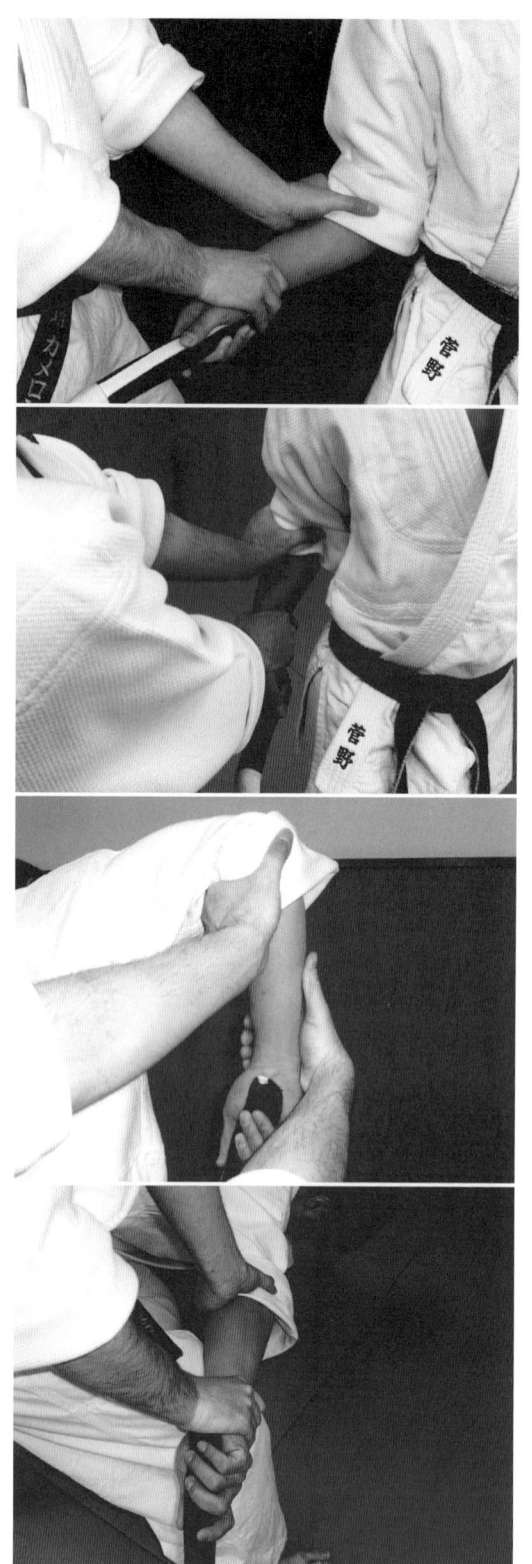

181

ii. Jōdan - gyakute

1. Stand in migigamae. Move forward and to the right off of the line of attack as tantō stabs and grasp his wrist with both hands in a reverse grip. Bring your elbows into your body, bend your legs and then extend them while leaning back slightly using the power of your leg muscles to bring him onto his toes and start moving him towards you. Do not lean back too much as this makes you vulnerable to counterattack or to losing your balance.

Once he is moving, turn to your right, extend your arms and make several tsugi ashi movements to keep him moving with his arm extended. Place your elbow under his arm to make it difficult for him to drop his elbow (picture right). It is safe to use your arm this way because his arm is rotated and you are applying pressure on the inside of his arm rather than on the elbow.

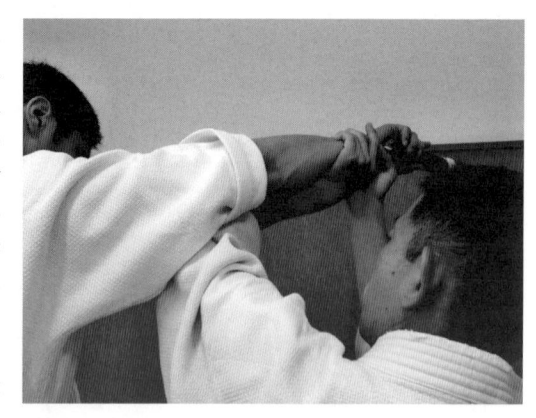

Stop after several tsugi ashi with your right foot forward.

2. Repeat the tsukuri as above and then apply waki gatame by releasing your right hand and continuing as in the basic technique.

iii. Gedan - junte (pictures page 185)

1. Stand in migigamae. Step with your right foot forward and to the right off of the line of attack as tantō stabs and grasp his wrist with both hands in a regular grip.

Step forward with your left foot to his right side while you open your left hand and slide it up to his elbow pushing it into the side of his body (picture below left).

Keep his elbow close to his body and rotate his forearm around his elbow as you pivot around his body almost 180° by sweeping your right leg back (picture below right). The further you

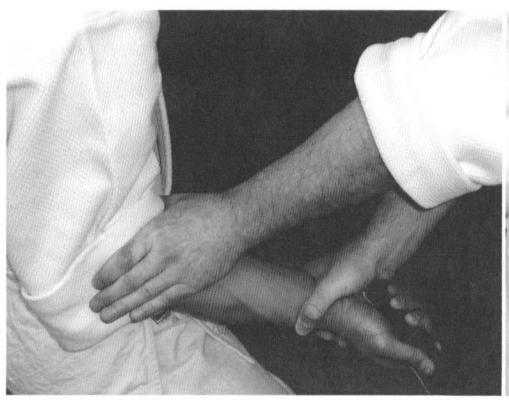

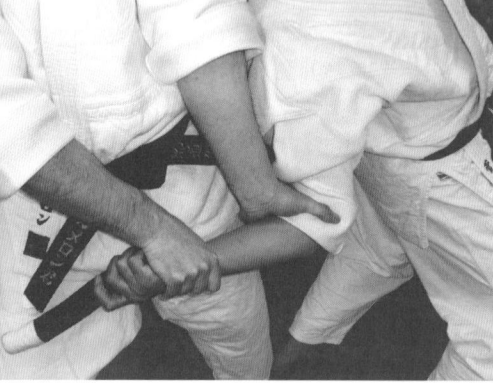

183

take his arm behind him the weaker his position becomes and the easier it is to get your weight on the top of his arm.

When you have finishing moving behind him your left arm is straight and you are keeping his arm low by applying your weight through your arm and shōtei on his forearm. Your arms are close to your body and in your centre. You have your right foot forward in a stance that is directed away from him along the line of his forearm.

Bend your knees to bring his arm low and make several tsugi ashi movements before stopping.

2. Repeat the tsukuri as above and then apply tenkai kote gaeshi by releasing the pressure on his arm allowing him to start to stand up. Slide your left hand down to his wrist step across in front of him and applying the technique as in the aigamae tegatana gedan no tsukuri (page 156).

iv. Gedan - gyakute (pictures page 186)
1. Stand in hidarigamae or migigamae. As tantō stabs step with your left foot forward and to the left off of the line of attack and control his stab with your right hand in an anti-clockwise sweeping movement close to your body similar to the kesa uchi movement (pictures 3 to 4) in tegatana dōsa so that your arm is between your body and his arm.

As you finish your arm movement turn to face the same way as him and slide your left hand down his arm so that you take a reverse grip on his wrist. Take a reverse grip with your right hand so that your thumbs are crossed on the back of the knuckle of his ring finger.

Sweep your right foot behind, keep your arms extended in front of you and pivot on the balls of your feet to facing the opposite direction breaking his balance by bringing your hands down low. As soon as you have finished your turn make several tsugi ashi movements before stopping.

2. Repeat the tsukuri as above and then apply kote gaeshi as in the basic technique.

Coaching point
You can stand with either foot forward to begin. Either way, you must turn your body and keep close to his arm as you step forward to avoid tantō's stab. Sweep your right arm across your body to get it between you and his arm but do not deflect his stab.

Once you have turned and taken your grip on his wrist it is very important that you do not apply any pressure on his elbow against the side of your body as you turn. Keep your arms extended and in your centre and draw him round in a circular movement so that his arm does not make contact with your body.

His balance is broken through the twist of your body along with bending your knees and bringing your hands low.

1

2

3

4

5

6

7

8

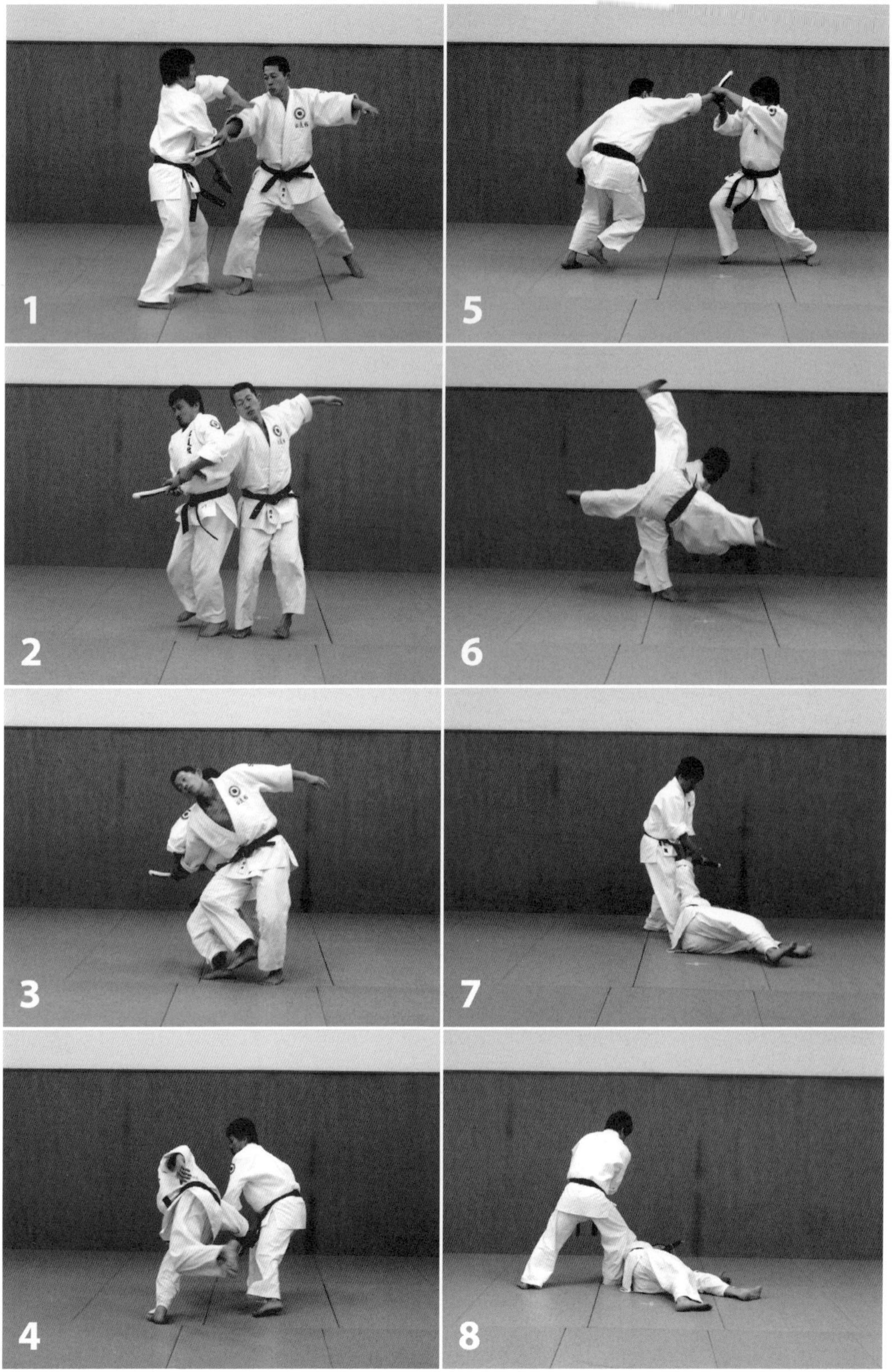
1
2
3
4
5
6
7
8

TIMING OPPORTUNITIES AGAINST TANTŌ TSUKI

The timing opportunities described for the atemi waza can also be used to apply kansetsu waza.

Okori o utsu

From your position separated from tantō you have to close the distance to grasp his arm before applying kansetsu waza. Consequently, it is not really possible to apply kansetsu waza at this timing point. However, you can close the distance and use your tegatana to control tantō's arm by placing it on his elbow or wrist which is a step towards applying kansetsu waza.

This corresponds to the kote (wrist) cut in kendo in the same way that the atemi waza relate directly to sword cuts. This movement is similar to the use of the hand blade on your partner's leg in the basic practice of tegatana no bōgyo (page 29).

Tsukitaru o utsu

When tantō stabs take a grip on his wrist as you avoid the line of his attack. The grips you can take are the same as described on page 178 just as tantō is finishing his attacking movement. The aim is to take advantage of his momentary immobility at the end of his attack, just as he fully extends his arm and places his foot down on the tatami, and immediately apply a kansetsu waza.

Four examples here demonstrate one technique for each of the four grips from page 178 although there are other possibilities.

i. Sumi otoshi (pictures page 188)
Stand in hidarigamae. As tantō stabs move forward and to the left off of the line of attack and grasp his wrist with both hands in a regular grip. Without stopping, turn your body to your left and bring your hands low into your centre as you take a deep step with your left leg to his rear right corner to break his balance and apply sumi otoshi.

ii. Tenkai kote gaeshi (pictures page 189)
Stand in migigamae. Move forward and to the right off of the line of attack as tantō stabs and

grasp his wrist with both hands in a regular grip. Immediately twist your hips to the right, turning on the balls of your feet, and bring your hands low into your centre to break his balance. Step through with your left leg and apply tenkai kote gaeshi.

iii. Kote gaeshi (pictures page 190)
Stand in hidarigamae. As tantō stabs move forward and to the left off of the line of attack, bring your right arm over the top of his arm (like the sweeping movement in the hiji michi no tsukuri but much smaller and faster) and turn towards his arm taking a reverse grip with both hands. Immediately step to his front left corner with your right foot bringing your hands low to break his balance. Sweep your left foot behind and apply kote gaeshi.

iv. Waki gatame

There are no pictures here for this technique because this timing opportunity is the same as in waki gatame for the jōdan gyakute movement from the hiji mochi no tsukuri described on page 182 with pictures on page 183.

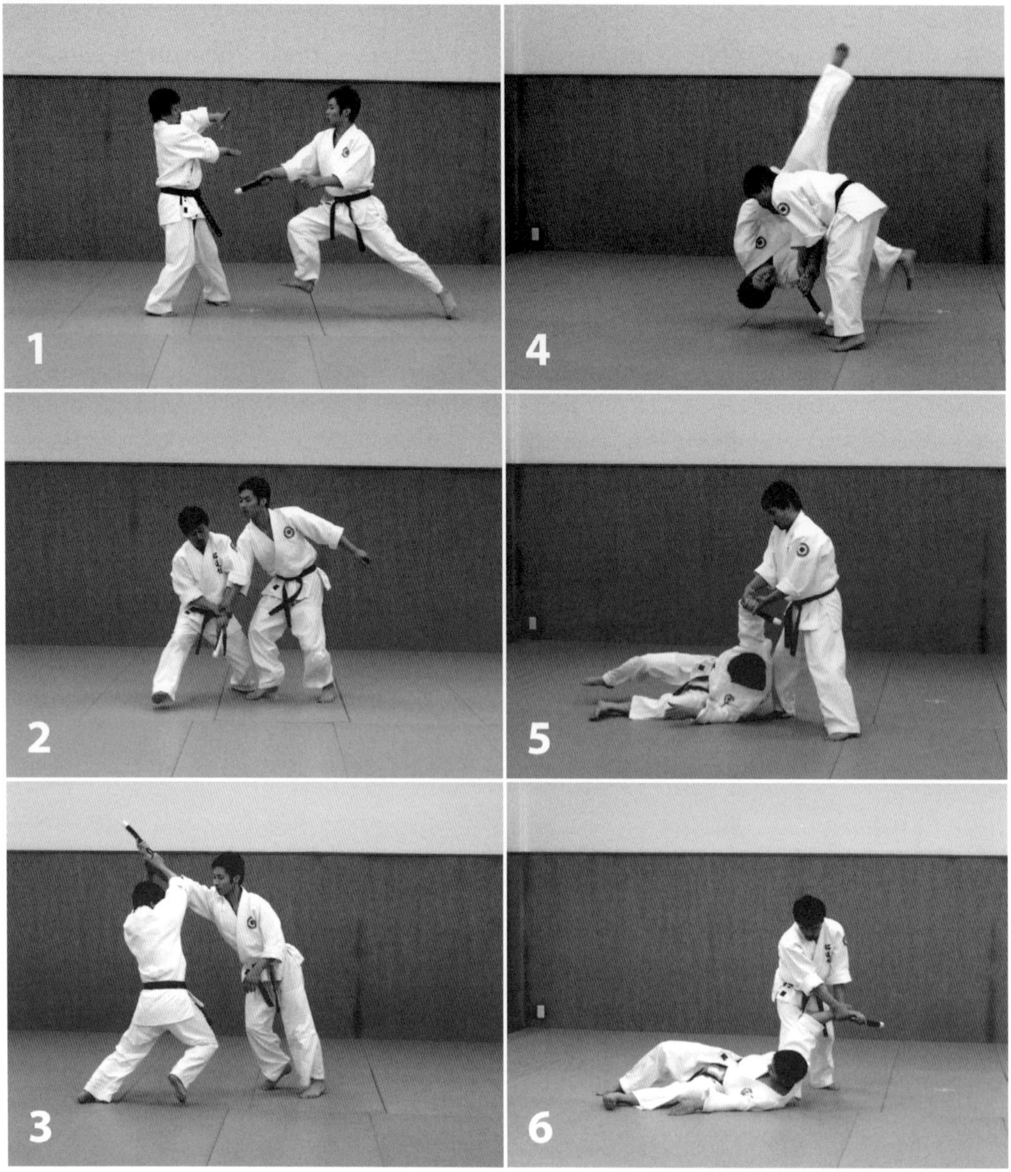
1
2
3
4
5
6

Hikiokori o utsu

This timing opportunity occurs after you have grasped tantō's arm and he pulls his hand back to bring his elbow close to his body where he has more control over it. To take advantage of this timing point you need to move quickly towards him to maintain your balance and use that movement to continue into a kansetsu waza.

The four examples here demonstrate one technique for each of the four grips from page 178 although there are other possibilities.

i. Oshi taoshi
This is applied exactly as for the jōdan junte movement from the hiji mochi no tsukuri described on page 180 with pictures on page 181. Your movement to close the distance to tantō after you have grasped his arm coincides with him pulling his elbow back close his body. Maintain your balance as he does this and continue your movement to push his arm behind him and finish with oshi taoshi.

ii. Tenkai kote gaeshi
This is applied exactly as for the gedan junte movement from the hiji mochi no tsukuri described on page 182 with pictures on page 185. Your step forward with your left foot after you have grasped tantō's arm coincides with him pulling his elbow back close to his body. Maintain your balance as he does this and continue your movement to take his arm behind him and finish with tenkai kote gaeshi.

iii. Kote gaeshi
This is similar to the gedan gyakute movement from the hiji mochi no tsukuri, described on page 184 with pictures on page 186, except that once you have grasped tantō's arm he pulls his elbow back to his body before you can turn. As he does this, move towards him to maintain your balance and then turn to your right and continue to finish with kote gaeshi.

iv. Waki gatame
This is similar to the jōdan gyakute movement from the hiji mochi no tsukuri, described on page 182 with pictures on page 183, except that once you have grasped tantō's arm he pulls his elbow back before you can pull him forward. As he does this, move towards him to maintain your balance and push his hand towards his face. Continue your movement to his left and extend his arm over his left shoulder to break his balance to his rear and finish with waki gatame (pictures page 192).

Ōjitaru o utsu

When tantō reacts to your attack or feint he moves away from you to maintain the distance between you. In this case you are effectively in the same situation as for the okori o utsu timing opportunity. You have far too much distance between you to be able to apply a kansetsu waza but you can follow his movement and close the distance to him controlling his arm with your tegatana as a transition to kansetsu waza.

KIHON URA WAZA

Ura waza (also called kaeshi waza) are counter techniques applied in response to an opponent's technique. In the current JAA rules tantō is allowed to apply atemi waza after his arm has been grasped by toshu using both hands. Toshu is also allowed to counter tantō's techniques.

There are ten basic counters to the 17 randori techniques: five against atemi waza and five against kansetsu waza summarised in the table below. Although the kansetsu waza counters are not valid within the current JAA rules they are nevertheless useful for understanding the connections between techniques and the timing needed to apply a counter. Practising these will benefit both toshu and tantō.

Group	Initial technique	Counter technique
atemi waza	shōmen ate	waki gatame
	aigamae ate	oshi taoshi
	gyakugamae ate	gedan ate
	gedan ate	aigamae ate
	ushiro ate	tenkai kote hineri
kansetsu waza	oshi taoshi	oshi taoshi
	hiki taoshi	tenkai kote hineri
	kote gaeshi	kote gaeshi
	tenkai kote hineri	waki gatame
	tenkai kote gaeshi	tenkai kote gaeshi

Ura waza can be viewed as linked techniques where there is a transition from your opponent's technique to yours. To apply these effectively you need quick, controlled body movement to draw your opponent into your technique when he moves to attack. To do this, maintain a natural, adaptable stance so you can move in all directions and deal with your opponent's attacks fluidly. Do not defend stiffly.

There are fundamental similarities in the theory and practice of counter techniques in aikido when compared to judo and kendo. These are outside the scope of this book but just as in judo and kendo you must attack positively and not wait passively for your opponent's attacks otherwise you will not improve. Take the opportunity to attack from start to finish, smoothly and spontaneously changing from one technique to another in your combinations and counter techniques.

1. Shōmen ate - waki gatame

Uke attempts shōmen ate as for the basic technique up to the point where he is about to push on your jaw. In this position he is at about a 45° angle to you and is aiming to push on that line.

At the moment he pushes make a tsugi ashi straight back to avoid his hand and bring your left hand up underneath his right wrist. Keep your elbow down and close to your body so that you can grasp his wrist as far underneath as possible. As you move back keep your torso upright and push up on his wrist to start to break his balance.

Turn to your right keeping his balance broken and his arm extended. At this point start to rotate his arm so that his elbow is on top. Keep your left hand high, move your body up towards his arm and place his wrist in the inside of your elbow with your left hand just to the outside of your arm.

Bring his arm down to your chest and continue for two or three more tsugi ashi movements in the same direction before stopping.

Your right arm is bent with your thumb pointing towards you so that it squeezes his wrist. His arm should be in contact with your chest with your left hand to the outside of your right arm as in the basic technique.

In the finish position he has his left foot forward and arm extended above his head. He is bent over with his head down so that his arm, shoulders and head are at about the same level. You stand with your right foot forward in a natural posture with your shoulders level.

This technique should lock his arm but not cause any pain.

Coaching points

The critical timing point where his technique changes into yours is the instant he tries to push on your jaw. At that time his line of attack is at an angle to you. If you move straight back just at the moment he moves forward to push you then you can avoid his technique.

The position of your hand on his wrist at the moment you move back to avoid his push is shown on the right. Your elbow is down so that you can get the palm of your hand as much as possible on the inside of his wrist which allows you to rotate his arm more.

195

2. Aigamae ate - oshi taoshi

Uke starts to apply aigamae ate by stepping forward with his left leg and trying to turn your arm over to break your balance.

Step back with your right foot as he steps forward maintaining your balance and distance from him and preventing him from applying his technique. At the same time bring your left hand over and take a reverse grip on his left hand.

Raise both arms at the same time bringing your right hand onto the inside of his left elbow as you lift his arm. Step forward with your right foot and push his elbow towards his left ear.

Once he has fallen to his hands and knees make a tsugi ashi movement to close any distance between your right leg and his armpit.

Step up with your left foot and step back and away from his body with your right foot. Place his arm on top of your leg just above the knee. The angle between your leg and his arm is 90°, the angle between his arm and his body is much greater than 90°. Your left leg is bent, right leg is straight. This is the same finish as in the basic oshi taoshi except for the position of your hands (picture below right).

Slide your right hand blade around the front of his elbow and pull his elbow round towards you while twisting your left thumb down.

Coaching points

The critical timing point is the instant that uke takes his first step forward. Step back with your right foot and avoid him and turn naturally to the right to take a reverse grip on his left hand (picture below left).

When you switch into applying oshi taoshi raise both hands together rather than lifting his left hand away from your arm. As you lift your arms your right hand naturally comes underneath his left elbow.

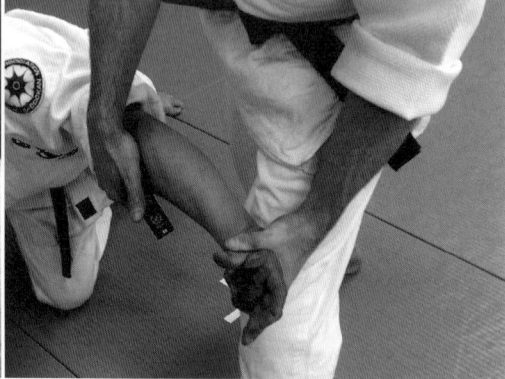

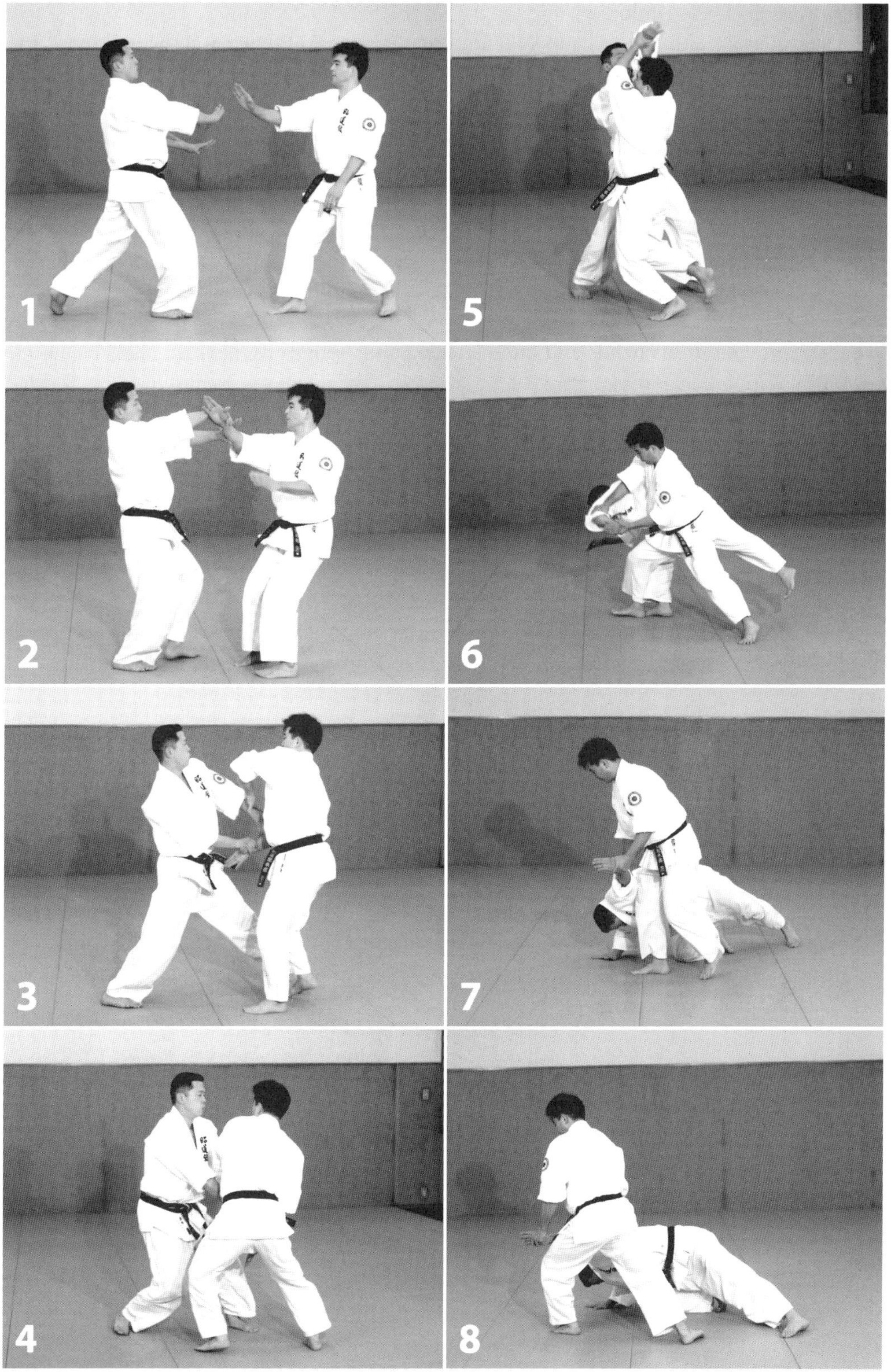
1
2
3
4
5
6
7
8

3. Gyakugamae ate - gedan ate

Uke starts to apply gyakugamae ate. When he steps forward with his left leg to bring his left arm across your chest raise your left arm to block it on your centre line and step back with your right foot deeply and slightly to the right. Bend your legs and keep your torso upright. As you do this rotate your right hand clockwise and drop it sharply to your centre with your fingers pointing downwards and hand blade towards your body to break his grip.

Raise yourself up and step to his left side with your right foot placing the inside of your right arm low across his body. As you do this, bring your left hand down so that it is also in front of you.

Push forward with your left leg to push him down and straight back. At the same time, turn your hips slightly to the right and draw your left foot up so that at the end of the technique you are facing your original direction in a correct posture.

Coaching points

The critical timing point is when uke steps in with his left foot to place his arm across your chest. Step back at the same time and block his left arm with your left arm.

His first movement when applying gyakugamae ate is to avoid to your right side. When he steps towards you to place his arm across your chest he stands just to your right. As you step back to avoid him make sure that you step slightly to your right rather than straight back. This means that you finish in front of him and this allows you to step to his left side more easily to apply gedan ate.

As in the basic technique, when you step to his left side to throw him, do not step behind him. You must allow him the freedom to step back to take an ukemi at his own pace.

4. Gedan ate - aigamae ate (pictures page 201)

Uke applies gedan ate in a slightly different manner than in the basic technique. In this case after he feints with his left hand (against which you raise your left hand) he moves directly with his left leg to apply gedan ate with his left arm.

As he moves in with his left foot step back with your right foot and bring your left arm down to block his arm. Without stopping, bring your left foot back and then forward to the outside of his left foot in a kind of V-shaped movement. Grasp his left arm at the same time and pull it over his head to break his balance.

Release his arm and, as he recovers his balance and turns towards you, bring your left hand under his left arm up to his chin and into your centre.

Push off with your right leg and move forward and slightly to the left to apply aigamae ate as in the basic technique.

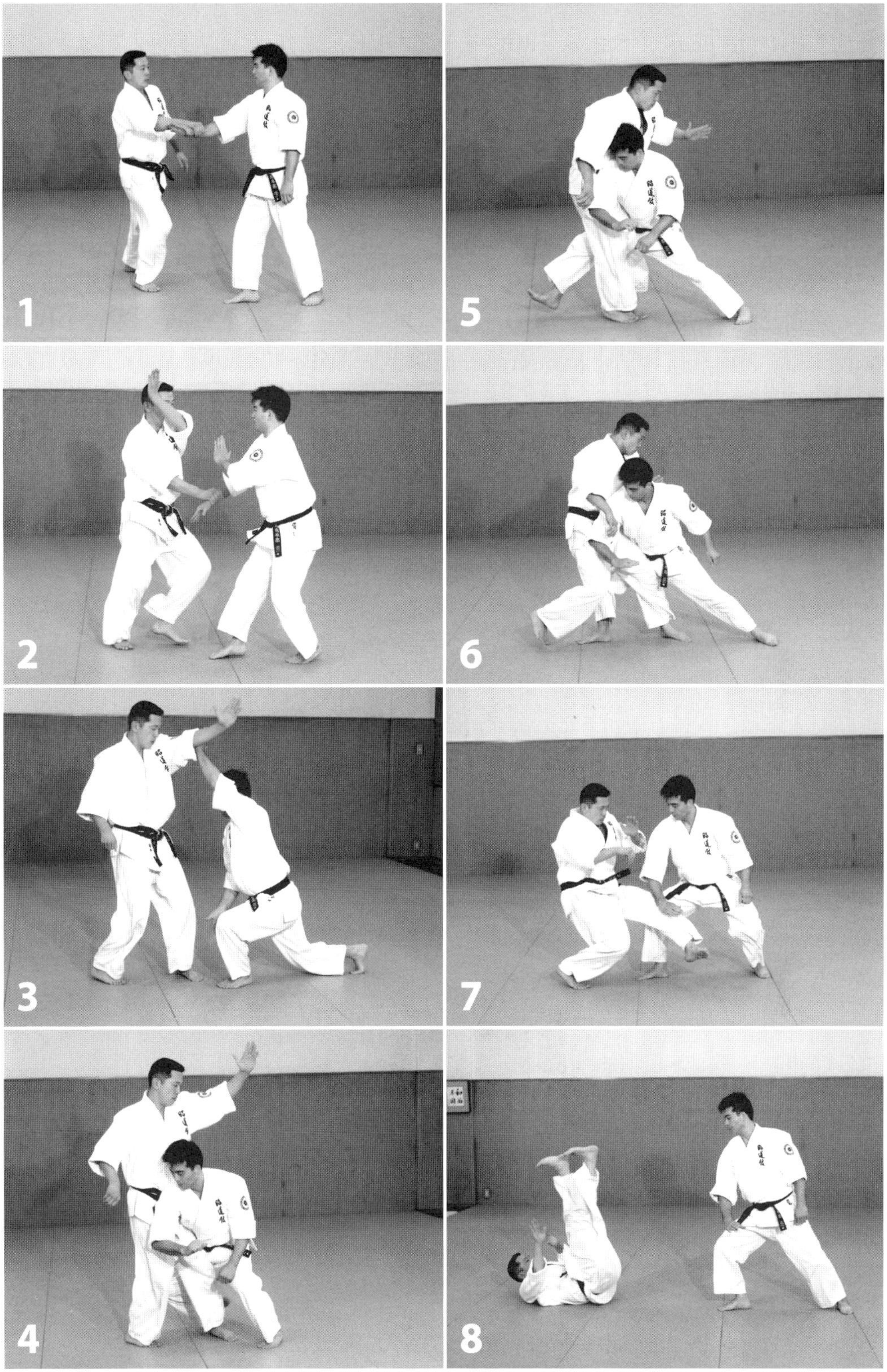
1
5
2
6
3
7
4
8

Coaching points
The critical timing point is when uke steps forward with his left leg to apply gedan ate with his left arm. Block his arm and step back to avoid his technique.

After you step back with your right leg you will find that his foot is alongside your left foot or even closer to you due to his deep step forward. You will need to bring your left foot back a little before bringing it forward to the outside of his left foot. This is the reason for the little V-shaped movement described above which follows on without stopping after you step back with your right foot.

When you pull his arm over the top is his head to break his balance this will turn his body. As you release his arm he recovers his upright posture and turns back to face you. It is at this point that you apply aigamae ate as he is momentarily immobile. He then takes a backward ukemi in the direction of your movement rather falling early when you have turned his body. If he falls when his body is turned this not only stops you from practising the full technique but is potentially dangerous as he may fall across your knee as you step through.

5. Ushiro ate - tenkai kote hineri (pictures page 203)
Uke uses his right hand blade to lower your arm. As he does this bring your left hand over the top of his right hand and grasp it while making a fast tsugi ashi to his right side far enough so that your shoulder touches the front of his shoulder.

Raise your hands on your centre line until they are above your head and turn to your left to face in the opposite direction.

Keep your left foot forward and turn slightly to your left to break his balance by twisting his wrist with your left hand assisted by the hand blade of your right hand. Maintain a natural posture and keep your hands in your centre.

Continue and finish as for the basic technique.

Coaching points
The critical timing point is as uke lowers your right hand. Grasp his wrist and move forward quickly before he can twist your arm.

Your forward movement needs to be very quick to prevent him from applying ushiro ate. Pass close to his body so that your right shoulder touches his right shoulder. It is also very important that uke applies ushiro ate correctly. He must not move his right foot to his right at the start of his technique as this places it directly in line with your movement and is likely to result in injury.

To help close the distance to his shoulder you can turn your right shoulder forward as you move towards him and then quickly turn under his arm to apply tenkai kote hineri.

1
2
3
4
5
6
7
8

6. Oshi taoshi - oshi taoshi (pictures page 205)
This is very similar to the counter technique used against aigamae ate except that the initial movement is in a different direction. Uke avoids to his left and then draws your arm away from you as he makes a short movement back. As he does this, move towards him enough to maintain your balance and distance from him, and grasp his left hand with your left hand in a reverse grip.

Raise both arms at the same time to lift his arm. As you do this bring your right hand onto his left elbow with your thumb underneath and fingers on top. Once you start to lift your arms step forward with your right foot pushing his elbow towards his left ear.

After he has fallen to his hands and knees make a tsugi ashi movement to close any distance between your right leg and his armpit.

Continue as for the counter technique of oshi taoshi against aigamae ate.

Coaching point
The critical timing point is when uke takes hold of your forearm and moves backwards. Move towards him to maintain your balance and grasp his hand (picture right).

Raise both hands together so that his left hand stays in contact with your arm and your right hand naturally comes into contact with his elbow.

7. Hiki taoshi - tenkai kote hineri (pictures page 206)
This is very similar to the counter technique used against ushiro ate except that the timing and depth of your movement are different. Uke grasps your arm aiming to apply hiki taoshi by pulling it down. Turn your elbow down just as he starts to pull and make a fast and deep tsugi ashi just to his right side so that your shoulder touches to the front of his shoulder. Grasp his right wrist with your left hand as you move.

Raise your hands on your centre line until they are above your head and turn to your left to face in the opposite direction. Continue as for the basic tenkai kote hineri.

Coaching points
The critical timing point is when uke pulls your arm down. Dip your elbow and quickly move forward to maintain your balance.

203

As in ushiro ate it is very important, from the point of view of avoiding injury, that uke applies hiki taoshi correctly. He must not move his foot to the right as he pulls your arm down.

The main difference between applying tenkai kote hineri as the counter to ushiro ate and hiki taoshi is the distance. In ushiro ate uke is pushing your arm towards you not moving back whereas in hiki taoshi he is pulling your arm and moving back to break your balance. This means that the distance you have to close to him when he applies hiki taoshi is much greater. This is not easy but is helped by turning your right shoulder forward to help close the distance to his shoulder before you turn under his arm.

8. Kote gaeshi - kote gaeshi (pictures page 207)
When uke pulls your hand down to break your balance before applying kote gaeshi as in the basic technique move towards him with your right foot to retain your balance.

When he sweeps his left foot back and twists your wrist, before your hand is twisted outside of your elbow, bring your elbow towards your body and turn your hand in an anti-clockwise direction underneath his hands so that your hand blade is towards his left side but on your centre line. Tsugi ashi in the same direction as you turn your hand down and grasp his right hand in a reverse grip. Once you have broken his grip take hold with both hands and take them low on your last movement to break his balance.

Pivot on your right foot sweeping your left leg behind and continue as for the basic technique.

Coaching point
The critical timing point is when uke tries to turn your wrist. Draw your hand towards you and turn it under his hands as you grasp his wrist and apply kote gaeshi.

The grip change is shown here (pictures 1-3)

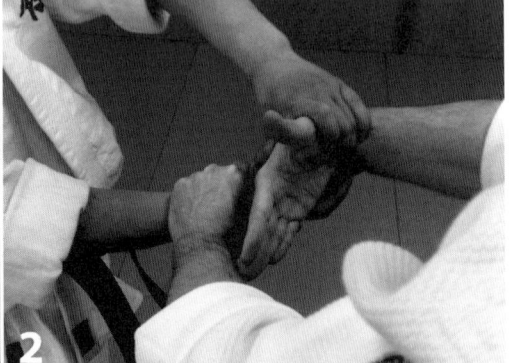

205

206

207

9. Tenkai kote hineri - waki gatame
Uke starts to apply tenkai kote hineri. Take a big step forward with your left leg the instant before he turns and lift your arm high over his head.

Bring your left hand up underneath his left arm and then between his arms as you pass by him.

Continue moving forward and to the front of him bringing your hands over and down in a big circle to the left side your chest. Your hands are open with uke maintaining his grip on your wrist.

Finish with your left leg forward, shoulders level with his arm across your chest squeezing his hand with the backs of your open hands (picture below).

Coaching points
The critical timing point is immediately before uke turns. Lift your hand and quickly move forward to take control of the technique.

It helps to slide your left hand up close to his body as you move but be careful to avoid taking your hand near to his face.

10. Tenkai kote gaeshi - tenkai kote gaeshi (pictures page 211)
Uke starts to apply tenkai kote gaeshi. As he brings your arm down, just before it reaches its lowest point bring your left hand between his wrists. Move your right foot towards him and slide your fingers around his left wrist as far as they will go. Straighten his arm by turning your right hand anti-clockwise and drawing your left hand back in the opposite direction. This locks his arm straight and stops his body movement.

Grasp his left wrist, pivot on your right leg and sweep your left leg behind turning to face the opposite direction taking your hands over the top of your head and bringing them down to shoulder height behind him to break his balance. Continue as for the basic technique.

209

Coaching points
The critical timing point is as uke brings your arm down from its start position. Use your hands to stop his movement before changing direction into your technique.

The pictures below show the action of your hands to stop his movement. The fingers of the left hand reach around his wrist as fas as possible (picture 1). Turn your left hand back in the opposite direction as your rotate your right hand anti-clockwise to extend his wrist. This moves the back of his hand towards the back of his forearm and locks his arm straight (picture 2).

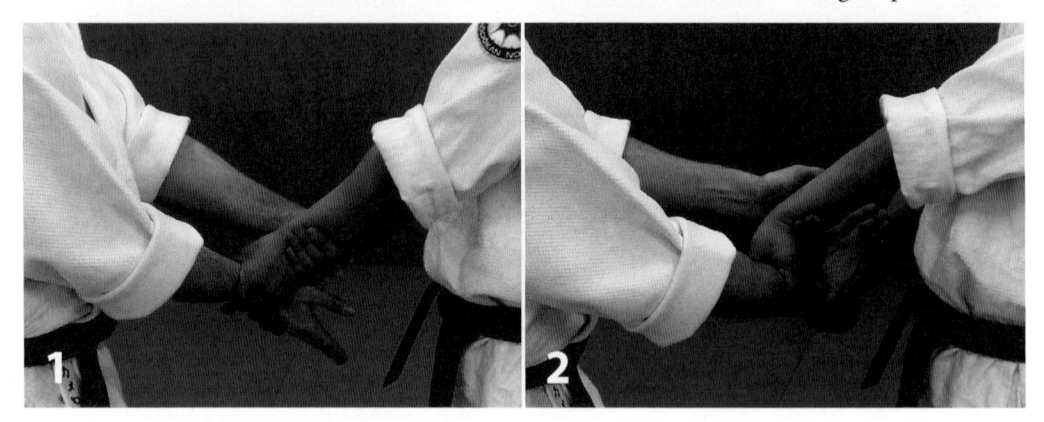

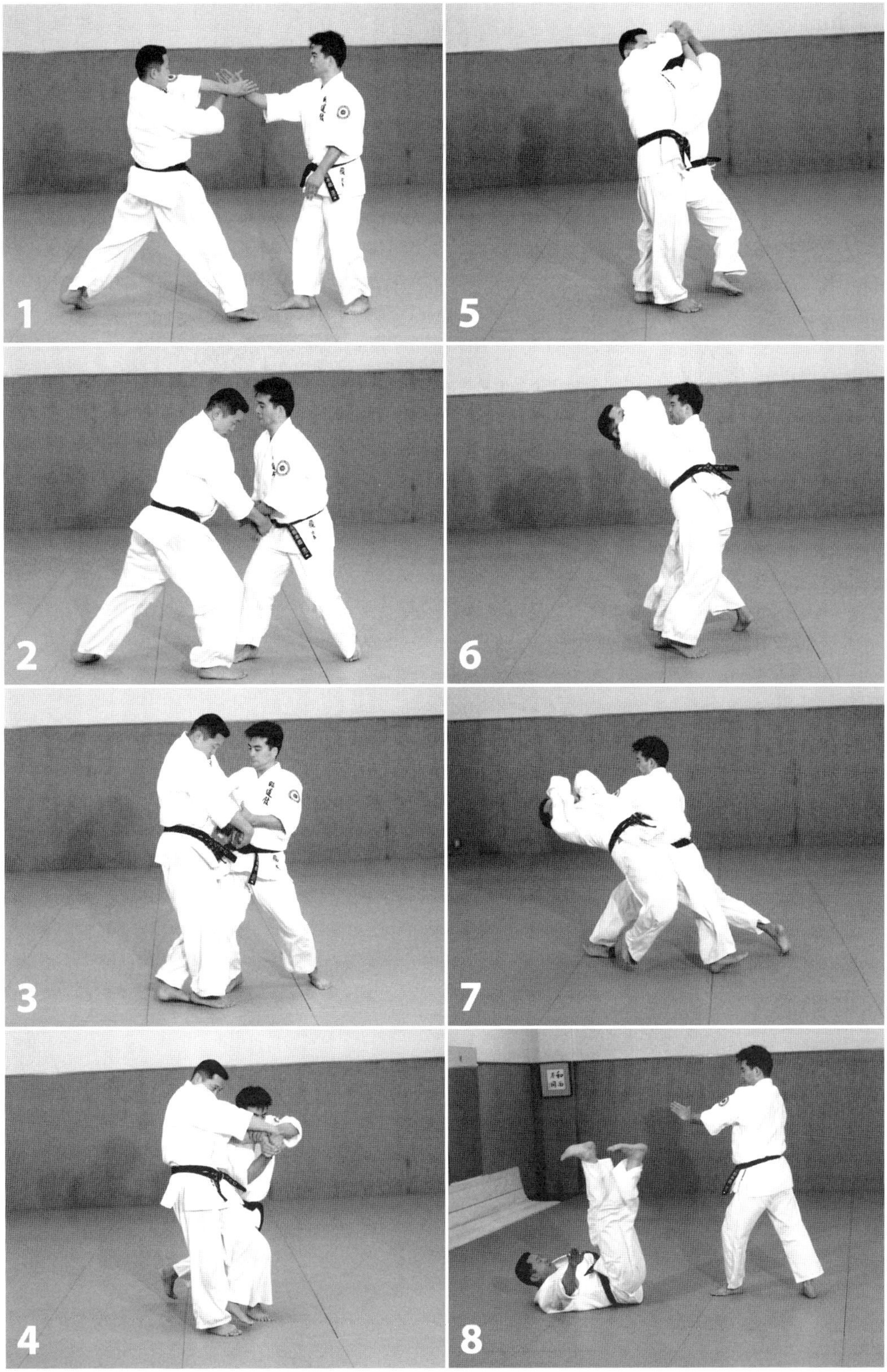
1
2
3
4
5
6
7
8

COMBINATIONS

Techniques are often most effective in combinations where you create an opening or get a reaction from your opponent that allows a second or even third technique. The first one can either be a genuine attempt or a feint as long as you get the desired reaction from your opponent. Repeated attempts at a technique or feints will often produce the same reaction in an opponent. This can reveal an opponent's habits which you can use to your advantage.

The following pictures show six workable combinations. They are only a small sample of the possibilities and no descriptions are given as you are encouraged to research and experiment to find combinations that work for you. Transitions from one technique to the next should be made as smoothly as possible.

Start off slowly and build up to a more realistic pace but remember that a combination done at a slow speed may not necessarily be feasible in a normal situation. You should note the way that tantō reacts or resists your techniques and determine the best way to change to another one. It is therefore important to test the feasibility of your combinations in competitive practices such as hikitate geiko and light randori training.

Combinations are allowed involving any of the 17 basic techniques although your position and stance, and that of uke, may limit your possibilities. Do not forget that you are also allowed to swap from applying kansetsu waza on one arm to kansetsu waza on the other.

Page 213: oshi taoshi to ushiro ate
Page 214: waki gatame to gyakugamae ate
Page 215: tenkai kote gaeshi to gyakugamae ate
Page 216: kote gaeshi to ushiro ate
Page 217: kote gaeshi to gedan ate
Page 218: kote gaeshi to tenkai kote gaeshi

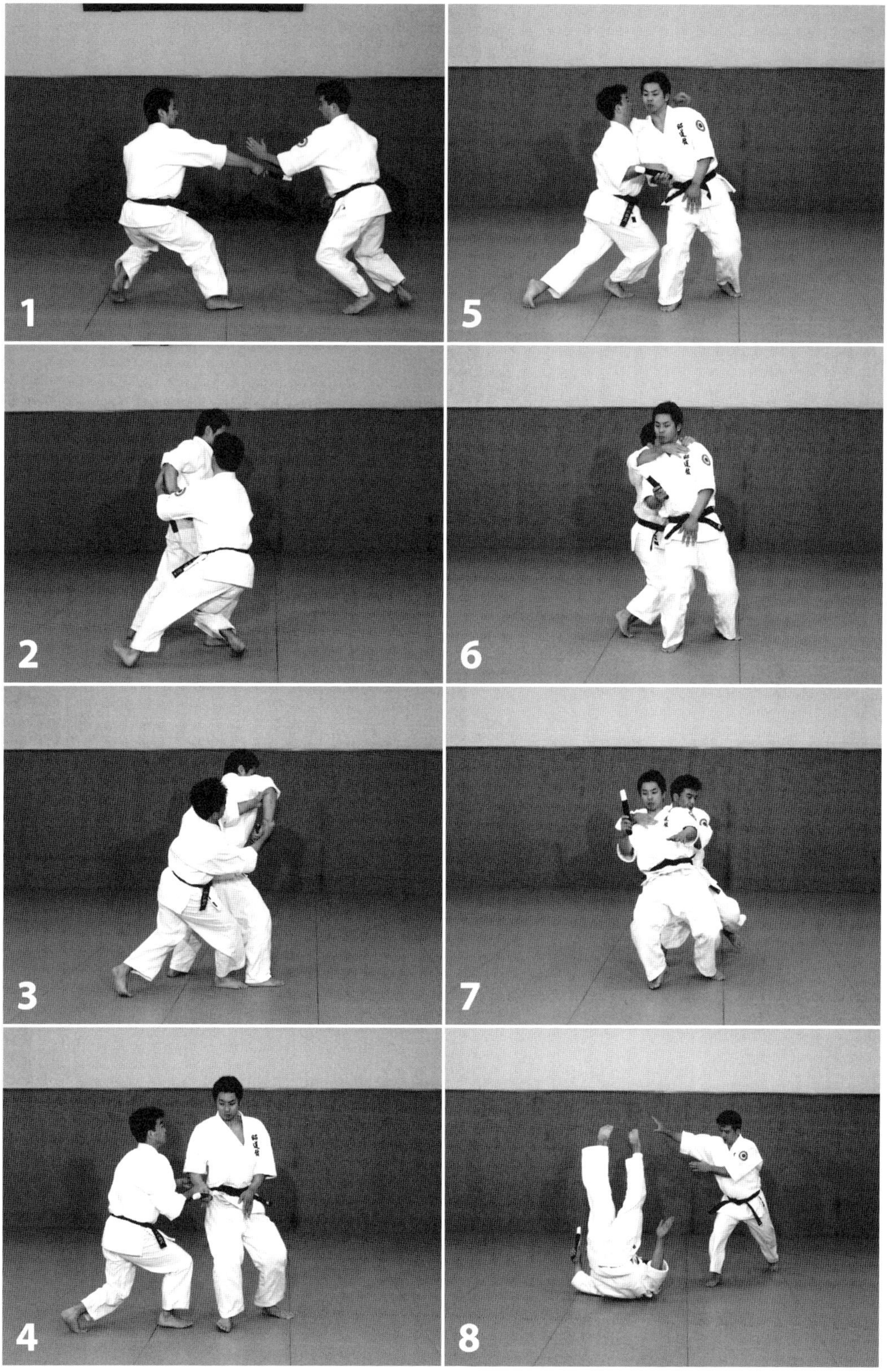
1
2
3
4
5
6
7
8

214

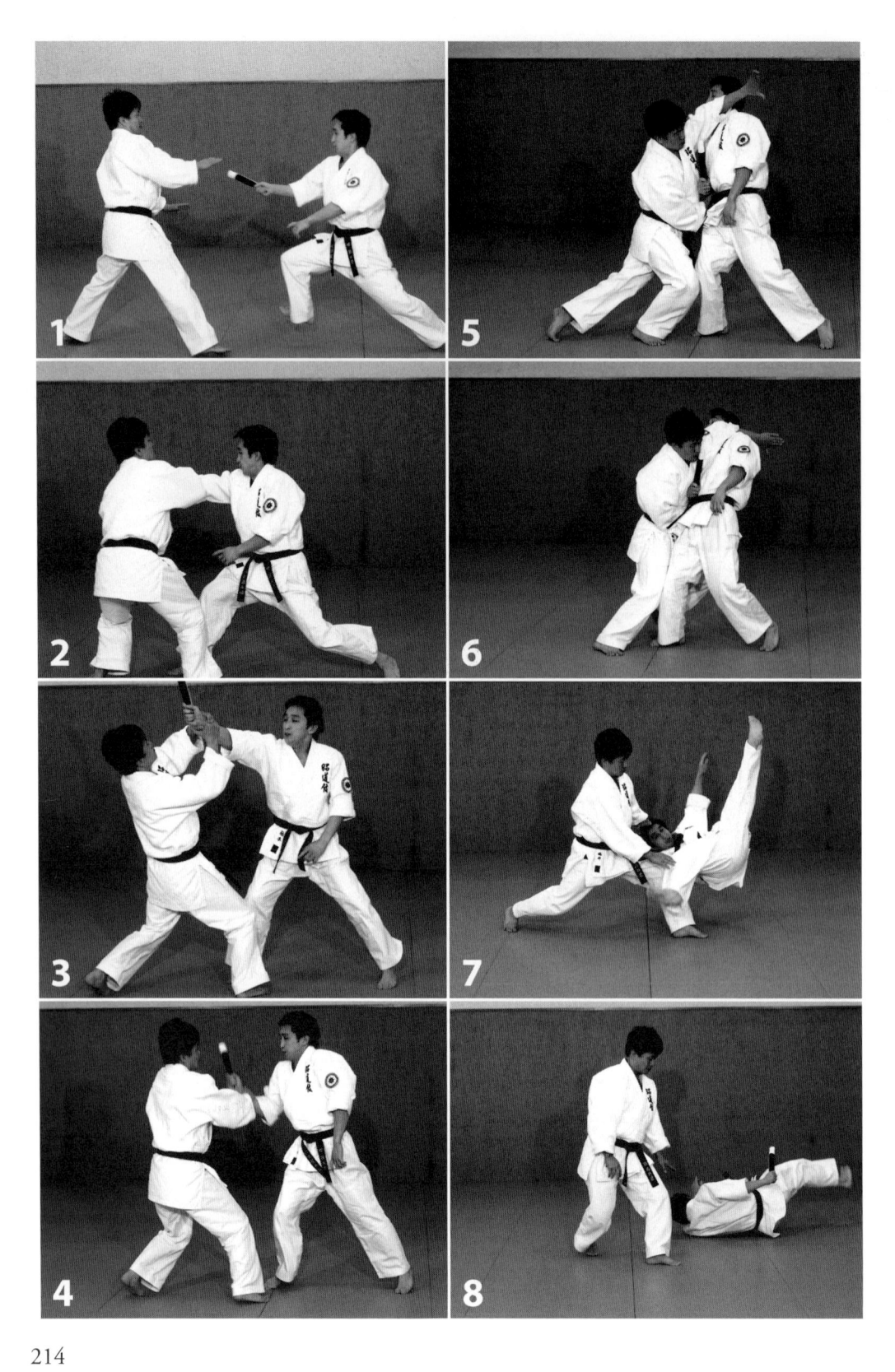

215

216

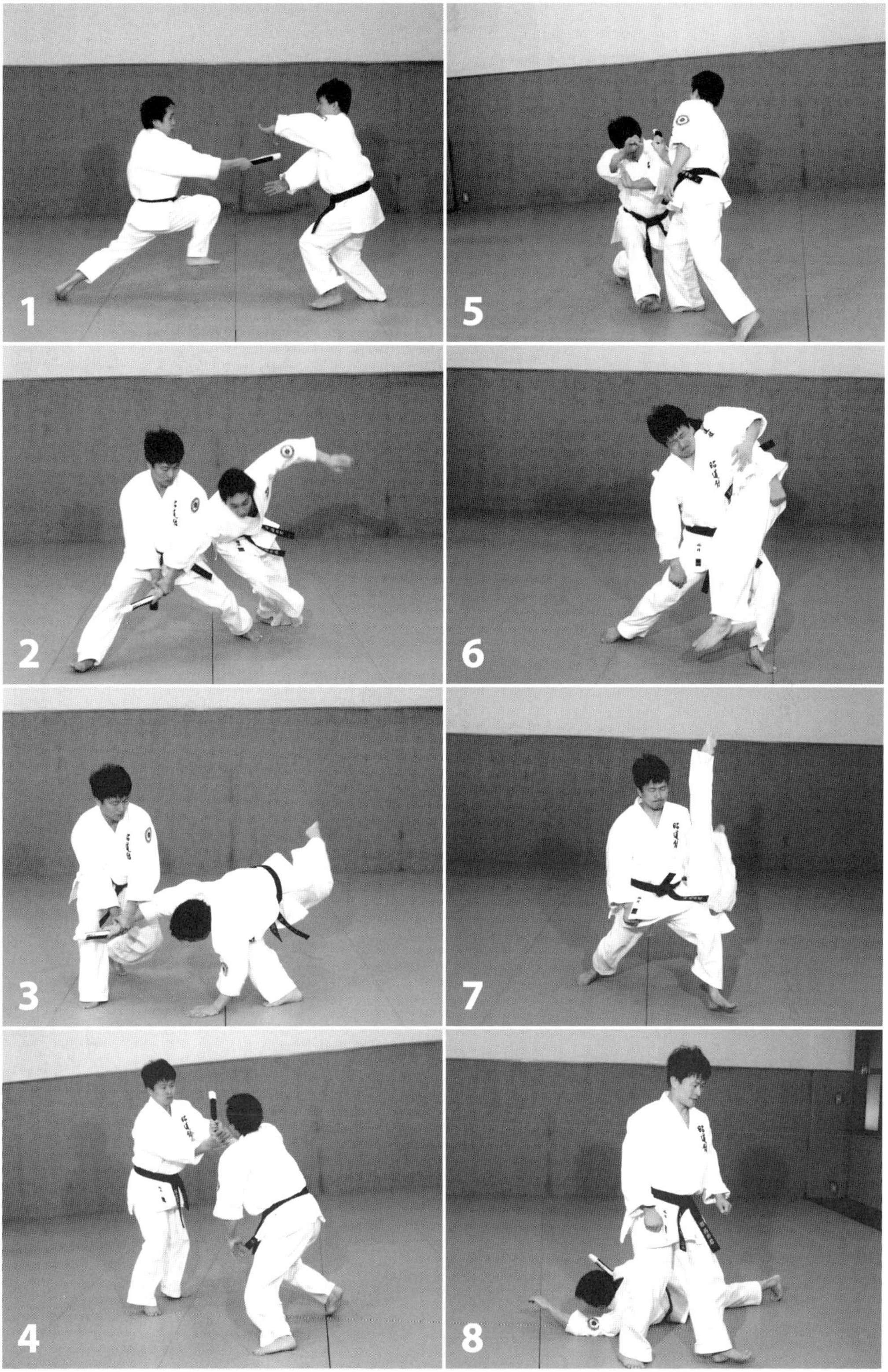

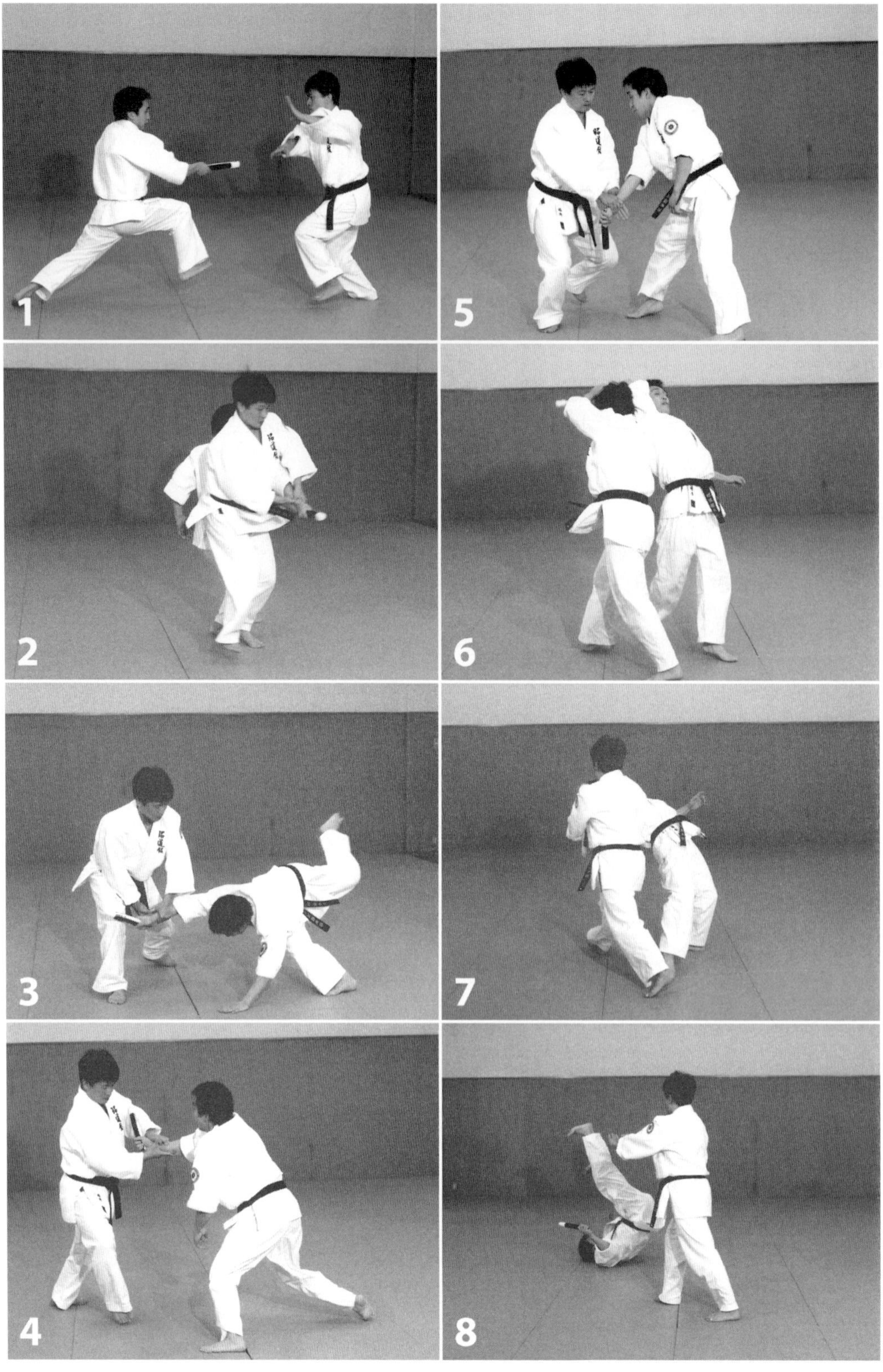
1
2
3
4
5
6
7
8

PART 3

TANTŌ

The tantō side of randori is often overlooked and the emphasis placed on the toshu side. However, the skills of both are fundamentally very similar when considered in depth from a technical viewpoint. This part looks at these similarities and introduces the techniques and skills used by tantō.

Tomiki's view of a complete judo encompassed two parts: kumi judo (grappling) which equates to Kōdōkan judo, and hanare judo (separated) which is aikido. We know that the combative distances in judo and aikido are different. A knife is used in aikido randori to prevent the correct distance from being ignored. Tantō's intention is to stab and toshu uses body movement and tegatana to control the attacks.

The concept of tantō tsuki comes directly from kendo and the use of tegatana in aikido randori is comparable to the use of a sword in kendo. By introducing the tantō we are immediately bringing concepts and skills from kendo into both sides.

In terms of the use of tegatana there are two aspects, how to use it and when to use it, which can be understood from both toshu and tantō sides.

The correct movements are practised in tegatana dōsa. For toshu these are used in kansetsu waza as the hand movements while avoiding the tantō tsuki, grasping tantō's arm, breaking balance and applying the final movement of the technique. In atemi waza they are used when avoiding the knife or applied directly as summarised in the table on page 64.

For tantō, he can stop toshu's movement to grasp his arm by using the tegatana of his empty hand. Also, when he is grasped he can use his free hand to break away from that grasp although he is not allowed to grip with his free hand.

Tantō's movement to stop toshu's grasp and toshu's hand movement to avoid tantō's stab are similar when examined. Tantō's movement to break toshu's grasp and toshu's balance break or final application also correspond.

The timing for using tegatana from the viewpoint of tantō is the same as the timing in the atemi waza:

- okori o utsu – the instant that toshu starts a movement to close the distance or apply a technique
- tsukitaru o utsu – the instant that toshu's technique misses or he fails to reach you
- uketaru o utsu – the instant that toshu withdraws after his technique misses or after tantō uses his free hand to break away from toshu's grip, or the instant that toshu senses and reacts to tantō's attacking movement or feint

Because of the similarity in skills between toshu and tantō, the exercises used for developing toshu skills are useful for developing tantō skills and vice versa. Of course, it is essential to practise both roles in your training.

THE TANTŌ AND TANTŌ TSUKI

The tantō used in aikido randori is 30cm long and made of sponge rubber in a black canvas cover. One end of the tantō is covered with a piece of white material and there is also a strip of white material running down its length (older style tantō were white canvas with black material).

The white end of the tantō represents the point and the strip of leather represents the back of the tantō, not the edge (picture page 221 top left). this corresponds to the string or 'tsuru' along the back of a bamboo shinai (picture page 221 top right). Hold the tantō with your little finger flush with the end and your fingers curled around the body of the knife rather than extended along it (picture page 221 bottom left).

It is always passed to another person with the white strip of material facing towards the receiver. The picture on page 221 (bottom right) shows the knife being passed from the person on the right to the person on the left.

In toshu randori (randori without a knife) the participants inevitably close to a distance similar to that used in judo. The leg and hip throws from judo are not allowed in aikido randori but Tomiki considered it important to avoid the close range where those kinds of techniques are possible. The knife was introduced to ensure a separated maai and encourage correct aikido training somewhat out of range of leg and hip techniques.

Tantō scores points by tantō tsuki (stab with a knife) to prescribed parts of toshu's body. The target area is the torso above the belt and below the horizontal line between toshu's armpits on the front, sides and back. A stab to his arm is also valid if that arm is held against his body.

For a valid stab tantō must have forward hip movement, his hips must be stable at the time the stab occurs, his torso upright and not twisted excessively. His arm must be extended and the angle of the stab at about 90° to toshu's body in the target area with the final one third or half of the knife bent. Whichever hand is used to hold the knife the same side foot must be forward at the start and end of the stab.

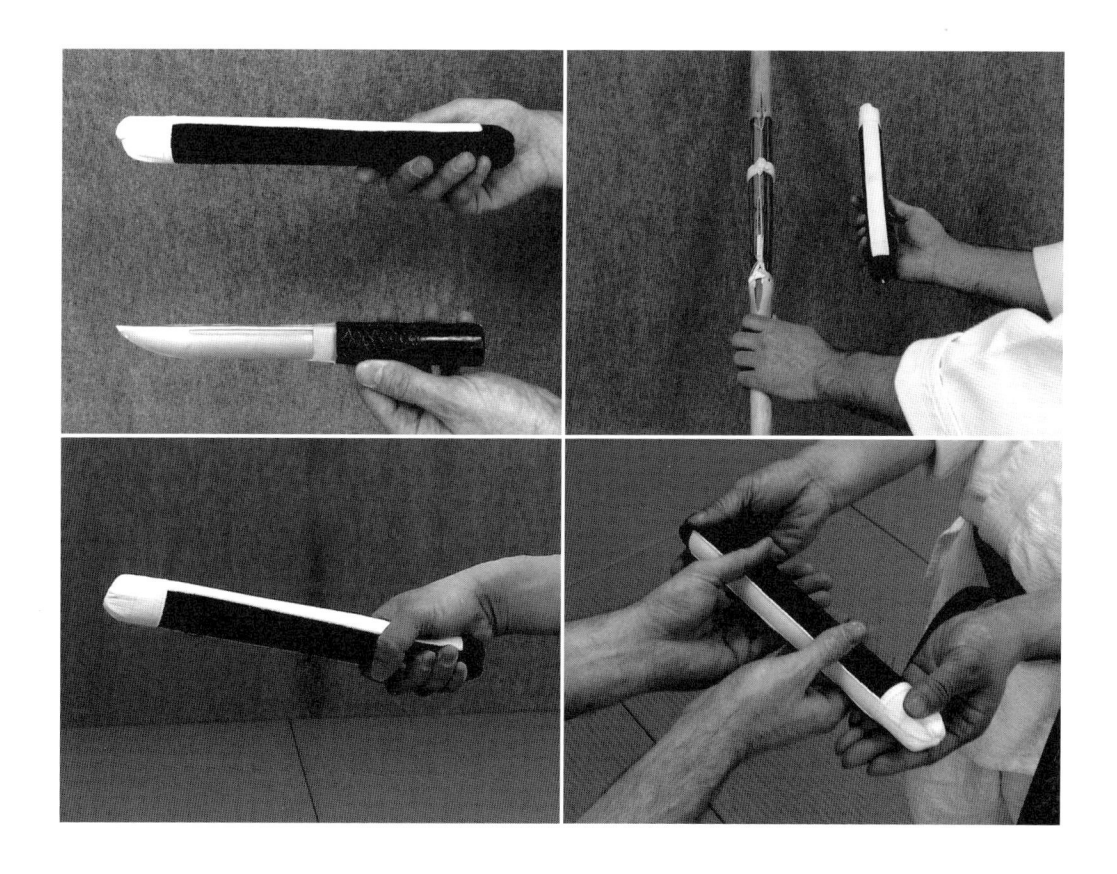

DEVELOPING TANTŌ TSUKI SKILLS

A series of drills and exercises to improve your tantō tsuki ability is presented below roughly in order of increasing technical difficulty.

Most people favour holding the knife in one hand over the other even though it can be held in either one. The drills described here are described for a person holding the knife in the right hand but as the skills of tantō and toshu are closely related there are benefits to practising tantō tsuki skills with both hands.

From toshu's point of view you have no control over which hand your opponent holds the knife. Therefore, it is very important to practise with people holding it in the right hand as much as in the left hand.

Tantō tsuki

To learn the basic tsuki and an appreciation of maai, stand facing toshu with your right foot forward and holding the tantō in your right hand at a distance from where you can reach him with one step.

Hold the tantō low and in your centre with your arm relaxed and slightly flexed. Push forward with your left leg and extend your arm so that your right foot comes down on the tatami at the same time the knife strikes toshu. Ensure it is consistent with the correct form as described above and pictured below.

At the end of your movement your feet are not too far apart that you are unable to move easily and not too close together that your stability is compromised.

Aim to move faster and from a greater distance from toshu as you improve. Your stab should always have the correct form, be well controlled and to the correct depth in the target area.

Although toshu is standing stationary in mugamae he can still gain an appreciation of maai from tantō's start position. He can practise metsuke by maintaining eye contact and observing the movements of tantō's body. It also gives him a chance to identify any weaknesses in tantō's stab such as the telltale signs as he starts to move.

You are allowed to rotate your hand so that your thumb turns down or palm turns up (pictures below left and right respectively) during the stab. This is called maki zuki and is related to the third tegatana dōsa movement and a useful skill in avoiding toshu's defences and in the application of tantō kaeshi waza (counter techniques against a stab). The stab is still a straight thrust and differs from mawashi tsuki where the line of the knife strike is outside the width of your shoulders.

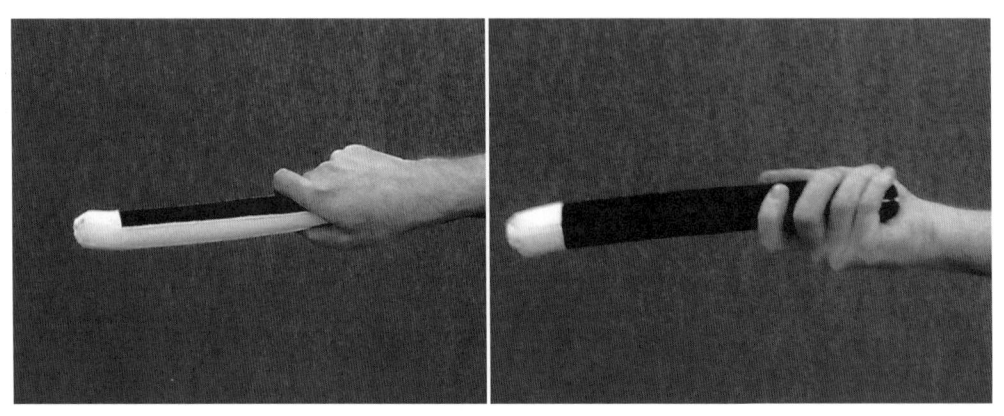

The pictures above show mawashi tsuki which is not allowed as the knife is brought outside the width of your shoulders in a large curved movement.

Extensions
The following are a selection of practices as an extension of the basic tantō tsuki.

1. Vary the starting distance
Stand at varying distances from toshu. Make every stab to the correct depth to improve your control and judgment of distance.

2. Maximise the starting distance
Stand at a distance from toshu that is slightly greater than the maximum distance that you can comfortably move in one movement. Make every effort to cover the distance with a correct stab to extend your effective maai and develop fast, explosive power.

3. Vary the target
Stab to different parts of the target area: high and low, left and right, with or without using maki zuki. This is to improve the control of your stab and ability to vary the angle and target of your attack.

4. Basic timing
Toshu jumps on the spot as in shōki no tsukuri. Tantō stands at the correct distance and makes his stab so that the knife makes contact with toshu's chest at the instant his feet touch, shoulder width apart, on the tatami. This is a practice for basic timing of tsuki taking advantage of toshu's immobility.

5. Advanced timing
You and your opponent each hold a tantō and freely move around the tatami taking opportunities to stab while at the same time avoiding any attack. Chances to attack occur:
- as the opponent makes his initial preparation to stab (okori o utsu)
- as he stabs (tsukitaru o utsu)

223

- as he withdraws after you have avoided his stab (hikiokori o utsu)
- as he moves in response to your feint or when he senses your attack and moves away (ōjitaru o utsu)
- at any time you gain an advantage by breaking the maai, changing your position, etc

You can allow the use of the tegatana of the free hand to defend against the stab or to disallow it which is a much harder practice.

6. Repeat stab
Start on one side of the tatami and make several stabs moving across to the other side of the tatami. This is to practice the ability to 'reload' and stab more than once moving forward. This can be done alone or with a partner who stands as your target and quickly moves back to the correct distance after each stab.

7. Stab and withdraw
Toshu stands in mugamae and tantō stands at the correct distance. He stabs, withdraws and then stabs again. This is to develop a fast recovery after an unsuccessful stab by moving back. You can vary this exercise by withdrawing straight back or at an angle.

Toshu can also be mobile in this exercise and practising tai sabaki. He avoids your first attack and then waits for you to withdraw and stab a second time.

8. Breaking a grip (ridatsu) and tsuki
Tantō stabs and toshu grasps his arm in a grip of his choice. Tantō then uses his arm and body movements to break the grip with or without the use of the tegatana of his empty hand (tantō is not allowed to grasp at all with his free hand). As soon as he has broken the grip he moves backwards or to an advantageous position to create room before attacking with a valid stab.

Create other practices that you feel will benefit your tantō tsuki. Generally, everyone favours one side over the other and will usually practise tantō skills holding the knife with the same hand. However, it is recommended that you practise using the both left and right sides.

TANTŌ KAESHI WAZA

Formerly, tantō was only allowed to score points by stabbing. His defence was limited to breaking free from a grasp to make a further attack or to using the tegatana of his free hand to prevent toshu from grasping. One good aspect of this was the speedy attack and defence which improved the technical level of the atemi waza. However, it created a few problems with posture and tai sabaki which are fundamentally important in budo.

In this situation the good characteristics of tantō tsuki were seldom seen. Poor posture started to appear as well as other things that are undesirable in terms of budo. This in turn resulted in a poor posture for toshu which tended to invite techniques that were applied with brute force. This kind of randori lacked skilful techniques and the merits of sudden change of attack and defence that are found in judo and kendo.

To improve on this situation the rules were altered while staying consistent with the nature of budo. If toshu holds tantō's free arm and tantō places the knife against toshu's chest for more than 3 seconds the referee can interrupt play and penalise toshu for not breaking tantō's balance.

This helped greatly in stopping both players becoming careless and getting too close to each other which is at odds with the correct maai in aikido. However, overuse of these rules could cause too many stoppages which interrupted the fluid offence and defence of both players.

A further fundamental change was made by introducing the atemi waza as counter techniques for tantō in certain circumstances. They can be used when:

- toshu has grasped tantō's knife-holding arm with both hands. In this case tantō can use either hand to apply atemi waza
- toshu has grasped tantō's free hand with both hands. In this case tantō can apply atemi waza only with the hand that is grasped

The atemi waza can also be applied as above at the instant toshu releases his grip.

The addition of these counter techniques for tantō puts more pressure on toshu's defence forcing him to improve his defensive skills which are a characteristic of budo. Toshu is of course then allowed to apply a counter technique to tantō's atemi waza which increases the likelihood of more active attack and defence.

In other words, with tantō's skills now including elements from toshu, the merits of attack and defence that we see in judo and kendo are introduced into aikido randori. This increases its value as budo and makes it more interesting for participants and spectators.

Practicc for tantō kaeshi waza begins with the basic ura waza (page 193) to understand the transition and timing between techniques and their counters. The atemi waza as counter techniques can only be applied once your arm has been grasped so the practice of atemi waza against single handed grasps (katate dori) are considered to be an important step because there are elements from them that are used in the tantō kaeshi waza.

The five atemi waza are practised in two groups:

- aigamae katate dori – you and your opponent stand in migigamae and he steps forward with his right foot to grasp your right wrist with his right hand. Or, you both stand in hidarigamae and he steps forward with his left foot to grasp your left wrist with his left hand.
- gyakugamae katate dori – you stand in hidarigamae, uke stands in migigamae and he steps forward with his right foot to grasp your left hand with his right hand. Or, you stand in migigamae, uke stands in hidarigamae and he steps forward with his left foot to grasp your right hand with his left hand.

AIGAMAE KATATE DORI
1. Shōmen ate
Turn your thumb down the instant before uke takes his grip on your wrist.

Keep your hand and wrist relaxed and roll it over in a clockwise direction so that the palm is up and the back of your hand is on the inside of his wrist. As you do this, move forward and to the right so that you are at about 45° from your original line. Your right hand is low and you are at a distance from him where your arm is straight and his hand is against his body at about the height of his belt.

Slide your hand up until it is level with his jaw. Turn your hand so that the palm is towards him with your elbow down, arm straight and U-shape between your thumb and forefinger uppermost.

Push off with your left leg so that your right foot slides between his feet pushing him back and down. As you push, your feet become further apart so your body will naturally lower. However, keep your hand in the same position relative to your body with your arm extended and use your whole body movement to throw him.

As soon as your right foot is placed bring your left foot up behind it to finish in a natural posture. He takes a backward ukemi.

Coaching points
Relax your wrist completely when you turn your hand over after uke's grasp. If there is any tension in your wrist you risk breaking his grip.

Uke should arch his back and wait as long as possible before falling. This allows you to practise the technique fully.

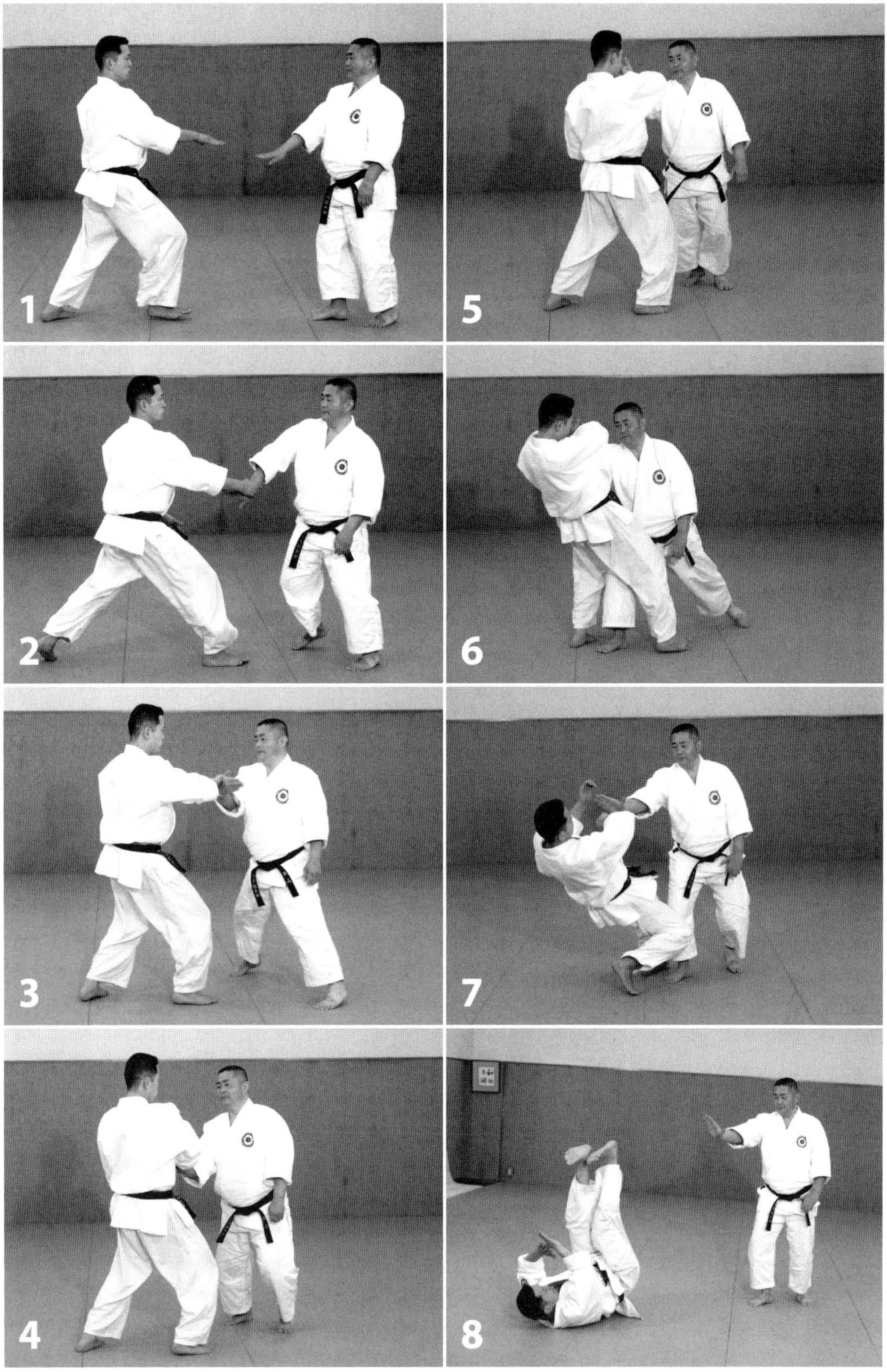
1
5
2
6
3
7
4
8

The picture on the right shows the position of your hand after your first movement. Your hand is relaxed so that it does not break uke's grip. The back of your hand is on the inside of his wrist with his hand against his body around the level of his belt.

2. Aigamae ate
Turn your thumb down the instant before uke takes his grip on your wrist.

Keep your hand and wrist relaxed and roll it over in a clockwise direction so that the palm is up and the back of your hand is on the inside of his wrist as for shōmen ate. As you roll your hand over move to the left stepping with your left foot first and then your right foot while keeping your right foot forward.

Keep your right hand low with your arm extended and push your hand blade into his body stepping forward with your right foot to his right side to maintain a good posture.

Slide your hand up until it is level with his jaw.

Turn your hand so that the palm is towards him with your elbow down, arm straight and U-shape between your thumb and forefinger uppermost. Place it against his chin and bring his head into your centre to break his balance.

Keep facing forward and push off with your left leg moving forward and slightly to your right to throw him as for the basic technique. Follow with your right foot to finish in migigamae.

Coaching points
Relax your wrist completely when you turn your hand over after uke's grasp so that you do not break his grip.

Uke should arch his back and wait as long as possible before falling. This allows you to practise the technique fully. You move slightly into him as in the basic technique to displace him rather than sharply twisting to the left to throw him.

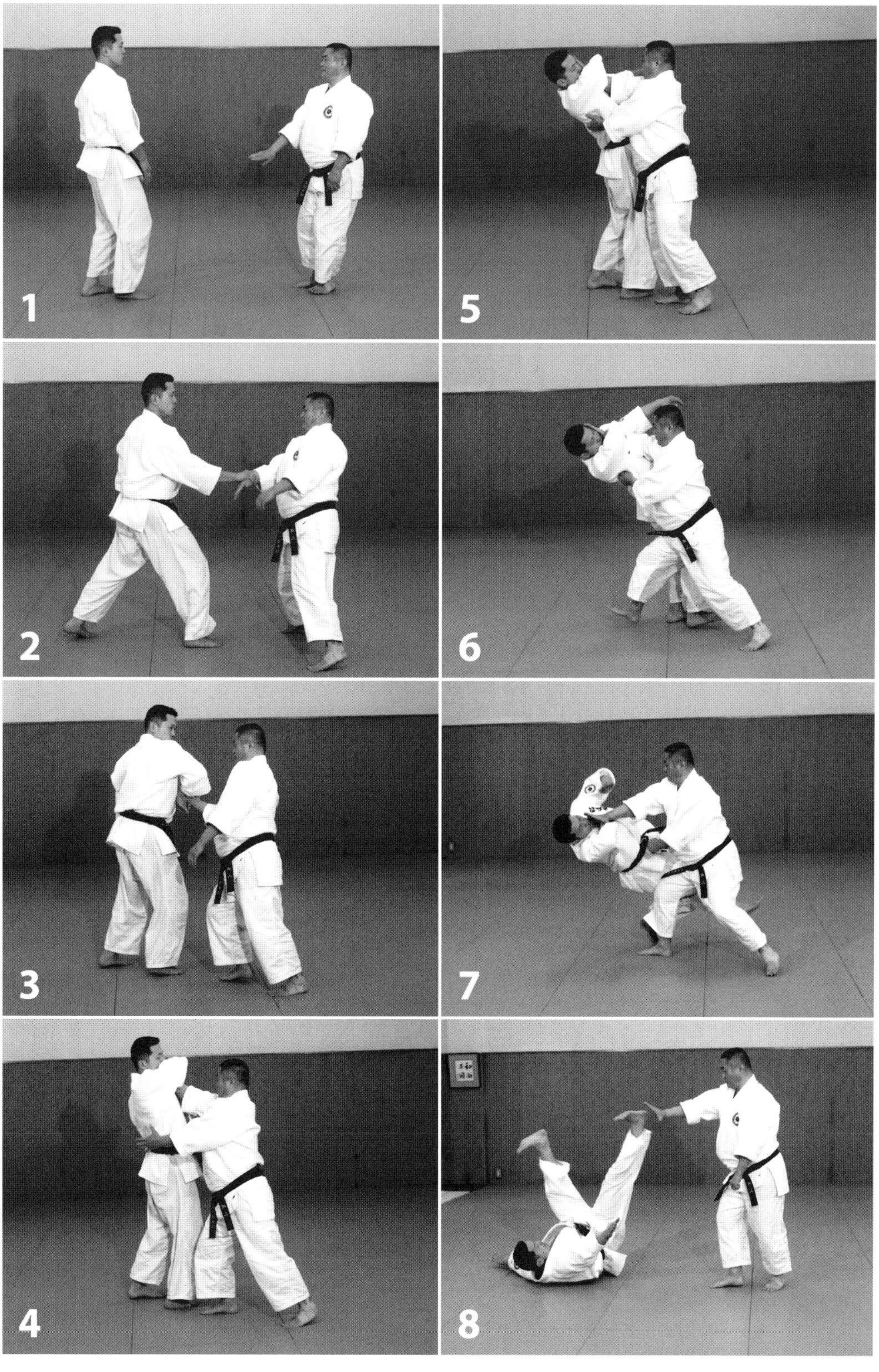
1
2
3
4
5
6
7
8

3. Gyakugamae ate
Turn your palm up the instant before uke takes his grip on your wrist.

Turn your palm down so that your hand is above his wrist. At the same time step forward with your left foot and slide your left arm, with palm up, along his right arm and across his chest. Keep your right arm straight and your hand open.

Turn your left hand so that your tegatana is away from you.

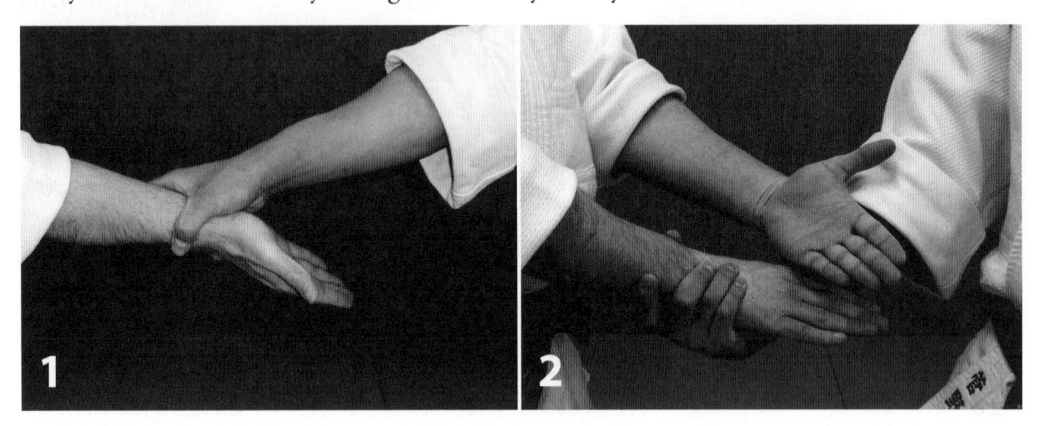

Keep your arms straight and turn your body so that you are facing in your original direction keeping your left arm into your centre to break his balance.

Push off with your right leg and move straight in the direction you are facing. Apply the throw by body movement rather than trying to throw simply by twisting your body. Uke falls after arching his back and waiting as long as possible.

The position of your hand just after he has grasped is shown in picture 1 above. Picture 2 shows your hand after turning your right hand over and bringing your left hand onto his arm just before sliding it up along his arm to his chest (picture 2).

4. Gedan ate (pictures page 233)
Turn your thumb down the instant before uke takes his grip on your wrist.

Move to the left stepping with your left foot first and then your right foot keeping your right foot forward. Dip your elbow as you move, turn your thumb up bringing your hand into your centre and then raise it towards his face stepping forward with your right to maintain a good posture.

Grasp his wrist at the end of your movement so that the palm of your hand is on the inside of his wrist. Keep your elbow down so that his elbow is uppermost.

231

Release your grip on his wrist. Turn to your right as you take a deep step with your left foot to the right of uke and place the inside of your left arm low across his body. As you do this, bring your right hand down.

As you push with of your left leg, to push him down and straight back, turn your hips slightly to the left and draw your right foot up so that at the end of the technique you are facing your original direction with your left foot forward.

Coaching point
Gedan ate is applied by a movement through uke to displace him rather than by remaining stationary and twisting your hips.

As in the basic technique, uke is thrown straight backwards and you must not bring your leg behind him to impede his fall.

The picture below left shows the orientation of your hand just after he has grasped, twisting your arm as much as possible without affecting your posture. The picture below right shows the position of his arm with his elbow up and the palm of your hand on the inside of his wrist.

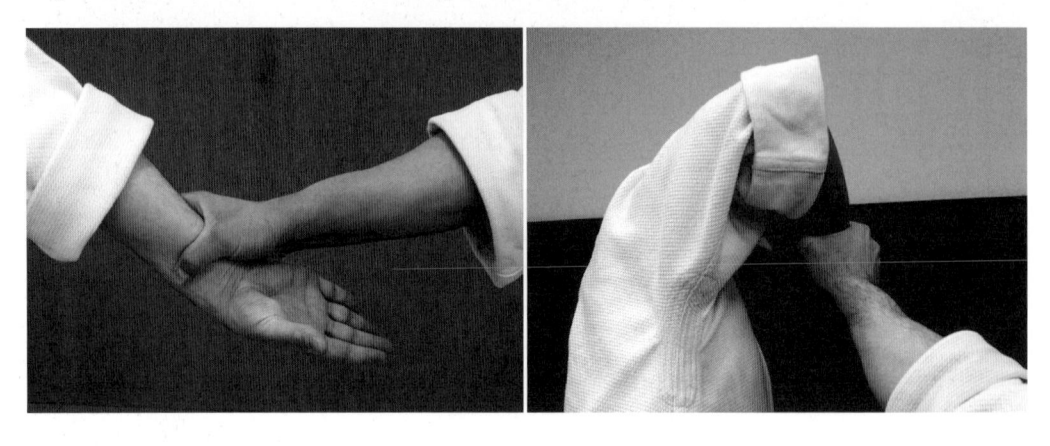

5. Ushiro ate (pictures page 235)
Turn your thumb down just before uke takes his grip on your wrist and then turn it back again as much as possible so that your hand blade is on the inside of his forearm. This is the same as the first movement from the go no sen no kuzushi (pictures page 38) except that you turn your hand much more when he grasps. At the same time, without moving back, twist your hips and shoulders 90° to the left and raise your hand straight up keeping it on the original centre line between you and uke.

Without stopping, and by turning on the balls of your feet, twist your body as much as possible in the opposite direction. As you do this keep your hand relaxed and drop in straight down. Draw your hand towards your centre as you turn more and then let it pass close to your body and through behind you as far as possible. This movement pulls uke towards you.

233

Step forward to his right side with your left foot once he is moving so that you are standing close behind him and bring your hands up to his shoulders. Keep as close to him as possible when you pass by each other.

Take two or three tsugi ashi movements back and to your left at 45° keeping your right foot forward. Pull your arms horizontally to your right side as you start to move and applying the throw using body movement rather than the strength of your arms. Uke falls straight back from his turned position which is 90° from the original line between you.

Coaching points
Breaking uke's balance is normally achieved only by your body turn and without stepping back. However, if he steps too close to you as he grasps then you may need to move back a little to regain the correct distance as you turn your body.

This technique is difficult for him to hold on when done fast so it is important to keep your right hand relaxed throughout so as not to break his grip. Turning your hand as much as possible as you turn your body to the left makes this more effective when you turn in the opposite direction.

Pull your hand through your centre and behind you to break his balance and get his body moving rather than shortening the movement and taking your hand away from your body to the side.

The position of your hand on the inside of his forearm after your body turn to the left is shown in the picture on the right.

235

GYAKUGAMAE KATATE DORI

1. Shōmen ate (pictures page 237)

Open your left hand and extend your fingers as uke grasps your wrist. At the same time move forward and to your right with your right foot following with your left foot so that you are at about 45° from your original position. Also bring your right hand straight up to his jaw with your elbow down and arm extended. Leave your left hand in its original position.

Without stopping, push off with your left leg and slide your right foot forward between his feet. Keep your arm extended and push him down. Bring your left foot up behind your right foot and finish in a natural posture.

Coaching points

It is natural that uke's grasp and the placement of his foot occur at the same time. As his foot comes down onto the tatami he is transferring his weight onto it and for a moment he will be unable to move it. Aim to place the palm of your hand onto his jaw at the same time as he commits his weight onto his front foot.

Leave your left hand in its original position so as not to pull him around to face you as you move. He keeps facing forward as you move so that your hand comes onto the side of his jaw. He arches his back and stays on his feet as long as possible before taking his ukemi.

2. Aigamae ate (pictures page 239)

As uke grasps your wrist open your hand and extend your fingers.

Move forward and to your left keeping your torso upright and bending your knees to place your hand blade on the inside of your left knee. At the same time bring your right hand up onto his jaw. Keep both arms extended with that his balance is broken backwards and slightly to the side through your movement and the position of your arms.

Step forward and slightly to the right behind him with your right foot. As you do this the side of your body makes contact with uke and he is pushed off of his feet by your body movement.

Bring your left foot up behind your right foot and finish in a natural posture.

Coaching points

Your centre is angled to the direction of your first step with your left foot so you must bring your right hand, and uke's balance, towards your centre. Keep your right hand in your centre with your second foot movement and change of direction.

This technique is applied by body movement to displace him rather than by a sharp twist to your left to throw him across your thigh.

For toshu to get the full benefit of this technique he should arch backwards as much as possible before taking his ukemi.

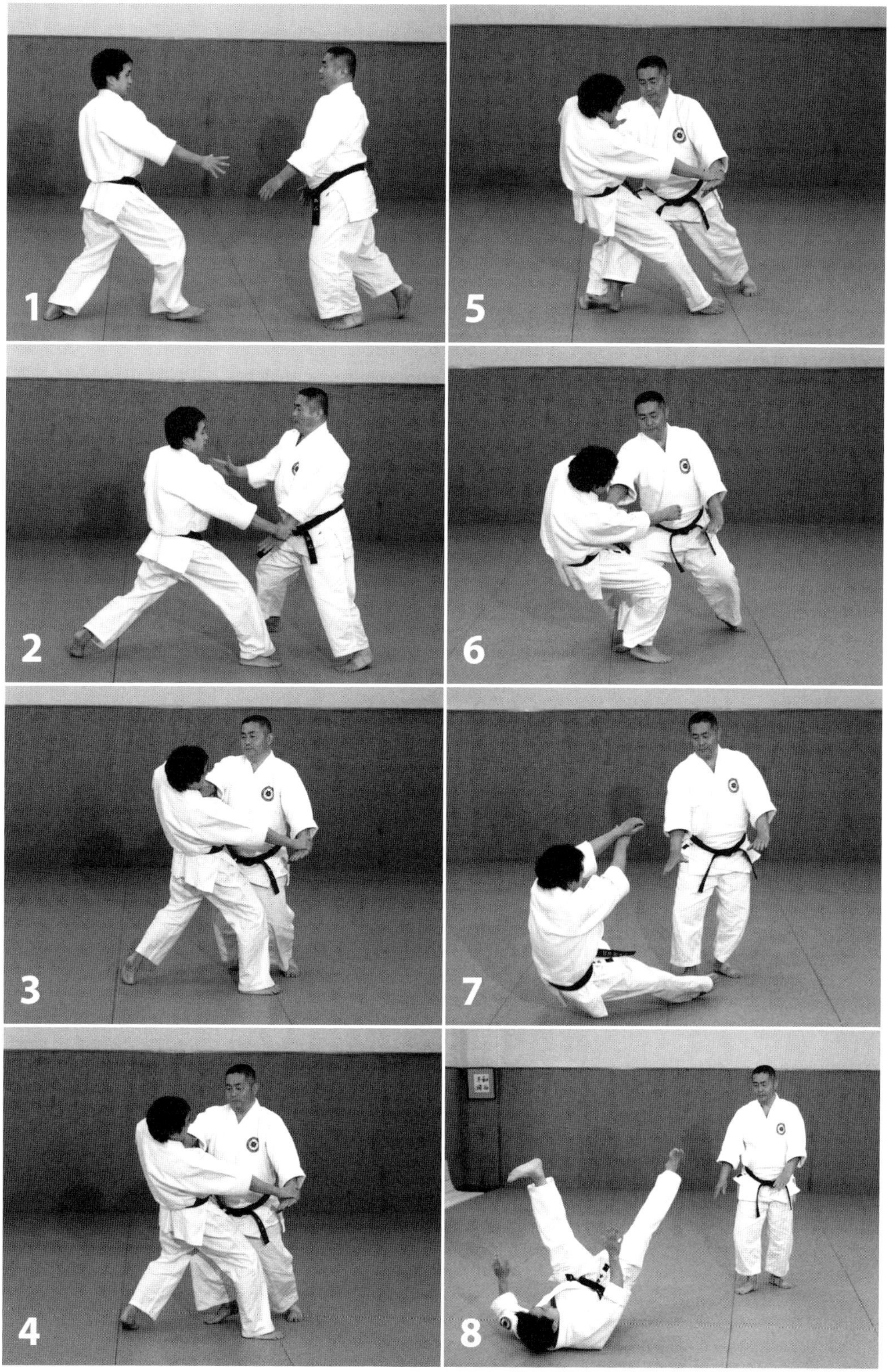
1
5
2
6
3
7
4
8

3. Gyakugamae ate (pictures page 241)
Open your right hand and extend your fingers as uke grasps your wrist.

Keep your hand in the same place and move your body towards it. First step forward and to your right with your right foot and follow with your left foot turning to your left as you complete your movement. Face to your left at 90° from your original position with your left foot forward, your hand blade towards you and your hand held close in your centre.

Keep your torso upright, bend your knees and drop straight down to affect his balance but do not let your knee touch the tatami.

Without stopping stand back up again and, as he also stands back up, bring your arm over in a large vertical circle so that it is across his chest with the back of your arm towards him. At the same time step to his left side with your right foot and close the distance to him.

Continue your arm movement bringing it down to chest height with your palm up as you complete your step and turn to face forward to complete the throw. Finish in a natural posture.

Coaching point
Your left hand does not push on uke's body to throw him. It is a single handed technique applied with body movement so bring your left arm close to you with your hand in your centre.

4. Gedan ate (pictures page 242)
Open your right hand and extend your fingers as uke grasps your wrist.

Keep your hand in the same place and move your body towards it. First step forward and to your right with your right foot and follow with your left foot turning to your left as you complete your movement. Face to your left at 90° from your original position with your left foot forward, your hand blade towards you and your hand held close in your centre.

Keep your torso upright, bend your knees and drop straight down to affect his balance but do not let your knee touch the tatami.

While your knees are bent turn your thumb towards you to break his grasp. With your hand still turned place your arm low across his body as you step to the left of him with your right foot.

Push forward with your left leg to push him straight back and down. At the same time turn your hips to the right and bring your left foot up to return to a natural posture facing in your original direction.

Coaching point
The direction of the throw is straight back moving through uke rather than remaining in

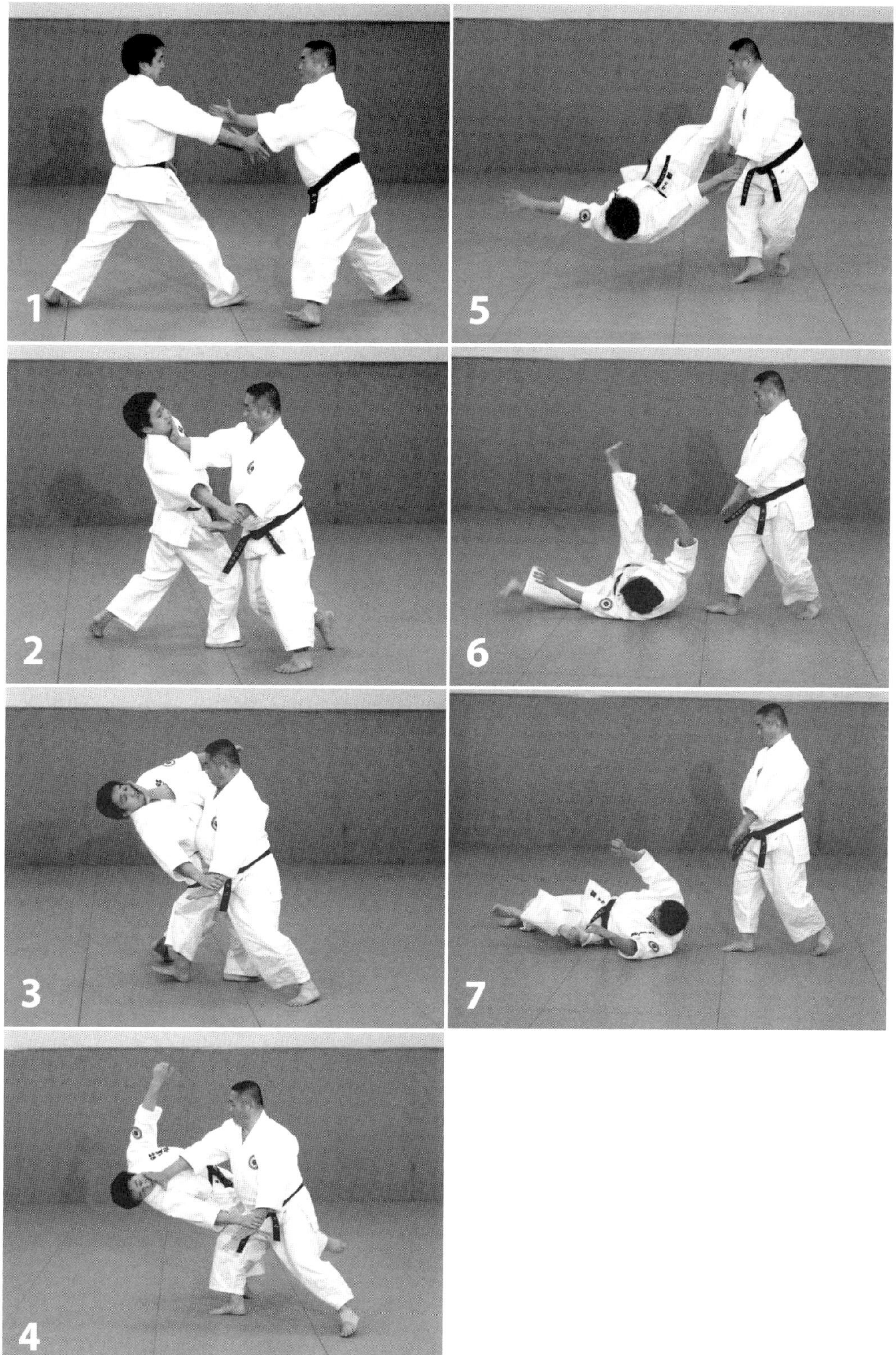
1
2
3
4
5
6
7

one place and only turning your body. Ensure that your right foot does come behind his left leg preventing him from stepping back and doing a straightforward backward fall. This is especially true when working with people who do not have a high level of skill in their ukemi.

The break of uke's grip is shown below. The picture of the left shows your hand in your centre and the picture on the right is just after you have turned your hand to break his grip.

5. Ushiro ate (pictures page 243)
As uke moves forward to grasp your right hand turn your hand blade down and tsugi ashi backwards to draw his balance forward. When he has taken his grip, tsugi ashi forward and turn your hand in the opposite direction to push the back of his hand towards the back of his forearm and lock his arm straight. Keep your arm extended and in your centre.

Step to your right with your right foot and follow with your left foot turning to your left as you complete your movement. Face to the left at 90° from your original position with your hand in your centre and left foot forward.

Bend your knees and dip your elbow to expose his hand. Bring your left hand over your arm and, with thumb uppermost, take a grip on his wrist so that your thumb is on the inside of his wrist and your fingers are along the back of his hand. As you do this turn your right hand away to break his grip. This is the same hand movement as in the pictures 1-3 from the gyakugamae tegatana gedan no tsukuri on page 160.

Turn his wrist and at the same time move to his right side placing your right hand on his right shoulder and extending his left arm vertically maintaining the twist on his wrist.

Slide your left hand down his arm to his shoulder and take two or three tsugi ashi movements back and to your right at 45° keeping your left foot forward. Pull your arms to your left side as you start to move and apply the throw using the movement of your body. Uke takes an ukemi straight back from his turned position.

241

242

243

TANTŌ KAESHI WAZA

The 14 techniques described here are split into two groups. The first seven are applied with the hand holding the tantō. The second seven are applied with the empty hand. These are only examples of the possibilities and you are encouraged to find other counter techniques that work for you within the framework and rules of randori.

Toshu's initial technique and reaction are predetermined in these examples so that your counter technique can be practised as intended. Toshu must apply his initial technique correctly so that tantō can also practise correctly. However, in randori an opponent is free to apply variations of techniques that may be unorthodox or he may react unexpectedly to one of your counter techniques. These are good reasons for researching alternatives.

If you practice with different people and try a variety of counter techniques you will have a much better chance of being able to adapt to different situations as they present themselves and use a suitable technique for your opponent's position and stance. The same applies to toshu when he applies combinations of techniques. This kind of disordered practice is developed in the next part of this book.

Most people consistently hold the tantō with the same hand so understandably tend to practise these counter techniques on one side. However, with the technical connections between these counters and other techniques in aikido it is always a good idea to practise on both left and right sides.

Hand used	Initial technique	Counter technique
hand holding the tantō	oshi taoshi	ushiro ate
	hiki taoshi	shōmen ate
	waki gatame	gyakugamae ate
	kote gaeshi	ushiro ate
	tenkai kote hineri	ushiro ate
	tenkai kote gaeshi	gyakugamae ate
	mae otoshi	gedan ate
empty hand	oshi taoshi	shōmen ate
	hiki taoshi	gyakugamae ate
	waki gatame	gyakugamae ate
	kote gaeshi	gedan ate
	tenkai kote hineri	ushiro ate
	tenkai kote gaeshi	gyakugamae ate
	sumi otoshi	shōmen ate

1. Oshi taoshi - ushiro ate (pictures page 246)
Toshu stands with his left foot forward. He avoids to his left using his left tegatana to control your stab.

He grasps your wrist with his right hand, slides his left hand to the inside of your elbow and closes the distance to you with his left foot forward taking your arm close to your body. He pushes mainly on your wrist to get your arm behind you before turning to apply oshi taoshi.

Once your arm is behind you he slides his left arm around your forearm just as he turns to face in the opposite direction and lift your arm. Bend your knees slightly and drop your weight the instant he slides his hand around your forearm and starts to turn. This stops his movement.

Without waiting, step behind him and bring your arm over his left shoulder. Keep moving back and slightly to your right using body movement to throw him.

Coaching points
Do not react too early to toshu's technique. You must wait until he has made a deep movement forward and your elbow is behind you. The critical timing point is just as he starts to turn which is when he slides his hand around your forearm which allows you to lift your arm up.

He will be momentarily unable to move at the instant you drop your weight to stop his technique. You must take advantage of this opportunity and move quickly to a position where you can start to affect his balance.

Once you are behind him with your arm over his shoulder you move back and slightly in towards him to make it harder for him to escape your technique.

2. Hiki taoshi - shōmen ate (pictures page 247)
Toshu avoids to your right side as you stab. He keeps his right foot forward and turns towards you to grasp your wrist with both hands.

He pulls your arm down in a large clockwise movement and makes a tsugi ashi back so that he is back on the original line of attack.

Keep your arm fairly relaxed as he pulls and drop your weight by bending your legs slightly. This stops his pull so that you maintain your balance.

As soon as you have controlled his pull roll your hand over in a clockwise direction and move forward and slightly to the right placing the back of your wrist on his chest.

Without stopping extend your arm and drive off with your left leg so that your right foot slides between his feet pushing him back and down. Follow up with your left foot to finish in a natural posture.

246

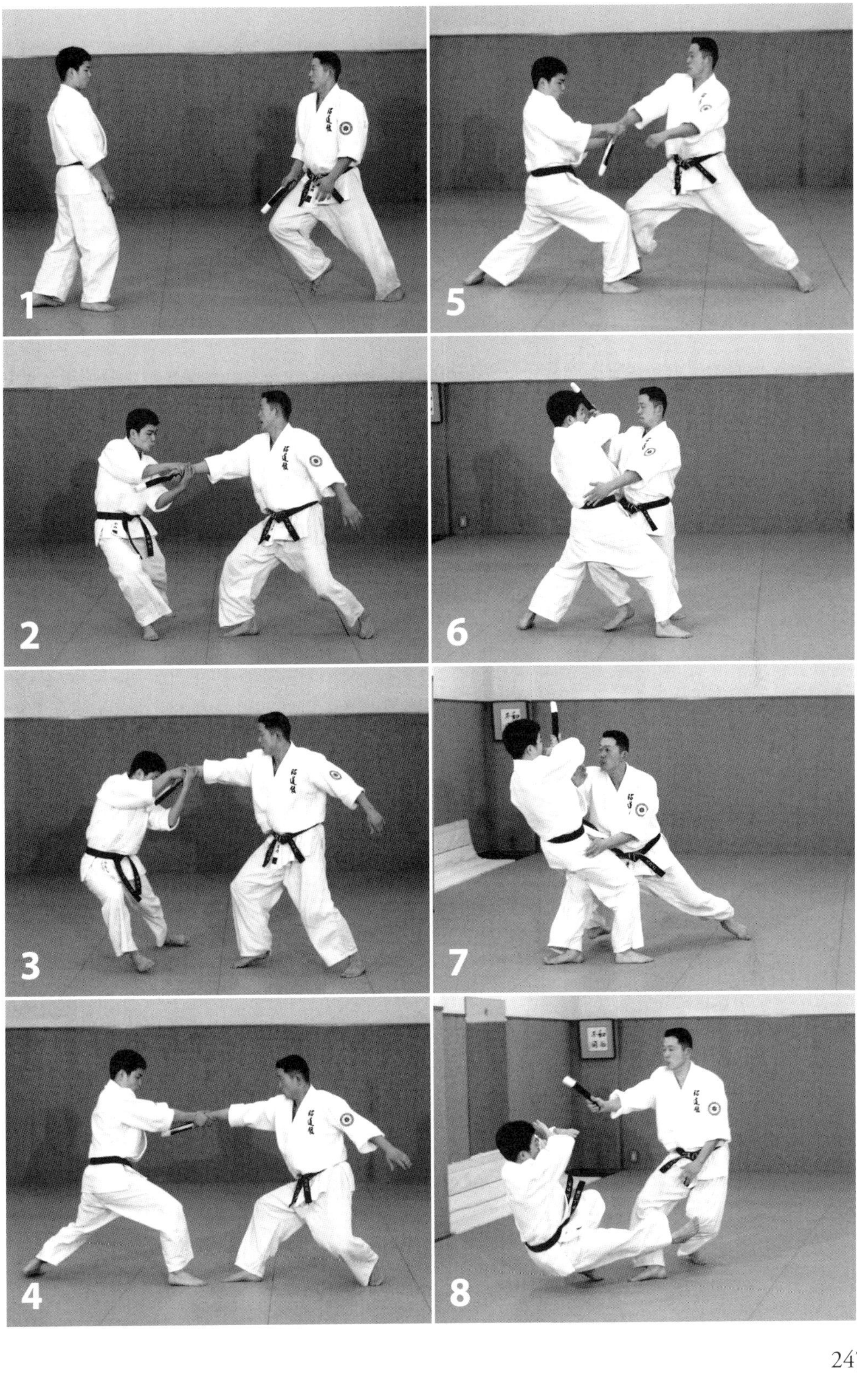
1
2
3
4
5
6
7
8

Coaching points
The critical timing point is when toshu pulls your arm to break your balance. Drop your weight but make sure that your hips are slightly forward of your shoulders, but not to the extent that you are leaning back, so that you are not pulled off balance. As you block his technique he is momentarily immobile which is the time to quickly close the distance to him and apply shōmen ate.

When you drop your weight to block toshu's technique you are also momentarily immobile. Picture 4 on page 247 shows that tantō and toshu are in almost identical positions. So, you must immediately take control and move forward to counter his technique otherwise he will regain his mobility and take the chance to apply a further technique.

If your timing is good enough your application of shōmen ate can be with the back of the wrist by simply extending your arm when you have closed the distance to him. Alternatively, once you have closed the distance you can turn your hand so that the inside of your wrist is towards him.

3. Waki gatamae - gyakugamae ate
Toshu's aim in waki gatame is to roll your arm over so that your elbow is uppermost. Turn your palm up as you stab to make this movement difficult and less effective for him.

He moves just to your left keeping his right foot forward and brings his hand blade onto your wrist followed immediately by his left hand, bending his knees and grasping your wrist from underneath.

Take a deep step forward with your right leg to the left of him as he tries to extend his legs and lift your arm to break your balance.

Turn your thumb down and place the inside of your arm across his body to apply gyakugamae ate.

Coaching points
Do not stopping toshu's technique when you switch into your counter. Take the initiative as he tries to lift your arm and move quicker than him to close the distance and continue through to apply gyakugamae ate.

Turn your thumb down as you apply gyakugamae ate to ensure that the soft part of the inside of your arm is placed against him to avoid striking him with your elbow.

Once you have closed the distance apply gyakugamae ate with body movement through him rather than by simply twisting your body.

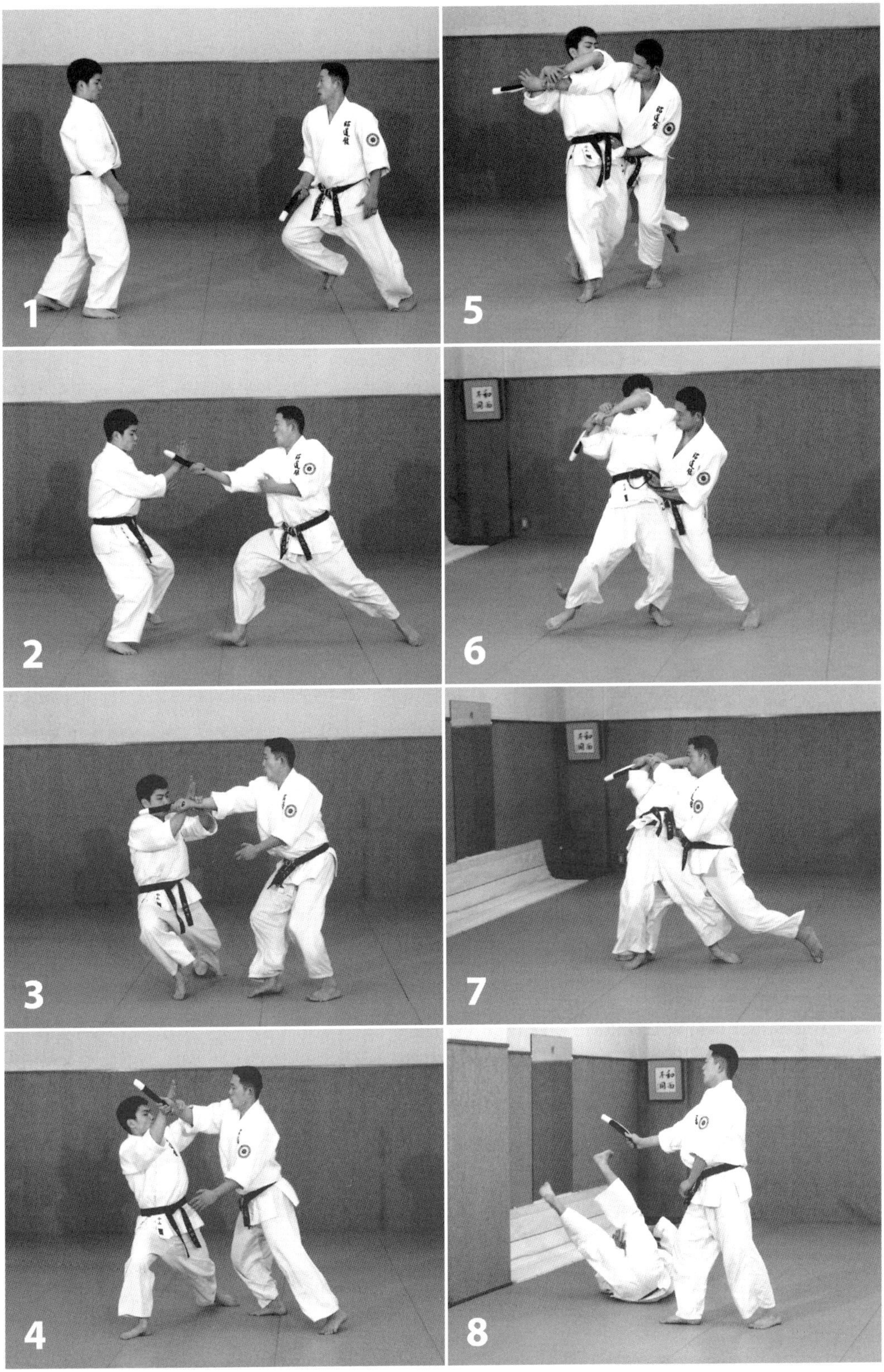
1
5
2
6
3
7
4
8

4. Kote gaeshi - ushiro ate

Toshu's aim in kote gaeshi is to twist your wrist out to break your balance backwards. Turn your thumb down as you stab to make this difficult and less effective for him.

Toshu moves to your right and sweeps his right hand in an anti-clockwise direction so that his arm is between his body and your arm. As he sweeps his arm he turns to his right and slides his left hand down your arm to your wrist to take a reverse grip with both hands.

Keeping his hands close to him he moves to your front left corner taking your hand down to break your balance. Move your right foot forward as he does this to ensure that you maintain your balance.

He sweeps his left foot back, pivots on his right foot and applies kote gaeshi. Before your hand gets turned further than palm up turn your body to the right to pull toshu towards you. Use the power of your hips and keep your arm relatively relaxed.

Once he is moving in your direction pull your hand close to you through your centre keeping it moving and step forward with your left foot as he passes by you.

Bring your right arm over his shoulder so that your forearm is on his chest. Place your open left hand on his left shoulder.

Stand with your right foot forward as close as possible to him so that he is unable to turn under your arm. Bend your knees to drop your weight so that his balance is broken backwards and he cannot bend forward to escape.

Take two or three tsugi ashi back and to your left so that he falls to your right side. Use your body movement to throw him rather than the strength of your arms.

Coaching points

The hip twist is much more powerful than pulling toshu towards you just by using your arm. As he passes by you, turn your thumb down so that his grip on your wrist does not break.

Your right forearm must be placed on his chest and safely away from his throat as shown in the picture to the right.

In this technique you turn your palm up as you stab. In waki gatame you turn your thumb down as you stab. Be aware that, in randori, if you make a mistake and anticipate the wrong technique the turn of your hand can assist him significantly.

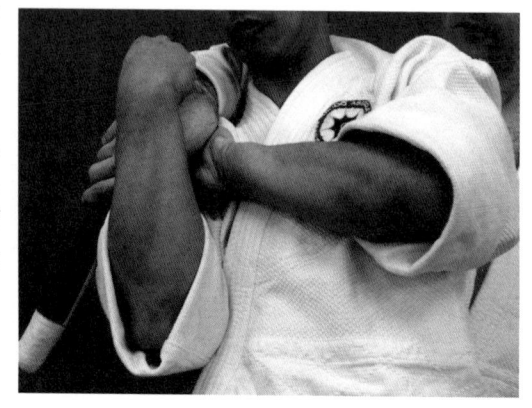

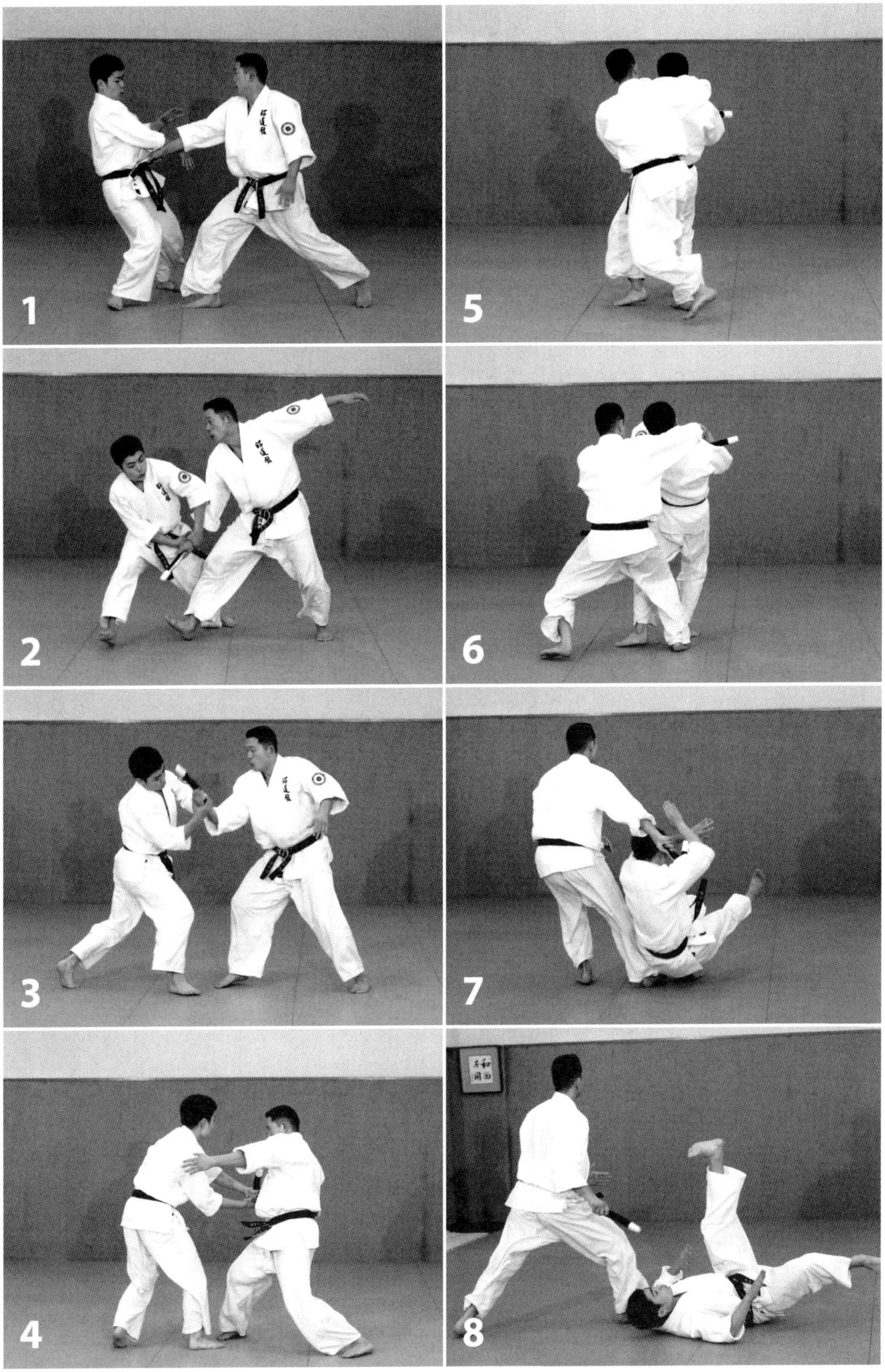
1
5
2
6
3
7
4
8

The picture on the right shows the position before throwing toshu. You should have complete control of him at this point. You must be close to him so that he cannot turn under your arm and sink your weight so that his balance is broken backward and he is unable to lean forward. Your right hand can assist as shown but you can only use an open hand.

5. Tenkai kote hineri - ushiro ate

Toshu stands in migigamae and steps forward and to your right with his left foot as you stab. He grasps your wrist with both hands in a regular grip as he moves.

He steps forward with his right foot to bring his right shoulder towards your shoulder before turning under your arm. Step forward with your left foot forward and around behind him as he steps forward with his right foot.

Keep yor right arm relaxed and bring it over his right shoulder placing your forearm onto his chest. Place your left hand blade on his left shoulder as support.

Stand with your right foot forward as close to him as possible so that he is unable to turn under your arm and drop your weight so that his balance is broken backward and he cannot bend forward to escape.

Take two or three tsugi ashi back and to your left so that he falls to your right side. Use body movement to throw him rather than the strength of your arms.

Coaching points

Bring your right arm over his shoulder with your arm bent and thumb turned down so that your forearm is across his chest. Be careful to avoid any contact with his throat.

Ushiro ate is primarily applied using the right arm in this technique and the previous one. Your left hand is assisting but you must use an open hand at all times.

You do not need to stop toshu's movement when you apply your counter technique. For him to apply tenkai kote hineri he must lower himself to get under your arm anyway so it is natural that your arm will move up over his shoulder giving you the chance to apply ushiro ate with body movement and good timing even against someone who is taller than you.

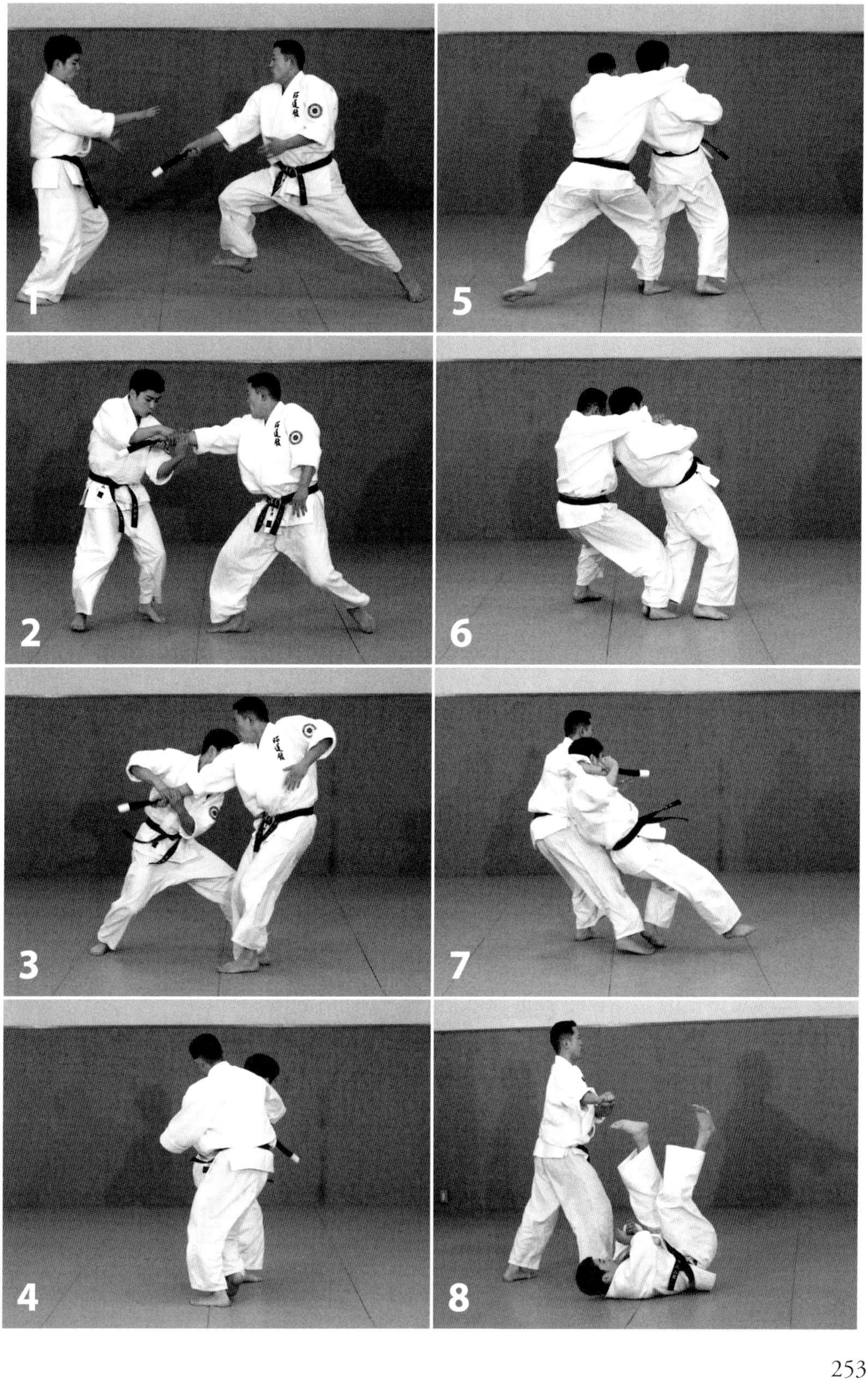
1
5
2
6
3
7
4
8

6. Tenkai kote gaeshi - gyakugamae ate

Turn your thumb down as you stab to make his technique harder for him. He avoids the knife by moving forward and to your left while grasping your arm with both hands in a regular grip.

He steps forward with his left foot and brings your arm down into his centre. As he does this, just before your hand gets to its lowest point take control of the movement and quickly bring your arm on a large vertical circle so that it finishes across his chest with your palm up. Make a fast tsugi ashi movement to close the distance to him as you move your arm. In this position he has his left foot forward.

Without stopping, move forward by pushing off of your left foot, lower your arm and turn slightly to return to a natural posture.

Coaching points

You do not need to stop toshu's movement to apply the counter. At the right moment you need to move faster than he does to take control of your arm and close the distance to him. At this point he is stepping through with his left foot so his weight in wholly on his right foot which limits his mobility.

As you bring your arm over turn it so that the back of your arm is towards toshu but be careful not to hit him with your elbow. Turning your arm ensures that his grip does not break.

Apply gyakugamae ate by body movement while dropping your arm. Turn to face him as you finish your movement but do not throw him just with a twist of your hips.

7. Mae otoshi - gedan ate (pictures page 257)

Turn your thumb down as you stab to make his technique harder for him. He avoids the knife by moving forward and to your left while grasping your arm with both hands in a regular grip.

He steps forward with his left foot, brings your arm down into his centre and starts to slide his left hand up to your elbow.

Just as his left foot passes by his right foot quickly move towards him with your right foot stepping deep behind him to close the distance. Bring your the inside of your right arm low across his body.

Without stopping make several tsugi ashi movements to his rear right corner to throw him.

Coaching points

Toshu applies mae otoshi by stepping forward with his left foot. This gives you the room to step behind him but the important point is the timing. Your step should be when he is at his most vulnerable which is when his left foot momentarily passes by his right foot.

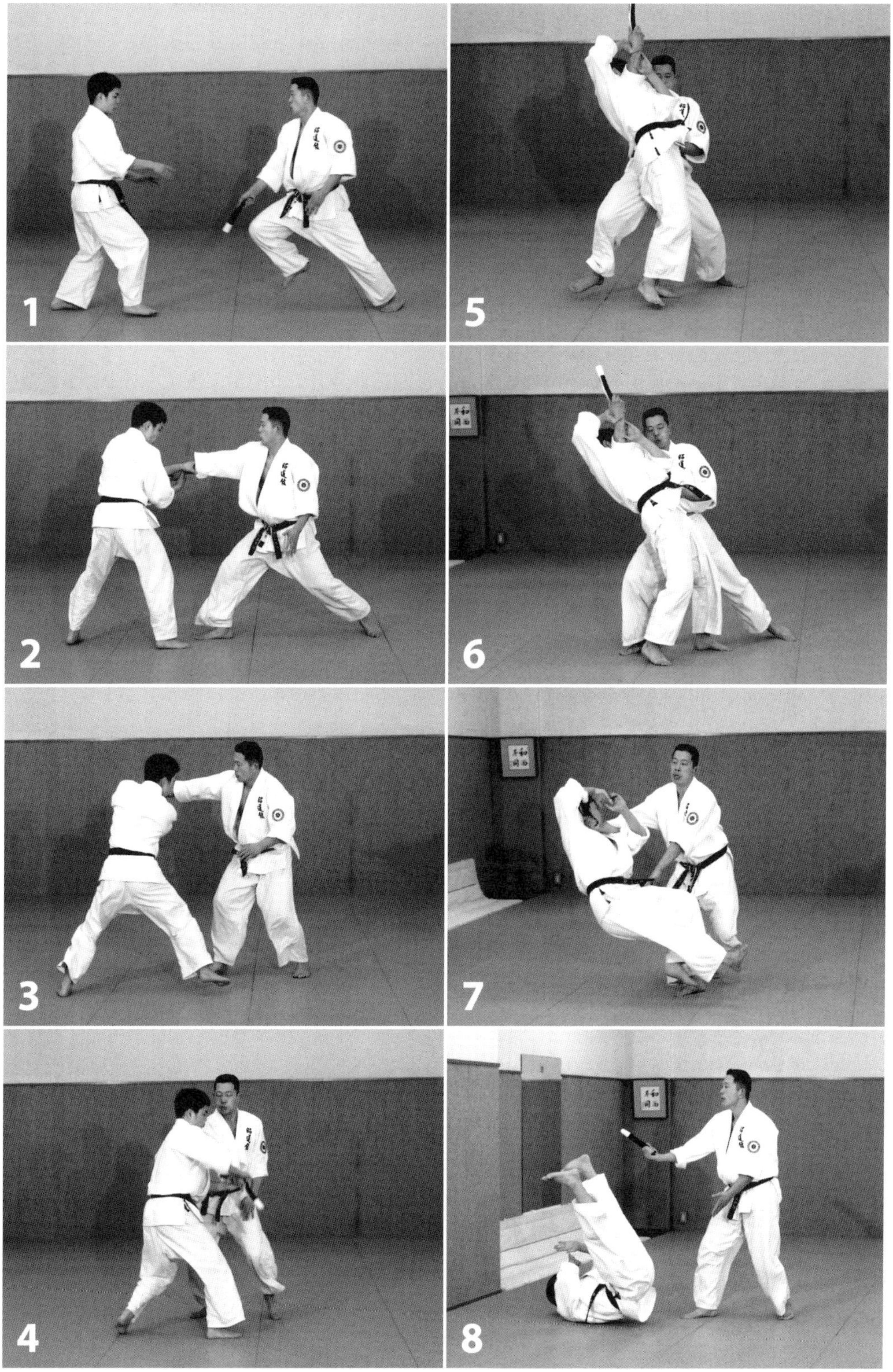
1
5
2
6
3
7
4
8

As you bring your arm across his body turn your thumb down so that the inside of your arm is against his body so there is less chance of striking him with your elbow.

Use quick body movement to throw toshu once you have closed the distance to him and caught him in his unstable position rather than using a twist of your body to throw him over your thigh.

8. Oshi taoshi - shōmen ate (pictures page 258)
Toshu stands with his left foot forward. He avoids to his left using his left tegatana to control your stab.

He grasps your wrist with his right hand, slides his left hand to the inside of your elbow and closes the distance to you with his left foot forward taking your arm close to your body. Stop him from taking your arm any further by pulling your elbow into your body and dropping your weight.

Bring your left hand up to his jaw and turn towards him quickly switching your feet by bringing your left foot up and right foot back at the same time. Your left foot points between his feet on his weak line at about 90° to your original position.

Without stopping push with your right leg so that your left foot slides between his feet to throw him back and down. Follow up with your right leg to finish in a natural posture.

Coaching points
Pulling your elbow tight into your body and dropping your weight momentarily prevents toshu from moving. This is the instant that you take the advantage and change your feet to apply shōmen ate.

Stay in the same spot and keep your centre low when you switch your feet. There is no movement across the tatami but simply a turn to face him. Avoid jumping as this takes longer and gives toshu an opportunity for a further technique much like the timing in shōki no tsukuri.

9. Hiki taoshi - gyakugamae ate (pictures page 259)
Toshu avoids to your right side as you stab. He keeps his right foot forward and turns towards you to grasp your wrist with both hands.

He pulls your arm down in a large clockwise movement and makes a tsugi ashi back so that he is back on the original line of attack.

Keep your arm fairly relaxed as he pulls and drop your weight by bending your legs slightly. This stops his pull so that you keep your balance.

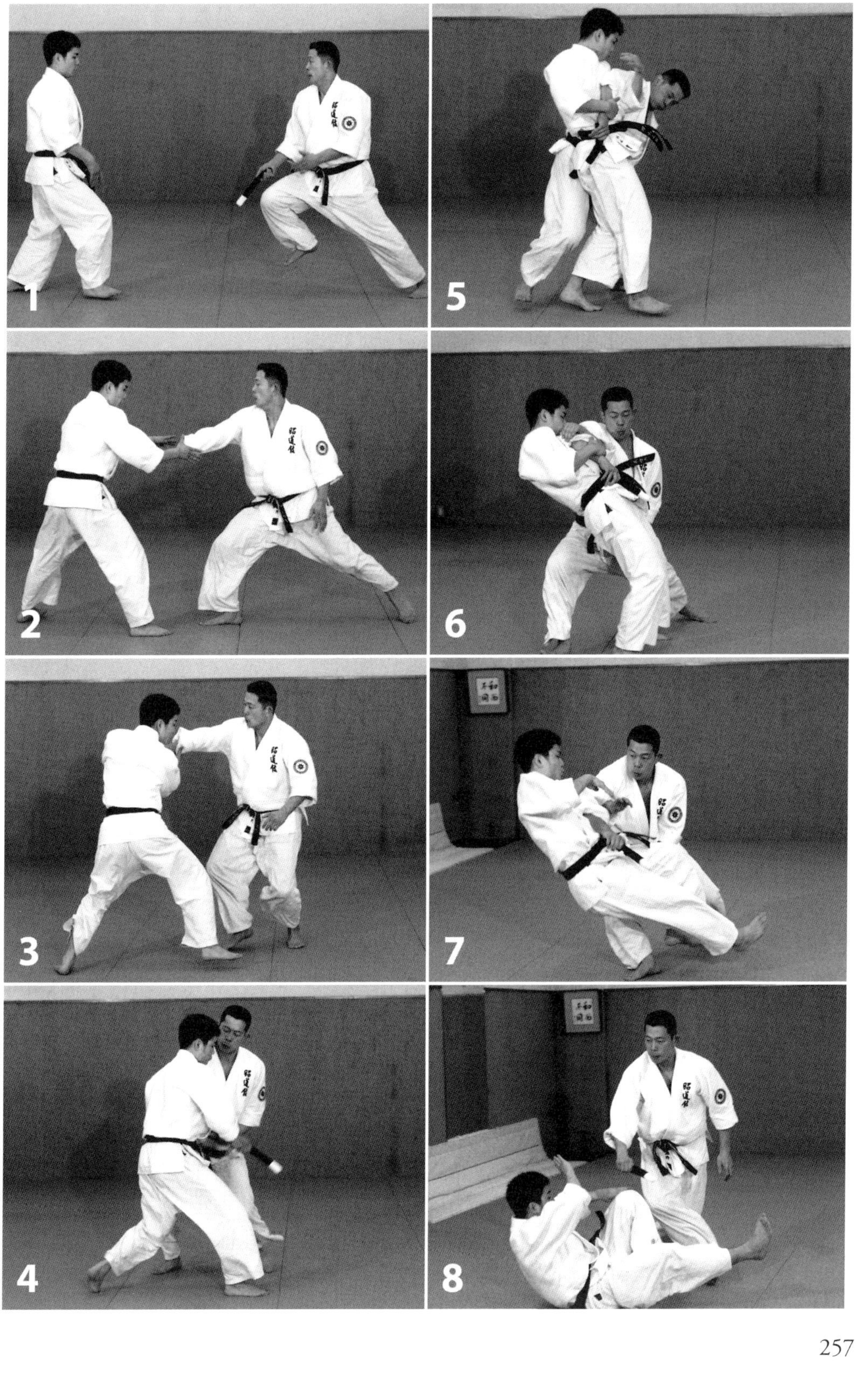
1
5
2
6
3
7
4
8

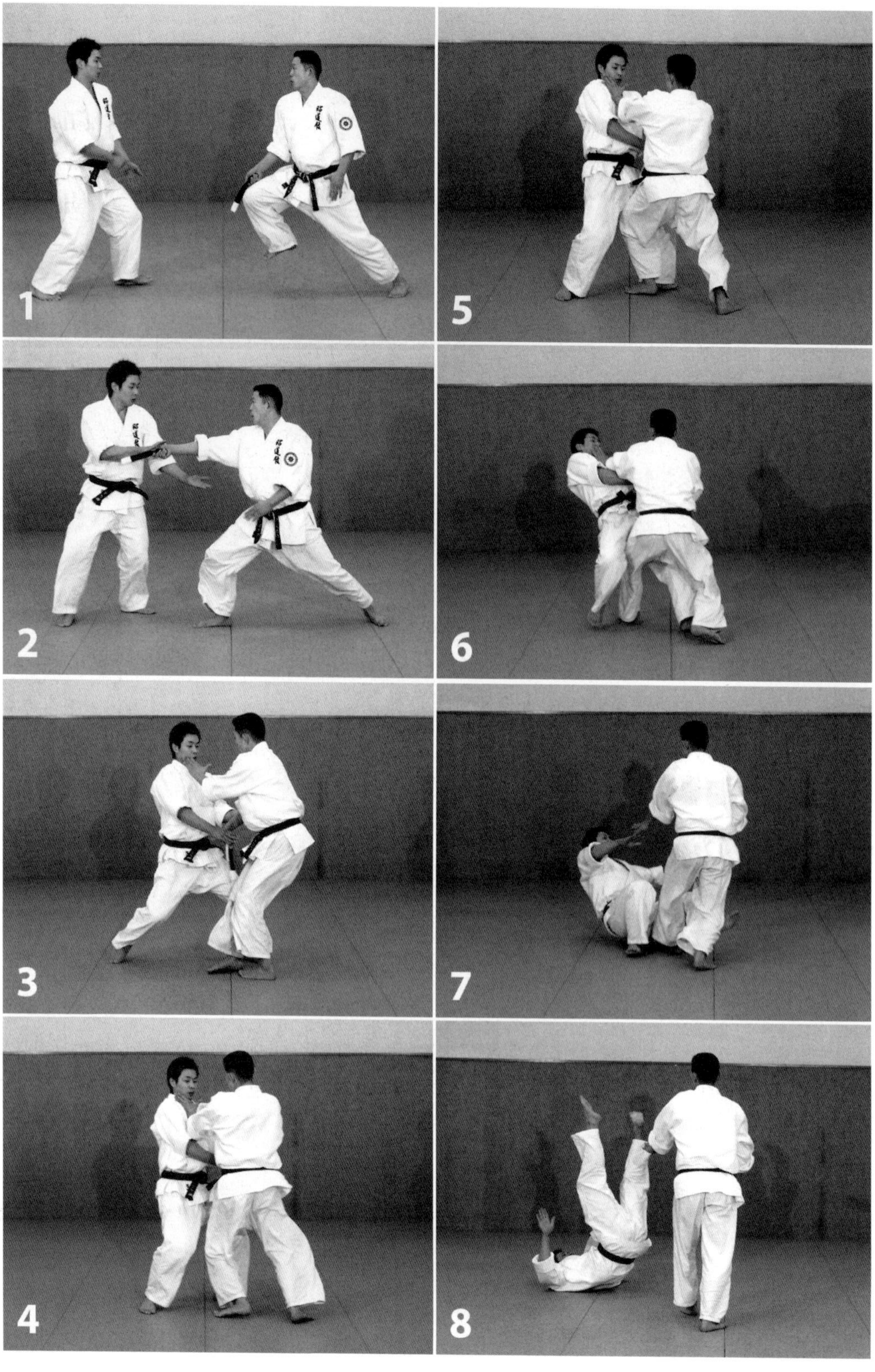
1
2
3
4
5
6
7
8

259

Step forward with your left leg as soon as you have controlled his pull and place the palm of your hand below the little finger onto his left temple.

Without stopping push off with your right leg to throw him and follow up with your left leg to return to a natural posture.

Coaching points
The critical timing point is when toshu pulls your arm to break your balance. Drop your weight but make sure that your hips are slightly forward of your shoulders, but not to the extent that you are leaning back, so that you are not pulled off balance. He is momentarily immobile as you block his technique which is the time to quickly close the distance to him and apply gyakugamae ate.

When you drop your weight to block his technique you are also momentarily immobile. So, you must immediately take control and move forward to apply your counter otherwise he will regain his mobility and take the chance to apply a further technique.

Throw him by body movement rather than twisting your body to throw him across your thigh.

10. Waki gatame - gyakugamae ate
Toshu moves with his right foot forward to your left side to avoid your stab and takes hold of your wrist with both hands in a reverse grip. He is aiming to roll your arm over so that your elbow is on top so turn your palm up as you stab to make it difficult to for him to apply waki gatame.

He brings his elbows in close to his body, bends his knees, leans back slightly and extends his knees to lift you forward and up onto your toes to break your balance.

Just as he extends his legs drop your weight by bending your legs. Keep your hips in front of your shoulders but not to the extent that you are leaning back. This stops him from pulling you off balance.

As soon as you have controlled his pull step forward with your left foot to his right side and place the palm of your left hand below the little finger onto his left temple.

Without stopping push off with your right leg to throw him and follow up with your left leg to return to a natural posture.

Coaching points
You stop toshu's lift by dropping your weight just as he extends his legs. This is the critical timing point and makes him momentarily immobile. Apply gyakugamae ate before he can regain his mobility and change to another technique. You are in the same situation as when

261

you drop your weight to counter his hiki taoshi where there is an instant where you are in similar positions. However, you have the slight advantage in that your movement is intentional whereas he is not expecting his movement to be stopped and he is likely to be slower to react not least because it is likely to break his concentration.

11. Kote gaeshi - gedan ate
Turn your thumb down as you stab to make toshu's technique more difficult and less effective for him.

He moves to your right and sweeps his right hand in an anti-clockwise direction so that his arm is between his body and your arm. As he sweeps his arm he turns to his right and slides his left hand down your arm to your wrist to take a reverse grip with both hands.

Keeping his hands close to him he moves to your front left corner taking your hand down to break your balance. Move your right foot forward as he does this to ensure that you maintain your balance.

He sweeps his left foot back, pivots on his right foot and applies kote gaeshi. Before your hand gets turned further than palm up turn your body to the right and extend your right arm above your head pushing it upwards towards his face and turn your hand in the opposite direction to his application of kote gaeshi. Keep your torso upright and bend your knees.

Take a deep step to his right side with your left foot. Place the inside of your left arm low across his body and use the forward movement of your whole body through him to throw him finishing on a natural posture with your left foot forward.

Coaching points
Redirect toshu's movement upwards with your arm rather than trying to block his technique.

Gedan ate is applied with body movement through him driving your hips up under his centre and displacing his whole body rather than simply remaining stationary and twisting your hips to throw him across your thigh.

12. Tenkai kote hineri - ushiro ate (pictures page 265)
Toshu steps forward and to your right with his left foot as you stab. He grasps your wrist with both hands in a regular grip as he moves.

He steps forward with his right foot to bring his shoulder towards your right shoulder before turning under your arm. Turn to your right as he steps forward with his right foot and step with your left foot so that it passes behind his right foot and in front of his left foot. You are stepping across his line of movement so that your left leg finishes between his legs. Place your left hand onto his left shoulder as you do this.

263

Keep very close to him and drop your weight so that you bend him back to break his balance and prevent him from turning under your arm.

Use body movement to pull toshu down so that he falls to your left side.

Coaching points
Good timing is required in your footwork because you are stepping across the line of his step. Once his right foot comes in front of his left foot the aim is to step just behind it and across his direction of movement so that your left foot finishes between his feet.

Keeping close to him with your weight low prevents him from turning under your arm or bending forward to escape.

Your left hand is used to apply ushiro ate but you must keep your hand open as you are not allowed to grasp (picture right).

Apply ushiro ate through body movement rather than twisting your body and pulling with your arm.

13. Tenkai kote gaeshi - gyakugamae ate (pictures page 267)
Toshu avoids the knife by moving forward and to your left while grasping with both hands in a regular grip.

Immediately after he has grasped your arm pull your elbow back into your body. At this time toshu will have his right foot forward as he has not had a chance to step.

Without waiting step forward with your left foot to his right side and place the palm of your left hand onto his temple. Push off with your right leg and step forward with your left foot to apply gyakugamae ate following up with your right leg to return to a natural posture.

Coaching points
Toshu is holding your arm at the moment you pull your elbow back so his body stiffens in surprise as a reaction to this movement which renders him immobile for a split second. Quickly take advantage and apply your technique before his regains his mobility.

Use the soft part of the palm of your hand beneath the little finger on his temple. Place it and push rather than making a hard contact.

265

14. Sumi otoshi - shōmen ate (pictures page 268)

Toshu starts with his right foot forward and avoids your stab to your right side stepping with his left foot. As he does this he takes hold of your arm in a regular grip with both hands.

He pulls you forward slightly and then turns his hips so that he is facing his original direction. He keeps his arms extended as he lifts his hands and draws his right foot close up behind his left foot. He then takes a deep step forward with his left foot and he brings his arms down to apply sumi otoshi.

Turn towards him just as he takes his deep step and bring your left hand onto his jaw. At the same time switch your feet by bringing your left foot forward and right foot back simultaneously so that you are at about 90° to your original position.

Without stopping push off with your right leg and slide your left foot forward between his feet to push him back and down.

Coaching points

Stay in the same spot when you switch your feet. Keep your centre low and turn towards toshu as you switch your feet. Avoid jumping as this takes longer and gives an opportunity for a further technique from him much like the timing in shōki no tsukuri.

He is vulnerable to counter attack when he makes his deep step forward to apply sumi otoshi. Take advantage of this opportunity and maintain your balance through good timing. Turn to face him, switch your feet and apply your technique by cutting across his line of movement without blocking his technique.

Aim to place the palm of your hand against the side of his jaw but be prepared to drop your arm and use your forearm on his chest if you miss with your hand.

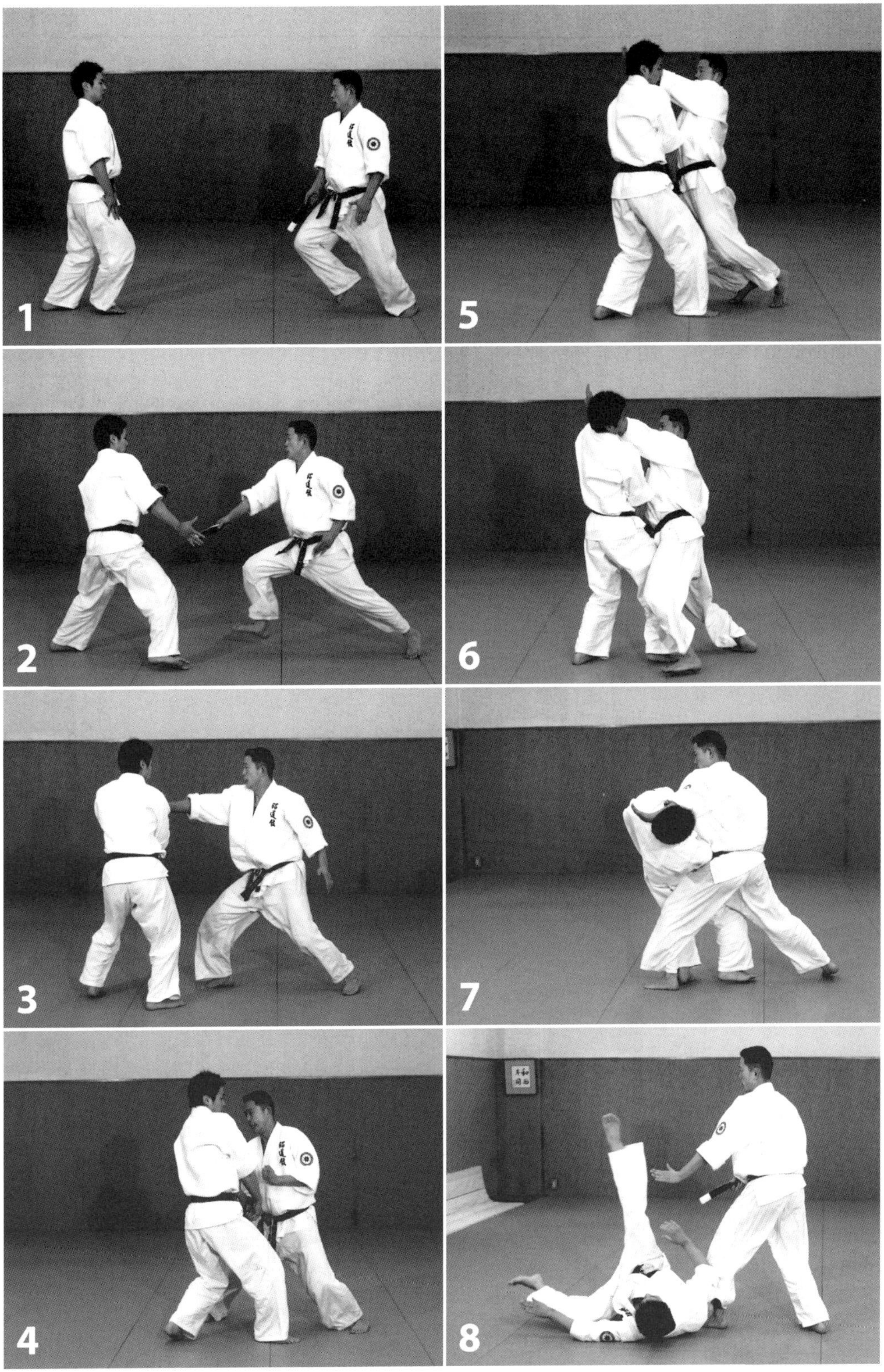
1
2
3
4
5
6
7
8

268

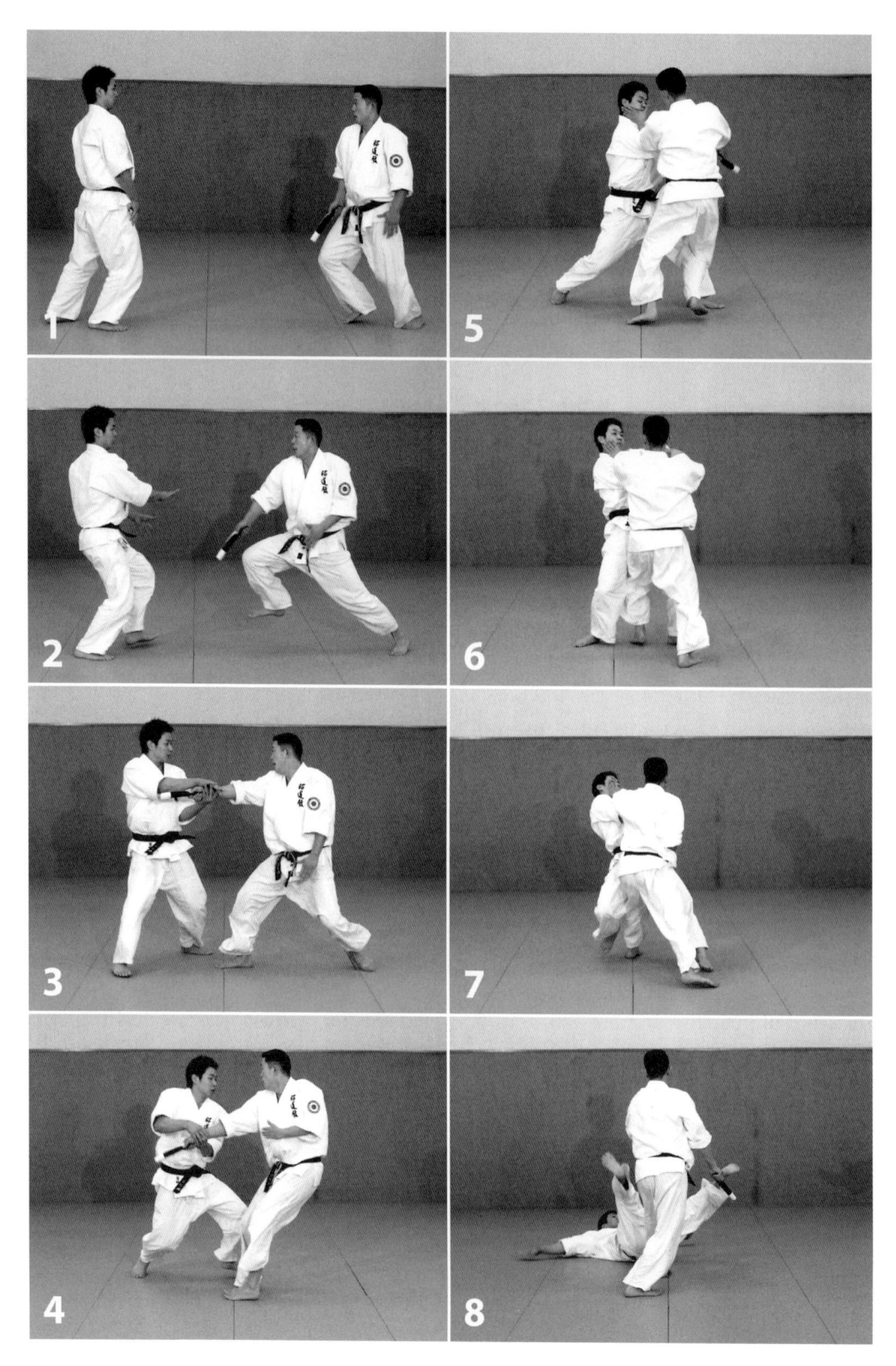

PART 4

APPLICATION

Aikido is primarily concerned with developing ourselves mentally and physically. From the viewpoint of a modern education in budo a system of randori practice is required based upon a training method that incorporates participation in both kata and randori. Both are equally important as over-specialisation in either one cannot result in a balanced development. The proper way to apply techniques in randori is practised through kata. Then, as a safe application of kata, randori ensures an understanding of their practical use. In fact, randori only occupies a tiny part of aikido and leaves a great many techniques that cannot be incorporated into it. The history and budo principles embodied in those techniques must be mastered through thorough kata practice.

Randori leads us closer to both the core principles of budo and the true power that they generate by letting us experience the techniques studied in kata against an antagonistic opponent which is similar to the way they were meant to be used. To this end, we work with others using a competitive environment to bring about the best in ourselves. The aim is for two people of similar attitude working for mutual benefit experiencing the movements, attacks, combinations and counterattacks in concentrated effort.

Randori is a study of movements conceived and executed with speed, precision and flair that requires a high level of skill and permits an element of creativity and personal expression. Doing this kind of aikido while remaining sensitive to your opponent's movements and capitalising on his weaknesses requires constant practice. It takes a lot longer to master than crude, heavy aikido but ultimately it is much more satisfying and the dividends are enormous. The greatest value lies in following the correct way through which, by perseverance, everyone can realise an improvement.

The patterns of movement in randori are complex and contain many variations which make us think about how to modify and fine tune techniques. The unpredictable nature is also a good way to test our strength of character and composure. We operate at the limits of our physical and mental abilities to continually expand our potential but we always do our best in the spirit of sportsmanship. Aggression has no place in aikido, only determination and commitment.

The competitive nature of randori naturally leads to the potential for matches but these are not the objective. Doing aikido just for the purposes of winning matches is wrong and generates an undesirable attitude of winning at all costs. A person focused on winning will never build a wide range of techniques and depth of understanding. In addition, simply reducing randori to a game reduces aikido to a less valuable discipline ignoring its historical and cultural significance.

The ideal of a balanced person, highly skilled in aikido is a much greater aim than a trophy or medal. That is not to say that competitions do not have their place and you should have no reservations about participating in them. However, success does not guarantee contentment in aikido afterwards and, of course, not everyone can win. So, the key to progress is practice for the sake of practice with the single idea of learning and not being concerned about being thrown.

Those of you who choose to participate in competitions must not let your standards drop. Do not think that any way to win is all right as long as you win. The way that you win is very important. To beat an opponent you must outwit him and be technically superior. Physical strength also has a part but not at the expense of poor technique just because skill requires more patience and practice. By relying on strength and power you inevitably pay less attention to speed, technique and timing. Superior technique should always prevail. If it does not, then more practice is required. It is as simple as that.

Randori will always be an invaluable and enjoyable practice for those who have no desire to enter competitions. Superior technique and the creative imagination needed to produce it are what is important, not winning or losing. So, the emphasis should be on the techniques themselves and whether you can do good randori and build real skill. Working to improve your old techniques and develop new applications is ultimately for everyone's benefit.

STAGES OF PRACTICE

The previous parts of this book considered the requirements for toshu and tantō separately, comprising prearranged drills (kata) with neither of you acting freely. This part brings these together into a series of applied practices beginning with tai sabaki and progressing towards full randori in three further stages:

1. Kakari geiko
This is the first step away from kata practise. In kata there is effectively an agreement where the order of techniques is fixed and ukemi are taken without resistance. In kakari geiko the order of the techniques is not fixed and they are usually applied in a basic form with tantō attacking with a straight stab and offering no resistance in order to help with the smooth execution of techniques and aid learning. This is kata but from toshu's viewpoint it is a kind of basic freestyle practice.

2. Hikitate geiko
In hikitate geiko toshu applies techniques freely and tantō has some freedom in his actions. His stabs can be more demanding for toshu involving feints or following toshu's movements. He offers a small amount of resistance when a technique has poor timing or ineffective kuzushi, or when determined by a particular drill. The aim is to use tantō's measured resistance as a cue to change to an alternative technique indicated by his movement and stance. This cultivates quick thinking and the ability to applying techniques, combinations and counters. Techniques that have good timing or kuzushi are accepted by your opponent and he takes an ukemi.

3. Randori geiko
Practices in randori geiko can be tailored as explained below but in general, within the framework of randori, neither you nor your opponent is restricted. Toshu can apply techniques at any opportunity and tantō is free to stab or apply counter techniques where allowed. The aim is to throw and avoid being thrown by using skill and timing rather than wrestling against force. You are free to defend against your opponent's attacks but if you are thrown then you must take an ukemi as these are an essential part of practice. Strictly speaking, only this third level is randori as hikitate geiko is still an applied method of kata.

Drills and their variations are targeted to specific techniques and skills or to a particular intensity so the boundaries between these three stages can sometimes be a little grey. In general, the more freedom you have in your actions the further you are along the path to randori. The aim is maintain the integrity of your aikido for mutual benefit whatever the level of practice you undertake.

The drills that follow are, on the whole, ordered from simple to more complex and low intensity to higher intensity in small steps to speed up learning and build confidence. You are free to choose from these according to your requirements or to create your own practices that you find useful in developing good randori skills.

These drills are intended to focus on particular skills so keep to the limits of each one in terms of intensity and technical content. Introducing things out of the context of the drill curtails your learning which will have an adverse effect on your randori. You cannot expect to be proficient at something as complex as randori without a thorough practice of its constituent parts to make these movements second nature.

Practice with different people
It is important to practise with people of different height, weight, strength and ability for example. Everyone is slightly different in their actions and reactions so you will develop a broader range of skills.

Regarding practice with people of different levels, there are three possibilities:

1. Practice with people not as good as you
This is not a chance for you to use your strength or to throw someone mercilessly to make you feel good. The aim is to practise with the correct attitude and use techniques as they should be done using the principles of aikido. If they do not work then do not use strength, take it as an opportunity to correct your weaknesses. Refine your techniques, work on subtle details, try new throws, combinations, etc but avoid your favourite ones because you will be training at a slower speed and this may dull them. You must also take ukemi as this assists in your opponent's learning and confidence building.

2. Practice with people of the same level
With two people of the same level practising together often the practice can escalate and become a competition with the intention of just beating the other person. Try to prevent this from happening and do not be defensive or worry about being thrown or losing. Attack with your best throws with speed and strength. Be constructive and try to develop counters against your opponent's full speed attacks to improve the standard of your aikido and his.

3. Practising with people better than you
In this practice you are likely to be thrown a lot or, against a tantō, stabbed a lot. Always take a positive attitude and attack as much as possible without thinking about losing. Your opponent is not interested in winning, he is there to improve his aikido and to give you advice.

In all three situations you are trying to improve yourself and your opponent using good aikido. Experiment to develop new techniques and don't even consider winning and or losing even though you are liable to leave yourself open to counter attack. This should be seen as to your benefit because it exposes flaws in your techniques which you then have to correct.

Posture in randori
Creative aikido starts with a sound posture. Without balance and stability you will be unsteady on your feet and have difficulty in moving. Your freedom of action and possibilities of movement in any direction will be severely limited. In short, a good posture is essential.

Your must be poised, neutral with no commitment in any direction and ready to attack or defend at speed. You are free to stand with either foot forward or in mugamae although this is not the most prepared of postures. Adopt the most mechanically favourable posture for your intended movement.

Do not let your posture deteriorate when you are under attack or if you are tired but if this does happen then it is vital to regain it as soon as possible.

Mental clarity is very important in translating quick decisions into controlled and fluent actions. Be physically active and dynamic; remain calm and undisturbed mentally but always alert.

Non-resistance in randori
As there are no weight divisions in practice or in competitions it is quite likely you will meet someone bigger and stronger than you. Do not rely on only your strength otherwise you will not succeed. If you do throw someone using strength alone rather than good aikido then you cannot count this as a success. Remember that what is effective is not necessarily good aikido.

Whether you are stronger than your opponent or not, giving precedence to your physical strength makes you insensitive to your opponent's movements and deprives you of the freedom to attack and defend. It is also a great waste of energy.

Stay relaxed but responsive in your randori. This is much more efficient in terms of conserving your energy and is also more effective. There are times when you may have to intermittently resist to keep your opponent from gaining an advantage but do not resist techniques rashly. Blocking techniques impulsively stops the natural flow of randori and removes your chances of counter attack.

Flexibility and adaptability to changing circumstances are the qualities of non-resistance. Fit naturally into the openings you find or create and aim for a clean, effortless technique. Acquiring this kind of sensitivity to an opponent's movements can only be achieved by repeated practice.

Non-resistance also applies to your mind. You must open your mind and let it flow freely, ready to change from defence to attack or from one technique to another without loss of mental equilibrium. With a flexible and positive mind you will be able to react more quickly and your movements will be faster.

Kuzushi in randori
Kuzushi is often considered as simply pushing or pulling to break your opponent's balance. However, it is more than just affecting his physical posture. Disrupting his concentration can also create a momentary opportunity for attack. This can be achieved by breaking rhythm, using feints or changing the maai for example.

The timing opportunities for applying techniques against tantō tsuki have been described previously. We can also consider the situation where the distance between you and your opponent has closed to where you can grasp his arm or he can grasp your arm.

If your opponent is applying a technique by pushing or pulling it is quite possible that his movement may cause him to lose balance by himself if you react to his movement correctly. In general, if he pushes then move out of the line of his attack rather than retreating directly; if he pulls then move forward at an angle which also avoids the line of his force. By applying a force while dissipating his attack you can take advantage of his unbalanced posture and even if he remains balanced while he applies a technique his momentary immobility at the end of his movement is a further opportunity.

If your opponent steps forward or steps back then by moving faster than him you will be able to break his balance as he commits his weight onto the foot with which he is stepping. The timing when he steps forward is the same as that for tsukitaru o utsu; when he steps back it is the same as hikiokori o utsu both of which have been described earlier with applications of atemi waza and kansetsu waza.

Another way to apply kuzushi is to take the initiative and setup or force your opponent into a weak position. The most common way to do this is by combinations where one technique gains a reaction in the opposite direction that can assist in another technique. The first technique can be a genuine one or a feint used to gauge his reaction. If he reacts the same way more than once then his is likely to do it again so you can anticipate it and set up a suitable combination.

Tsukuri in randori
In Jigorō Kanō's words, "To apply a technique easily an opponent's balance must be broken and you must be suitable positioned. This is known as tsukuri. Applying a technique from this position is called kake". This idea from judo applies to aikido in all techniques and is very important as it gives you the window of opportunity to apply a technique.

This statement shows that you must be in control of your opponent and yourself. Correct and subtle tsukuri using controlled body movement and precise timing is difficult to master but is vital for a high level of aikido.

Kuzushi and tsukuri in judo can easily be seen as two parts of a technique. In aikido there is more overlap between the two so do not focus just on breaking your opponent's balance. Your movement to position yourself is also important. The longer you can control the tsukuri by maintaining the balance break and your correct positioning, the greater chance you will have of applying a technique. Techniques are difficult without adequate tsukuri and you will only be able to apply them using strength or with the help of your opponent.

Against an opponent who is resisting you will find that movement in one direction may not be effective. In this case you must immediately change to the opposite direction to build an opportunity to apply a technique. Practising changes between high and low, right and left, forward and backward will greatly improve your skill.

RENZOKU TAI SABAKI

Renzoku tai sabaki is a good starting point in the application of the skills described previously to randori practice in a lesson. It involves practising repeated tai sabaki freely moving around the tatami rather than from a static position.

1. Without using tegatana

The simplest tai sabaki practice is using only footwork to avoid a tantō tsuki.

Stand in a natural posture of your choice. Tantō approaches to the correct distance where he stands ready to stab with the knife in one hand and the same side foot forward. Immediately, or after a slight pause, he makes a straight tantō tsuki. Avoid the attack only through footwork based on the six directions of movement shown on page 93.

After tantō has made his attack he must make a further one or two tsugi ashi movements forward to create some distance between you before turning and approaching you for his next attack.

Tantō should also use high attacks as well as straight stabs (pictures below). He changes the grip on the knife and raises it knife high to the left or right and brings it down slowly in a large diagonal movement as he steps forward. As he lifts the knife take a deep step forward (with the right foot when moving to tantō's left and left foot when moving to his right) to the same side that the knife is raised. Bend your knees and keep your torso upright and, as he finishes his movement, turn to face the same way as him keeping as close as possible. As above, tantō steps forward to create some room between you before his next attack which can be either a stab or high attack.

Tantō's attacks should be continuous without letting you have much of a break but the speed and pressure of the attacks can be adjusted to your ability.

Objectives

In this practice you use continuous footwork in a less static situation that requires better judgment of maai and timing of your movements. You use the six directions of avoidance from a straight stab or the two deep forward movements against the high attacks. This is not a practice just for toshu, tantō also has to judge maai for his stab as well as correct form, depth of attack and target area.

The entering movements in response to the high attacks are a basic practice for tsukuri used in kansetsu waza that require good body control to close the distance, move behind tantō and turn to keep close to him.

Coaching points

Tantō must make a straight stab at the correct depth to where you are standing and not deviate from that line or depth of attack even when you have moved. This ensures he has the correct form and control over the knife and allows you to judge the effectiveness of your movement.

To sharpen your timing wait as late as possible before moving and never turn your back towards tantō.

Extension

To increase the pressure on you to give you less chance of a break, two people can hold knives and alternately make repeated attacks. Here it is particularly important for you to be aware of where both attackers are and not turn your back to either of them.

2. Using tegatana

The next step is to add in the use of tegatana. You can use the six directions of tai sabaki while making contact with tantō's arm with the tegatana of one or both hands to prevent the stab from reaching its target (bottom four pictures on page 277).

In the case of a high attack, use the tegatana of both hands to block his arm by moving towards him as he is lifting it. Step with your right foot forward when moving to tantō's left side and left foot forward when moving to his right side (pictures top of page 277). Keep your hands in your centre and move into a stable, upright posture.

Top two pictures: using tegatana against a high attack.

Lower four pictures: various tai sabaki using tegatana. Your tegatana is held in your centre and turned towards uke's arm. Two hands can be used as a basic practice and one hand as a more advanced method. Either hand can be used as long as your posture is not compromised, you are at the correct distance from tantō and are controlling the attack. The pictures above show an avoidance to the outside of tantō's attack but mirror images of these movements can be used when avoiding to the inside.

After each attack make room between yourself and tantō as in the previous practice before continuing.

Coaching points

Try not to push tantō's arm away from its line of attack when he stabs. The aim is to control his arm using a soft contact with your tegatana bringing it between your body and his arm to prevent it from reaching its target but to keep it within range as a step to grasping his arm.

Try to avoid using your tegatana directly on his wrist. Draw your hand down his forearm keeping your hand in your centre as you turn your hips to avoid his attack. Always ensure that your tegatana is towards his arm as this is the focus of your power and your point of contact.

Extensions

1. Practice against two attackers.

2. Allow tantō to make feints as well as genuine attacks. In this case he is not allowed to do high attacks, only tantō tsuki. You should try to either ignore the feint or take the opportunity to close the distance to him and use your tegatana on his wrist or inside of his elbow to control his arm in a similar movement to that used against a kick in the basic practice of tegatana no bōgyo.

3. Using grasps

Once you have successfully avoided the stab one aim is to grasp tantō's arm which is a starting point for kansetsu waza or combinations based on them. It also prevents him from using the knife but does allow him to use atemi waza counter techniques.

Practise this in the same way as you practice zenzoku tai sabaki using tegatana against a stab but instead of using your tegatana use both hands to grasp tantō's wrist just as his stab finishes. The priority is still to avoid the stab through body movement.

There are four grasps as described on pages 176 and 178 with pictures on page 179. Tantō stops after you have taken your grip before you let go and then continues with one or two tsugi ashi before turning to attack again.

Do not attempt to grasp tantō's wrist every time. Use your tegatana as you avoid the attacks and grasp his wrist every two or three attacks.

Ensure that your feet are positioned so that your centre is towards tantō and you have to ability to make a further movement.

KAKARI GEIKO

Kakari geiko is, in general, the first step away from kata where there is still a kind of agreement between toshu and tantō with techniques being applied in a basic style but in no fixed order.

Tantō uses a basic, straight knife strike and learns the elements of a valid tantō tsuki from the correct distance with the necessary control of the knife. He offers no resistance to toshu's techniques.

Toshu uses basic techniques with freedom of movement and choice of technique against straight stabs. His techniques have good timing but with a considerable reduction in power because tantō is offering no resistance.

1. Basic practice
Tantō attacks as for the basic renzoku tai sabaki practice using stabs but no high attacks. Toshu avoids and uses tegatana but he applies a basic technique on every second or third attack after which tantō takes an ukemi.

Coaching points
When tantō attacks he pauses briefly giving toshu the chance to apply a technique. If toshu does not apply one then tantō makes one or two more tsugi ashi forward before turning to attack again.

Variations
Toshu can be limited to a group of techniques (atemi waza only, for example), a single technique or a selection chosen by the instructor.

2. Atemi waza timing practice
This is specifically targeted to practicing the timing opportunities for atemi waza. Tantō is free to make any of the three following movements:

   i. Emphasise the start of the tantō tsuki to allow toshu to practise okori o utsu timing. Tantō does not have to make a stab but can do if toshu does not react to this movement in which case toshu should avoid the stab.
   ii. Normal tantō tsuki to allow the practice of tsukitaru o utsu timing. This is the same as the basic practice above.
   iii. Normal tantō tsuki (which toshu avoids) then tantō emphasises his withdrawal in preparation for a second attack. This allows toshu to practise hikiokori o utsu timing.

In all of these cases, toshu can apply a technique or stop short of the throw depending on the lesson plan. Either way, tantō offers no resistance so takes an ukemi if he is thrown.

In addition, toshu can feint an atemi waza and apply a technique as tantō moves away. This is to practise the uketaru o utsu timing opportunity.

3. Kansetsu waza timing practice
This follows on from the use of grasps in renzoku tai sabaki. Tantō attacks as for the basic renzoku tai sabaki practice using stabs but no high attacks. Avoid the knife as he attacks and grasp his wrist with both hands as the stab finishes. As tantō retreats and pulls his arm back keep hold of his wrist and match his movement to close the distance to him.

Your footwork and timing have to be correct to allow you to close the distance without losing balance. This is a practice for closing the distance as a link between avoiding the knife to the application of a technique. This should be practised lightly and toshu should not attempt to grasp tantō's wrist every time.

HIKITATE GEIKO
Hikitate geiko is the next step towards randori with a level of agreement between toshu and tantō but both players having more freedom in their actions which means more scope for creating drills and practices.

In general, tantō makes his attacks more difficult to deal with and he is allowed to resist some of toshu's techniques or apply counter techniques. However, his aim is to encourage the development of your skills as well as his own.

1. As a first step tantō may follow toshu's movements during his attack, use feints to disrupt toshu's rhythm and generally put more pressure on toshu. Toshu has to deal with the more difficult attacks and respond by applying single techniques with tantō offering no resistance.

This allows toshu the chance to explore the possibilities of applying techniques which are not necessarily done as in the basic kata. The aim is to move away from the basic form but retain the underlying principles and start to develop applications that are effective in an unrestricted and fast moving environment.

2. The next step is to allow tantō to resist some techniques. This encourages toshu to research what options there are for combinations where there is a transition from one technique into another. The aim is to make a quick seamless change from one technique into another.

Tantō only resists against techniques which he feels have been ineffective either because of incorrect timing or insufficient breaking of balance for example. If this happens he resists with about 20% of his power which acts as a signal to toshu to change technique. Toshu should then move to another rather than use strength to continue the current technique.

Generally, tantō should not resist the second technique but the practice can be structured so that tantō resists more than once to force a chain of combinations from toshu.

3. A further step is to allow tantō to apply kaeshi waza. He should not counter a technique that toshu applies with good timing and sufficient balance breaking. However, when toshu's

application is inefficient, tantō can switch into a kaeshi waza to which toshu may or may not resist depending on what is decided before the practice starts.

After tantō resists against toshu's technique there is a point where he will be aiming to apply a kaeshi waza and toshu will be aiming to switch into a combination. Do not offer more than about 20% resistance and go with the general flow of the movements so that it does not escalate into a wrestling match of strength against strength. This should be an opportunity to learn.

These are examples of many varied practices that can be used according to the goals of the lesson. Create and use others if you find that they improve your aikido.

RANDORI GEIKO

With the idea of randori practice for mutual benefit you can simply practise randori that is restricted only by the rules with both players free in their actions and choice of techniques, combinations and counter techniques.

Alternatively, with the same idea in mind, practices can be targeted by restricting the options of the participants. This can make it more interesting and enjoyable which encourages learning leading to technical and tactical improvements. The following are some methods you may incorporate into lessons either individually or in combination. It is not an exhaustive list but gives you an idea of the possibilities. Use others if you find that they benefit your aikido. This kind of approach is not restricted to randori, some of these also apply to kakari geiko and hikitate geiko.

1. Limit the techniques
Toshu can be limited to:
- a single technique which tantō may or may not know about
- a group of techniques, for example atemi waza
- a selection of techniques
- a single technique and no combinations
- two or more techniques in combination
- a specific technique to finish a combination

Tantō can be limited to:
- tantō tsuki and no kaeshi waza
- kaeshi waza against specific techniques

2. Limit the intensity
Set a limit on the intensity of the practice. A light randori practice is considered to be hikitate geiko but the tendency is for participants to gradually increase the intensity to avoid being thrown. Use this in combination with longer periods of randori to promote economic movement and to conserve energy.

3. Limit to left or right side
Tantō can be limited to using the knife only in his left hand.
Toshu can be limited to:
>kansetsu waza only on the arm the knife is held
>kansetsu waza only on the empty hand
>atemi waza with the left hand or right hand

4. Limit the role
Limit participants to be only toshu or tantō for one lesson.

5. Limit the score
Continue until a predetermined value of technique has been scored. Or exchange the tantō each time a tsuki is scored.

6. Limit the start position
Start from a specific grasp on tantō's arm.

7. Limit the time
Limit the time of a bout. Shorts periods (20 seconds) for intense attack and defence, or longer periods (a few minutes) for conservation of energy and defence. Rounds of unknown length can also be used.

8. Limit the scoring technique
Limit to only one technique that can score. Combinations are allowed as long as they finish with the scoring technique but other techniques do not count.

9. Limit the space
Limit the size of contest area used.

10. Limit the activity
Allow bursts of activity for 5 seconds and then slow down.

11. Limit the participation
In a group the winner of a bout stays on for the next bout. Or, as an alternative, the winner is allowed to rest and the loser stays for the next bout. Either way that person is replaced by another. In addition, each bout can be limited in the ways mentioned above.

Randori and mock competition (mohōjiai) are opportunities to research and develop your techniques. They also allow referees to practice their judgment and management of a match. The regulations for randori are included in the last part of this book.

PART 5

A PAPER BY KENJI TOMIKI

This is a translation of Tomiki's last published paper to the Japanese Academy of Budo concerning the importance of tsukuri in aikido. It is written from the viewpoint of judo regarding the atemi waza and kansetsu waza that are part of judo although not included in judo randori. These techniques comprise aikido so the points here are relevant.

The importance of tsukuri in atemi waza and kansetsu waza

Preface
Practise of atemi waza and kansetsu waza is vital to fully understand the basic structure of judo and to experience the practical use of shizentai. However, these techniques are often neglected because the majority of them are part of kata practice. There are two reasons for this:

1. The exclusion of kata techniques from competitive practice methods.
2. A perception that an improvement in skill cannot be realized by practising kata alone and that it is not possible to make practical use of these techniques.

This paper clarifies that with knowledge of the meaning and method of tsukuri in atemi waza and kansetsu waza, as with nage waza and katame waza, you can develop real ability and an understanding of practical application.

1. The essential points of old jujutsu are mentioned in this quote, "A natural posture (mugamae) is an expression of a pure and clear mind (mushin). The principle of jujutsu lies in softness prevailing over strength".

Jigorō Kanō (1860-1938), who modernized jujutsu and established Kōdōkan judo, explained this in simple terms as three general principles:

1. Shizentai no ri (principle of natural posture) concerning posture that allows unrestricted attack and defence.

2. Jū no ri (principle of non-resistance) concerning quick tai sabaki and te sabaki to nullify an opponent's ability to attack.

3. Kuzushi no ri (principle of balance breaking) concerning the breaking of an opponent's balance and creating the opportunity to win.

These principles were deduced from the techniques and fighting styles of old jujutsu without favouring any particular school. Kanō stated that they are the foundation for techniques and also a means of cultivating one's mind. This 'mind' is the pure and clear mind (mushin) mentioned above but imperturbability, equanimity, flexible mind and presence of mind all have the same meaning. He taught the importance of tsukuri, which is the suppression of an opponent's offensive ability and the creation of a chance to apply a technique, as the key point in extending from the principles into techniques. The basic structure of tsukuri is learned first and then put to effective use in all nage waza, katame waza, atemi waza and kansetsu waza. The essence of 'softness prevailing over strength' is also found in tsukuri.

2. Judo randori (using nage waza and katame waza) begins with the practice of kata to learn the techniques and the correct use of power. Progress is made to randori and then competition. If we think of kata as the grammar of a sentence, randori practice is an application of that grammar with the strength of that usage expressed objectively in a match.

Kata is a one-sided practice with a compliant partner whereas techniques in randori are against an opponent offering some resistance. The intensity of this resistance increases as you move away from soft randori and closer to competition. Accordingly, most of the effort of judo practitioners is put into how to overcome this resistance and apply a technique. Kanō eventually realized that breaking balance an instant before applying a technique is the easy way to apply it. He called this chance of winning 'tsukuri'. He analyzed it scientifically regarding the postures of both particpants and organized a system of practice.

Judo depends on the skill of tsukuri through tai sabaki and te sabaki. In other words, judo practice should be focused on tsukuri rather than the application of a technique. We can go so far as to say that shiai (a match) is a competition of tsukuri rather than the application of techniques. Skilled players concentrate on this point.

3. Kata were devised as a way to practise old jujutsu safely. This was the only way of practising bujutsu in olden days which were focused entirely on actual combat and valued only victory. So, in the past, people would move directly from practising kata to life or death situations in real combat. They learned techniques and diverse fighting styles through kata practice to deal with all kinds of attacks. Consequently, this took many years. Moreover, much emphasis was placed on aiuchi (simultaneous strike), the secret to success in combat; students were encouraged to wait right up to the moment of their opponent's strike. Even in kata they made great efforts to maintain their strength of spirit and orientation towards actual combat.

However, in modern budo, greater value is found in the physical exercise itself and the fostering of social skills through personal relationships rather than focusing on fighting. This is a natural consequence of the development in educational principles as times change. Nevertheless, it cannot be denied that the strength of spirit found in the training of old budo is only realized through the experience of matches. Budo spirit comes from calming your mind and dealing with the mental conflict experienced when standing at the crossroads between life and death. Turning bujutsu into a sport by establishing a place for competition is the only way to test real ability within modern budo. This can only be achieved by limiting the number of techniques and standardizing the format. These changes are inevitable if education in budo is to be coordinated, particularly when the period available for such education is limited. As a result, Kanō stressed the importance of atemi waza and kansetsu waza, which were not included in competitive judo, and taught that they should be learnt through kata practice. This approach was central to the formation of modern judo.

4. When an investigative attitude regarding competitive principles is absent in kata such practice degrades into a stage performance with exaggerated movements, cut off from reality and reduced to a mere shell. This is the pitfall of kata. The way to avoid this is to compete in the form of a match. You must make use of this experience and have the same attitude and scientific approach when practising atemi waza and kansetsu waza in kata.

For this reason it is necessary to study in depth the basic framework derived from atemi waza and kansetsu waza. This is the same structure and foundation as the nage waza and katame waza but with te sabaki and sword principles absorbed into it. The characteristics of these techniques are the use of throws and pins while defending against an opponent's punch, strike or kick, and also against a cut or thrust with a weapon. If you pay attention to the practice of focussing your power through your tegatana and maintaining a flexible body then you will be able to keep your ability in these techniques throughout your life. Continue this as a lifelong practice and the depth and breadth of these techniques will be revealed. This was also Kanō's intention.

Summary
The points discussed above are shown in the diagram overleaf which acts as the summary for this short paper.

theory

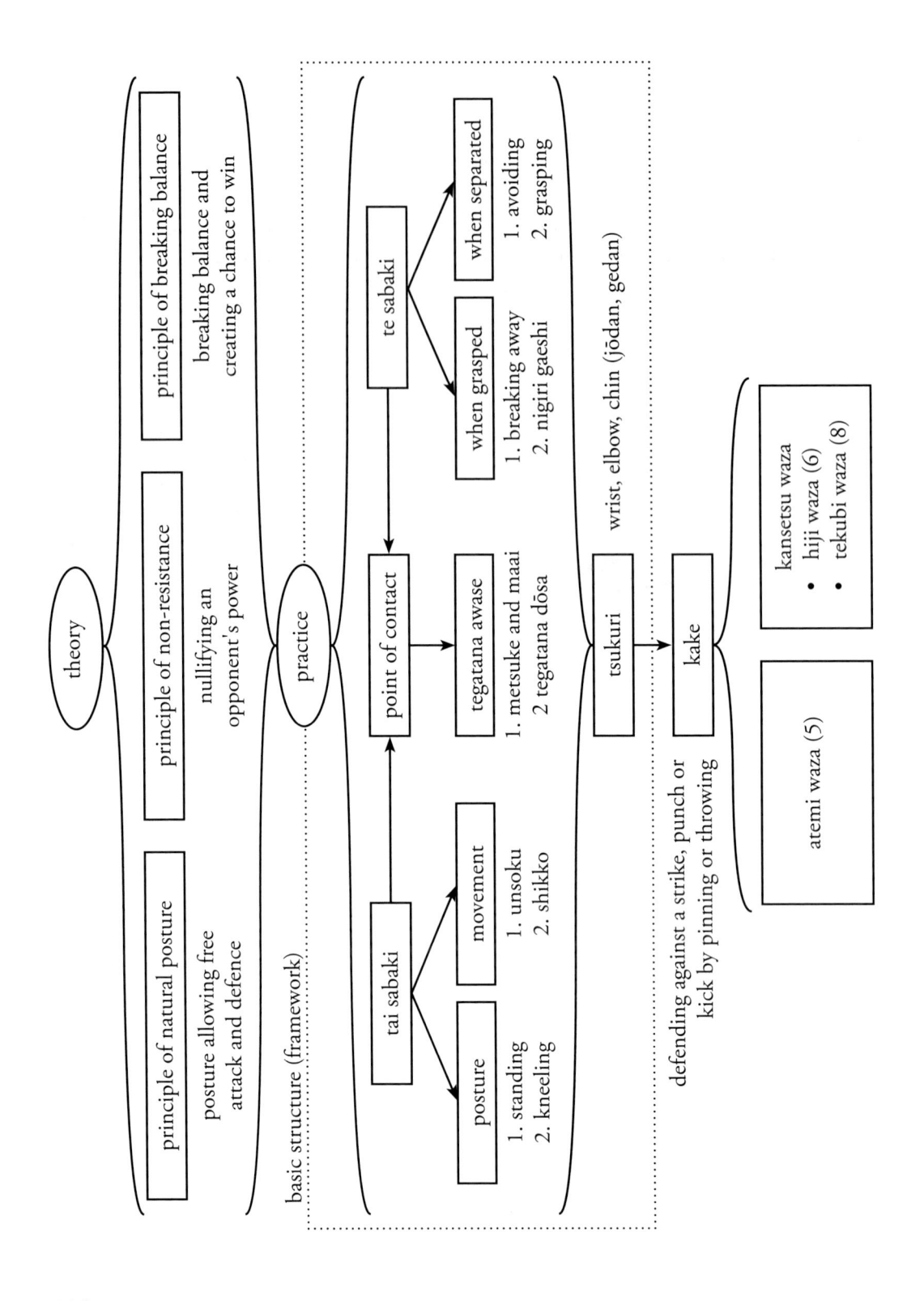

- **principle of natural posture** — posture allowing free attack and defence
- **principle of non-resistance** — nullifying an opponent's power
- **principle of breaking balance** — breaking balance and creating a chance to win

basic structure (framework)

practice

tai sabaki
- posture
  1. standing
  2. kneeling
- movement
  1. unsoku
  2. shikko

↓

point of contact
- tegatana awase
  1. metsuke and maai
  2. tegatana dōsa

↑

te sabaki
- when grasped
  1. breaking away
  2. nigiri gaeshi
- when separated
  1. avoiding
  2. grasping

→ **tsukuri** → **kake**

wrist, elbow, chin (jōdan, gedan)

defending against a strike, punch or kick by pinning or throwing

- atemi waza (5)
- kansetsu waza
  - hiji waza (6)
  - tekubi waza (8)

PART 6

REGULATIONS FOR RANDORI

Preface
Competitive aikido was created by Kenji Tomiki, the first president of the Japan Aikido Association (JAA), from his research into reorganising aikido from an educational viewpoint. He explained the necessity of randori practice, where players compete against each other with mutual free will, along with the more traditional kata practice to help in modern education and to increase aikido's value as a cultural asset. Randori not only has the technical depth that can be understood by just practising kata but it is also very good for learning how to deal with the highs and lows of competing. These points must be remembered because it is important not to fall into the trap of simply trying to win. These minimum regulations were established to put this kind of attitude into practice.

Article 1   Competition area
a. The competition area is a square of five tatami lengths (approx. 9.09m) on each side. This covers an area of 50 tatami.
b. Start lines are marked two tatami lengths apart (approx. 3.64m) in the centre of the competition area.
c. A matted safety zone of at least one tatami length (approx. 1.82m) in width is provided outside of the competition area. The edge of the competition area is clearly defined.
d. If a supervising referee is present, a place away from the competition area shall be established where those people with the right to question judgments (team managers, coaches, etc.) may do so.

Article 2   Uniform
a. Dōgi
   i. Players wear dōgi approved by the JAA. One player wears a red sash and the other wears a white sash tied over their belts.
   ii. Women wear a white t-shirt under their jackets; men wear nothing under their jackets. Body protectors, etc. made from plastic are not allowed for men or women.
b. Dōgi approved by the JAA satisfy the following criteria:
   i. The jacket is long enough to cover the buttocks when the belt is tied.

ii. The sleeves, when loose, cover at least one third of the forearms.
iii. The trousers, when loose, cover at least half of the lower legs.
iv. The belt is used to secure the jacket so it is tied moderately tight. Once tied, the ends of the belt are approximately 15cm in length.
v. The dōgi is clean and any damage repaired.

Article 3   Competition process
a. Duration of a match
   A match comprises two halves with each half lasting one minute thirty seconds excluding stoppages.
b. Starting, interrupting and ending a match
   i. Players stand on the start lines facing each other and bow at the same time. In this position when looking towards shōmen the player on the right is aka (red) and the player on the left is shiro (white).
   ii. A match starts when the chief referee calls 'hajime' (start). Play is interrupted by calling 'mate' (break) and both halves of a match end by calling 'yame' (stop).
   iii. At the end of each half, or if play is interrupted, the players quickly return to their start lines and await instructions from the chief referee.
   iv. After 'hantei' (decision) has been called the players bow to each other and leave the competition area.
c. Competition format
   i. One player is empty-handed (toshu) and the other player (tantō) holds a sponge rubber knife. Players attack and defend using prescribed techniques and tantō tsuki (stab).
   ii. The knife is made from sponge rubber approved by the JAA.
   iii. Players exchange the knife at the end of the first half.
   iv. Players can hold the knife in either hand. However, swapping the knife from one hand to the other is allowed only after the players have returned to their start lines during a break in play.
d. Competition techniques
   Toshu uses techniques included in Kenji Tomiki's 1978 publication 'Aikido kyōgi ni tsuite' (Concerning competitive aikido) which are five atemi waza, nine kansetsu waza and three uki waza. Tantō uses tantō tsuki and five atemi waza (as for toshu) as kaeshi waza (Article 5).

Article 4   Judging toshu's techniques
a. Techniques that score points are judged in three categories: ippon, waza ari and yūkō. The criteria for judging each technique are tabulated at the end of these regulations.
b. All techniques (including tantō tsuki) applied after one or both players have stepped outside the competition area are invalid. A player is judged to be outside the competition area when both feet are completely outside the area.
c. Techniques have an order of precedence. When one player applies a technique worth yūkō or more and the other player applies a counter technique also worth yūkō or more then the counter technique is invalid.

d. If a player, during a sequence of movements, applies more than one technique worth yūkō or more then only the highest scoring technique is recognised.

Article 5   Kaeshi waza
a. Kaeshi waza referred to in these regulations are atemi waza applied by tantō when toshu has grasped one of tantō's arms with both hands, or when toshu is applying kansetsu waza or uki waza. When toshu has grasped tantō's arm or hand that he is using to hold the knife, tantō can apply kaeshi waza with either arm. When toshu has grasped the arm or hand that tantō is not using to hold the knife, tantō can apply atemi waza with that arm only.
b. Kaeshi waza can be applied when toshu has grasped one of tantō's arms with both hands or when he is applying kansetsu waza or uki waza but they cannot be applied at the moment toshu touches tantō's arm. Grasping is defined as when the fingers are used to hold the arm. If toshu releases his grip or stops his technique at the moment that tantō applies a kaeshi waza then this technique is valid.

Article 6   Judging tantō tsuki
a. Tantō tsuki that score points are judged as tsuki ari. They apply the concepts of the stab and straight cut from kendo and the principle of kikentai no itchi (unity of mind, sword and body). They are an extension of tegatana dōsa that also use sword principles. Based on these points, tsuki ari satisfy the following conditions:
    i. Tsuki are to the valid target areas which are the front, sides and back of the body between the level of the armpits and the belt (but not including the belt). The arms are included where they are in contact with this area of the body.
    ii. Upright torso and stable hips at the instant the tsuki finishes.
    iii. Tsuki are approximately perpendicular to toshu's body. However, this does not apply if toshu has an irregular posture or has fallen.
    iv. Tsuki are safe. In particular, the knife is not turned so that the fist can strike toshu. This does not apply if toshu closes the distance to tantō without using tai sabaki at the time of the tsuki.
    v. Tsuki start by stepping forward from issoku ittō distance.
b. Maki zuki (where the hand is turned thumb down or palm up during the stab) are valid if they satisfy the criteria above.
c. If toshu has fallen a tsuki is valid if it is made quickly in the first movement and satisfies the criteria above.
d. When a tsuki ari and a technique scoring yūkō or more occur at the same time the tsuki ari takes precedence.
e. Mawashi zuki (stab with a wide, curved arm movement not in front of your body) are invalid because they deviate from the centre line.

Article 7   Penalties

Penalties are judged in three categories: hansoku make, chūi and shidō. They are judged by the chief referee according to the following criteria:

a. General cases for hansoku make
   i. Life threatening techniques are used, in particular those that are likely to cause a hard impact to a player's head. For example, in shōmen ate or gedan ate when the lower half of a player's body is held and lifted without any concern for the safety of his head.
   ii. A player, through foul play, injures either himself or the opponent and the match cannot continue.
   iii. The total of penalties through shidō and chūi amounts to four points.
   iv. The intention is to punch or strike the opponent with force using tantō tsuki or atemi waza.

b. General cases for chūi
   i. The fingers, neck or leg joints are attacked.
   ii. A punch or strike occurs using tantō tsuki or atemi waza.
   iii. Techniques other than those mentioned in Article 3d are used, such as judo or wrestling techniques.
   iv. A player deliberately leaves the competition area without making an effort to engage with the opponent.
   v. Where the penalty is a shidō as described in Article 7c but it is judged to be dangerous, or when a penalty occurs several times and the player does not or cannot obey the chief referee's instructions.
   vi. A player does not act with dignity when the chief referee makes his judgments.

c. General cases for shidō
   i. A player stands in a posture that deviates from shizentai as taught by Kenji Tomiki.
   ii. A player sacrifices his own posture to apply a technique (sutemi waza). Therefore, as a general rule atemi waza, kansetsu waza and uki waza are applied while standing or on one knee.
   iii. A player applies direct and sudden pressure to a vital point or elbow of the opponent without movement across the tatami.
   iv. A player grasps the other's dōgi.
   v. A player uses both hands to encircle the opponent or to control the opponent using one hand on each arm.
   vi. A player has both feet completely out of the competition area.
   vii. A player is disrespectful to the opponent in either speech or conduct, or makes meaningless sounds or movements.
   viii. A player kneels down, leaves the competition area, etc. without the permission of the chief referee or wilfully acts to cause the interruption of play.
   ix. Tantō stabs while not holding the end of the knife.
   x. Tantō stabs to areas outside of those specified in Article 6a.i.
   xi. Tantō ignores Article 6a.v and stabs from an inappropriate distance. Therefore, tantō tsuki is prohibited when toshu is holding tantō's arm and tantō stabs without breaking away.
   xii. Tantō is passive and has no intention of stabbing or he deliberately stalls his attacks.
   xiii. In defending against toshu's attack, tantō holds toshu's arm, clings to him, leans

forward or places his arm in toshu's armpit. It is also prohibited for tantō to place his hand on toshu's face or in a dangerous position with no intention of applying a technique.

- xiv. Tantō applies a kaeshi waza before toshu has grasped his arm.
- xv. Tantō intentionally or carelessly drops the knife or toshu intentionally pulls it from tantō. Tantō is penalised when toshu accidentally pulls the knife from him during a correct technique.
- xvi. Toshu ignores the knife and recklessly closes the distance to tantō without using tai sabaki (it is prohibited to ignore the nature of budo).
- xvii. Toshu hits tantō's arm or hand hard while avoiding the tantō tsuki.
- xviii. Toshu attacks and tantō places the knife within the valid area of toshu's body as defined in Article 6a.i for three seconds or more. Or, tantō repeatedly places the knife within the valid area even if each time is for less than three seconds. However, this does not apply if tantō has placed his arm around toshu and is preventing him from moving away.

Article 8   Calculating the score

a. Techniques that score are awarded points as follows:
   - i. ippon — four points
   - ii. waza ari — two points
   - iii. yūkō — one point
   - iv. tsuki ari — one point
b. Penalty points are awarded to the player not being penalised as follows:
   - i. two shidō (guidance), equivalent to one chūi   one point
   - ii. chūi (warning)   one point
   - iii. hansoku make (disqualification)   eight points
     If four penalty points have been awarded then this is judged as hansoku make with the award of eight points.
c. When a match finishes through hansoku make or a player is unable to participate (fusenshō) the winner will receive eight points and the loser zero points irrespective of any score during the match.
d. Itami wake is the decision the chief referee makes when either or both players are accidentally injured and unable to continue. When a match finishes this way and the scores are equal this is judged to be hiki wake (draw).

Article 9   Dealing with itami wake, hansoku make, etc.

a. Itami wake when a match cannot continue due to accidental injury to one or both players:
   - i. When only one player is injured and the match is in the individual competition, the uninjured player continues to the next round. In the team competition, the winner is decided on the score at the time of the injury.
   - ii. If both players are injured and unable to continue to the next round the opponent in the next round goes through on a bye (fusenshō). Substitutes take their places in

the team competition.
b. Hansoku make when a match cannot continue due to injury that is judged to be intentional:
   i. At the time the match cannot continue, the player responsible for the injury is disqualified. That person cannot participate in any event in the rest of the tournament. However, where the disqualification has occurred through accumulation of penalty points (Article 8b.iii) the player is allowed to participate in other events.
   ii. In the individual competition if the player who progressed to the next round because of the disqualification of his opponent is unable to participate in the next match then that opponent goes through on a bye (fusenshō). This does not apply if the player can continue. In the team competition a substitute takes his place.

Article 10   Determining the winner
a. The winner is determined according to the total score from both halves of a match.
b. If the players have the same score the winner is determined according to the following precedence:
   i. The greater number of ippon scored.
   ii. The greater number of waza ari scored.
   iii. The greater number of yūkō scored.
   iv. The greater number of tsuki ari scored.
c. If the winner cannot be determined by the precedence above then marginal differences apply according to the following precedence:
   i. The greater number of techniques close to scoring yūkō.
   ii. The lesser number of shidō.
   iii. Overall judgment of posture, tai sabaki, positive attitude, sportsmanship, etc. during the match.
d. Conditions for curtailing the first or second half of a match:
   i. The first half finishes if the difference in the scores is eight points or more.
   ii. The second half finishes if the difference in the scores is twelve points of more including the points from the first half.

Article 11   Referees
a. Referees have absolute authority in matches in which they are involved. Nobody other than the competition's head referee can overrule them. However, as specified in Articles 12a and 12e, if there is any doubt about a judgment a supervising referee can stop the match, discuss with the referees and request that the judgment be corrected.
b. Referees are impartial and fair in the management of matches and their judgments.
c. Referees comprise the chief referee and a number of assistant referees. The number of assistant referees is determined by the refereeing method chosen for the competition.
d. The chief referee stands in the competition area facing shōmen and is responsible for the management of the match. According to the refereeing method being used, the assistant referees stand in positions where they can assist the chief referee in the management of the match.
e. In spite of the previous regulation they have equal authority in their judgments.

Article 12   Refereeing method

a. A two referee (mirrored style), three referee or four referee system may be used. A supervising referee may be present to monitor the refereeing.
b. In the two referee system the assistant referee stands opposite and facing the chief referee. Both referees continually move according to the players' movements so that they are in the best position to make judgments. Neither referee uses flags to signal their judgments.
c. In the three referee system each assistant referee holds a white flag in his right hand and a red flag in his left hand. They are positioned outside the competition area in the corners opposite to, and facing, the chief referee.
d. In the four referee system the established method is to have one chief referee and three assistant referees.
e. One or more supervising referees may be present at the competition area to ensure the accuracy of the referees' decisions.

Article 13 Chief referee and refereeing team
a. A competition has a team of referees including a head referee appointed by the head of the JAA refereeing division.
b. The competition's head referee may be consulted for accuracy if a referee has some doubts about the regulations during a match.
c. In any competition associated with the JAA, regardless of Article 13b, the head of the JAA refereeing division has absolute authority in terms of refereeing and may be consulted for accuracy if there are doubts about the regulations.

Article 14 Management of a match
a. The chief referee ensures that the players have bowed to each other. He holds his right hand in front of his chest and pushes his tegatana forward while taking one step forward and calls "hajime" to start the match.
b. When play must be interrupted the chief referee quickly calls "mate" and the players return to their start lines. The chief referee can step between the players or touch them if necessary to ensure that play stops.
c. If a player moves outside the competition area during play the chief referee quickly calls "mate" to interrupt play and return the players to their start lines.
d. When the competition area does not have a sufficient safety area around it and the players are in contact but in a stalemate close to the edge of the area then the chief referee can call "mate" to interrupt play and move them to the centre of the competition area without separating them.
e. When a player tries to apply a technique that may cause injury because of his posture the chief referee can quickly called "mate" to interrupt play and ensure safety.
f. When the chief referee has awarded shidō or chūi against a player and that player continues in a manner that could easily lead to injury then, regardless of Article 7a, he can call "hansoku make".
g. At the end of the second half the chief referee calls "yame" followed by "sore made" to announce the end of the match.
h. If a supervising referee suspects a refereeing error then he raises a yellow flag in his right

hand straight above his head. When the chief referee is aware of the signal he immediately interrupts play. The referees consult the supervising referee and the chief referee then issues the correct judgment.
i. The supervising referee can reject an appeal if he considers it unwarranted.
j. If the chief referee is overruled by a supervising referee then the chief referee cancels the preceding judgment and signals the new judgment.

Article 15   Signals for awarding points

a. At the end of a match or when it is interrupted and the players have returned to their start lines the chief referee indicates the judgment by the relevant signal and announcement at the same time. A match is restarted by a call of "hajime".
b. Ippon – the chief referee uses his arm nearest to the player being awarded the points. He holds it straight above his head with the fingers extended and palm facing in and calls "ippon".
c. Waza ari – the chief referee uses his arm nearest to the player being awarded the points. He holds it straight and horizontally to his side with the fingers extended and palm down and calls "waza ari".
d. Yūkō – the chief referee uses his arm nearest the player being awarded the point. He holds it as for waza ari but at an angle of 45° to his side and calls "yūkō".
e. Tsuki ari – the chief referee uses his arm nearest to the player being awarded the points. He extends his arm and his fingers slightly forward and at an angle above his head with his palm facing in and calls "tsuki ari".
f. Fujūbun (where a technique or tantō tsuki is judged as not being effective) – the chief referee crosses his hands (open, with palms down) twice in front of his hips and calls "fujūbun".
g. Mukō (where a technique is effective but it is not within these regulations or not in the spirit of these regulations) – the chief referees holds his forearms, with the fingers of each hand extended, crossed in front of his chest and calls "mukō". The player that applied this technique is then penalised by shidō or chūi accordingly.
h. When players apply a technique the assistant referees signal their judgments to the chief referee clearly. The assistant referees continue to signal until the chief referee has made his judgment.
i. When the assistant referees signal their judgments and the chief referee calls "mate" to interrupt the match, the assistant referees continue to signal until the chief referee has made his judgment.
j. When a player scores a technique worth yūkō or waza ari and there is the possibility of a higher valued technique occurring, the referees continue to signal their judgments while the match continues.

Article 16   Managing disagreements in judgments

a. For a two referee system:
    i. When the chief referee and assistant referee disagree in their judgments, the chief referee's judgment takes precedence.
    ii. When the chief referee is standing in a blind spot and is unable to see the players' actions the assistant referee's judgment, as a general rule, is accepted.
    iii. When the chief referee sees a judgment from the assistant referee during a match but decides that nothing has occurred then he can signal and announce "fujūbun" and let the match continue uninterrupted.
b. In the three or four referee system when a technique has been applied and the chief referee's judgment is the same as one or more of the assistant referee's judgments then in general the majority decision is taken. However, if the chief referee has doubts about an assistant referee's judgment he can call for a discussion where opinions are heard and a decision taken which is generally the majority judgment. When the decision is split between any two referees the judgment is decided by the chief referee.
c. When an assistant referee judges it necessary to interrupt play he must signal. Once play has been interrupted he can express his opinion to the chief referee.

Article 17   Signals and calls for penalties and to announce the winner

a. After the players have returned to their start lines the winner can be announced. The chief referee uses his hand nearest to the winner holding it straight in front of his chest with the palm facing in. He then raises it up at an angle towards the winner and at the same time calls "aka" or "shiro". He then makes sure the players bow to each other.
b. Hiki wake and itami wake are announced after the players have returned to their start lines. The chief referee brings his extended right arm down from above his head to horizontally in front of his chest and at the same time calls "hiki wake" or "itami wake".
c. For hansoku make the players first return to their start lines. The chief referee explains the reason to the disqualified player and then announces "hansoku make". He then signals and announces the winner as in Article 17a.
d. For chūi, the chief referee turns to the penalised player, points his index finger to above the player's head and calls "chūi". For shidō, the chief referee remains facing forward, points his index finger to above the player's head and calls "shidō".

Article 18   Team randori competition format

a. In general a team has five regular members and three substitutes but this can be changed according to circumstances.
b. The winning team is determined by the total number of wins from all of the team members' matches.
c. The result of each team member's match is determined by its score. When the scores are the same the match is decided on precedence but not on marginal differences.
d. When the number of matches won for each team is the same the total accumulated points for all matches are compared. If they are equal then the precedence of the accumulated points is compared. If the winning team still cannot be determined there is a play-off

between one appointed player from each team. This winner of this match decides the winning team and can be determined by marginal differences if necessary.
e. The format can be a knockout, league or a combination of both.
f. In the league format, if the number of wins and losses on each team is the same the winning team is determined by the following: the points for the winner of each match are added up and compared. If they are equal then the points for all players are added up and compared. If these are the same then the winning team is determined by the precedence of these points.
g. Where a team has less than the full complement of players the matches with the vacant positions are placed at the top of the team order. However, when there is less than half of a full team on one side the matches cannot take place.

Article 19   Players' rights and spectators' responsibilities
a. When there is a feeling that a player is not being safe or sportsmanlike the chief referee can, generally through the manager of the team or organisation that the player belongs to, demand an improvement in the standard of play.
b. For each match a player may appoint one person with the right to question judgments to do so at the place specified in Article 1d if there is a supervising referee present. This applies to individual and team competitions.
c. Spectators must not insult the referees or players.
d. Spectators must not enter the competition area except at the request of the chief referee. Refreshments, etc. in particular must not be provided for the players.
e. Spectators must not communicate to the players the length of time remaining in the match and must not be unsportsmanlike in their speech and conduct.

Article 20   Match officials
a. The referees are assisted in the running of a match by official scorekeepers, a timekeeper and an announcer.
b. In general there are two scorekeepers, one who records on the scoreboard the points the chief referee awards and at the same time another who writes the score on a form for the tournament record. It is the second scorekeeper's duty to hand this record to the responsible official at the end of the competition.
c. In general there is one timekeeper who notifies the chief referee by a whistle, horn, etc. when the first and second halves have ended. Also, when there are interruptions during play the timekeeper stops the clock and indicates that it is stopped by raising one hand.
d. The timekeeper may alert the chief referee by a whistle, horn, etc. if the supervising referee's raised yellow flag goes unnoticed.
e. One of the scorekeepers is in charge of announcements. Before the start of every match he announces the names of the players just before they enter the competition area.

Criteria for judging toshu's techniques

For the atemi waza, toshu also refers to tantō (when applying kaeshi waza) to avoid verbosity.

yūkō	waza ari	ippon
1. Shōmen ate		
Toshu has a stable posture and breaks the opponent's balance significantly.	Toshu throws the opponent vigorously but does not have a stable posture or he has a stable posture but the throw lacks force.	Toshu has a stable posture and throws the opponent vigorously onto his front, side or back. As a general rule, toshu's other hand can be used on the back or buttocks of the opponent.
As a general rule toshu must remain standing but it is acceptable to do a forward rolling breakfall after throwing the opponent. It is acceptable to place the other hand on the back or buttocks of the opponent.		
2. Aigamae ate		
As for shōmen ate.	As for shōmen ate.	As for shōmen ate.
3. Gyakugamae ate		
As for shōmen ate.	As for shōmen ate.	As for shōmen ate.
4. Gedan ate		
As for shōmen ate.	As a general rule, the same as shōmen ate. Toshu does not make a continuous movement across the tatami and takes two seconds or more to throw the opponent.	Toshu stands in a stable posture and in an instant throws the opponent or throws him vigorously by a continuous movement across the tatami.
It is prohibited to apply gedan ate as a sacrifice technique or to use the fingers to hold and lift the opponent.		
5. Ushiro ate		
Toshu has a stable posture and breaks the opponent's balance significantly.	As for shōmen ate.	As for shōmen ate.
It is prohibited apply ushiro ate by holding and lifting the opponent or by using your leg as a fulcrum and throwing him over it with no foot movement.		

6. Oshi taoshi		
Toshu maintains a stable posture and breaks tantō's balance through 'jōdan no tsukuri' for two seconds or more without the possibility of counterattack or tantō is forced from the competition area.	Toshu pushes tantō down so that he touches the tatami with at least one part of his body ie. hand, knee, etc.	As for waza ari but toshu controls tantō's elbow for two seconds or more without the possibility of a counterattack.
7. Ude gaeshi		
Toshu has a stable posture and breaks tantō's balance significantly.	As for yūkō but maintained for two seconds or more using body movement, or toshu throws tantō but fails to maintain a stable posture during the technique.	As for yūkō but toshu maintains his balance as he throws tantō.
Applying ude gaeshi in the same manner as kote gaeshi by turning tantō's arm away from his body is prohibited because of the risk of injury.		
8. Hiki taoshi		
Toshu has a stable posture and tantō's balance is broken so that his head brought down very low.	As for yūkō but toshu makes tantō touch the tatami with at least one part of his body ie. hand, knee, etc.	As for waza ari but toshu maintains control of tantō for two seconds or more.
9. Ude hineri		
Toshu has a stable posture with tantō's arm entangled and balance broken so that his head is down very low.	As for yūkō but toshu then makes tantō touch the tatami with at least one part of his body ie. hand, knee, etc.	As for yūkō but toshu maintains control of tantō for two seconds or more. Or, during the technique tantō does a breakfall.
10. Waki gatame		
When the technique is applied tantō's arm is straight and his balance is broken. Toshu is generally moving at this time.	Toshu instantly pins tantō's straight arm while keeping a stable posture.	As for waza ari but toshu maintains control of tantō for two seconds or more.
It is prohibited to stand still and apply force directly to tantō's elbow by leverage. However, it is acceptable to apply pressure to break balance while moving in order to apply the correct technique as in the basic kata.		

11. Kote hineri		
Toshu has a stable posture and breaks tantō's balance significantly.	As for yūko but toshu makes tantō touch the tatami with at least one part of his body ie. hand, knee, etc.	As for waza ari but toshu maintains control for two seconds or more.
12. Kote gaeshi		
Toshu maintains a stable posture and completely twists tantō's wrist to break his balance.	As for yūko but toshu makes tantō's knee touch the tatami.	As for waza ari but toshu maintains control for two seconds or more. Or, from yūko or waza ari tantō is thrown.
13. Tenkai kote hineri		
Toshu maintains a stable posture and twists tantō's wrist causing a significant balance break. Or, after toshu has turned, tantō is forced from the competition area.	As for yūko but toshu pulls tantō down making him touch the tatami with at least one part of his body ie. hand, knee, etc.	As for waza ari but toshu controls tantō for two seconds or more.
14. Tenkai kote gaeshi		
Toshu has a stable posture, controls tantō's wrist and turns to the side breaking tantō's balance significantly. Or, after toshu has turned, tantō is forced from the competition area.	As for yūko but toshu makes tantō touch the tatami with at least one part of his body ie. hand, knee, etc. Alternatively, toshu controls tantō's wrist and turns to throw him or maintains a balance break while forcing him out of the competition area but fails to keep his own stable posture.	Toshu maintains a stable posture when he throws tantō.
15. Mae otoshi		
Toshu is standing in a stable posture and breaks tantō's balance significantly. It is acceptable to use the hips in this technique but not to carry tantō.	As for yūko but toshu makes tantō touch the tatami with at least one part of his body ie. hand, knee, etc.	As for waza ari but, using body movement, toshu controls tantō for two seconds or more or makes him do a breakfall.
It is prohibited to use sutemi waza (sacrifice techniques) or katsugi waza (carrying techniques).		

16. Sumi otoshi		
Toshu has a stable posture and breaks tantō's balance significantly.	Tantō is thrown or falls onto his buttocks but toshu fails to maintain a stable posture.	As for waza ari but toshu stays standing and throws tantō with force. After the technique toshu maintains a stable posture (he is allowed to go down on one knee).

17. Hiki otoshi		
Toshu has a stable posture and breaks tantō's balance significantly. Toshu is allowed to go down on one knee during the technique.	As for yūkō, toshu throws tantō but does not maintain a stable posture.	As for yūkō but toshu throws tantō and maintains a stable posture.

Notes
1. The standard of judgment above has been drawn up with the following objectives:
    a. To enhance the technical qualities and safety of competitive aikido. Also, to make a competitive budo that is a distinct part of Japanese culture.
    b. To establish a standard through which the skills of players, having practised correct aikido and acquired technical competence, can be judged appropriately. This is particularly relevant for the judgment of 'yūkō' where an effective balance break is considered as a valid score in both atemi waza and kansetsu waza.

2. Standard of judgment and spirit of the regulations for atemi waza.
A player takes advantage of an opponent's disrupted posture or immobility and attacks a vital point with controlled power using movement in one direction to throw him. Techniques are applied with the intention of causing no injury. The standard of judgment includes the stability of the player applying the technique, the way the opponent's balance is broken and the force of his fall. It is acceptable to place the other hand on the back or buttocks of the opponent when applying a technique.
    a. Ippon – the following two criteria are fully satisfied:
        i. the person applying the technique has a stable posture, either standing or on one knee, when the technique is applied.
        ii. the opponent is thrown vigorously.
    b. Waza ari – either of the two requirements for ippon above are seen to be lacking but the opponent is still thrown.
    c. Yūkō – the first criterion for ippon is fully satisfied but the opponent is not thrown. However, the opponent's balance is broken significantly and the technique is clearly effective.

3. Standard of judgment and spirit of the regulations for kansetsu waza and uki waza.
Toshu takes advantage of tantō's disrupted posture or immobility and attacks his wrist or elbow

to break his balance and throw or pin him. Techniques are applied with the intention of causing no injury. The standard of judgment includes the stability of toshu's technique, the way that tantō has been thrown and the degree of control applied. However, in spite of these criteria, if tantō signals his submission then toshu can be awarded ippon.

The stability and standing posture (including going down on one knee) of toshu does not include cases as in Article 7c.iii where there is no movement across the tatami and direct and sudden pressure is applied which are prohibited.

The degree of control required is such that when tantō has been thrown he has placed his hand, knee, etc. down firmly to support his body and he is uninjured but incapable of resistance.

Uki waza are generally the same as kansetsu waza but use a body movement across the tatami along with turning of the body one way and then the other to raise up tantō and then throw him. Judgement of kansetsu waza and each technique of the uki waza are tabulated above.

4. Supplementary items
   a. Techniques other than the basic randori kata of seventeen techniques and their applications, and tantō tsuki as defined in these regulations are prohibited. In particular judo, wrestling and traditional kata techniques are all prohibited.
   b. In the standards for judging techniques a certain number of seconds are specified. Referees are trusted in their judgment in the same way that the three second rule in basketball is successfully applied.
   c. Leg holding, tripping, sacrifice techniques, judo techniques, etc. will be dealt with strictly.

Japan Aikido Association
Referees' Division

21st June 1992
Revised 10th September 2005
Revised 30th August 2008